A HISTORY

A Narrative for the Middle School

GENERAL EDITOR

DENIS RICHARDS, M.A.

Formerly Principal of Morley College
Senior History and English Master, Bradfield College,
and Scholar of Trinity Hall, Cambridge

VOLUME III

BRITAIN UNDER THE TUDORS
AND STUARTS

A HISTORY OF BRITAIN

General Editor: Denis Richards

Also by Denis Richards

An Illustrated History of Modern Europe
An Illustrated History of Modern Britain
(with J. W. Hunt)

BRITAIN UNDER THE
TUDORS AND STUARTS

By

DENIS RICHARDS, M.A.
Formerly Principal of Morley College

LONGMAN

LONGMAN GROUP LIMITED
London

*Associated companies, branches and representatives
throughout the world*

© Denis Richards, 1958

First published 1958
Reprinted 1979

ISBN 0 582 31484 4

*Printed in Hong Kong by
Yu Luen Offset Printing Factory Ltd*

FOREWORD TO TEACHERS

THE History of which this volume forms a part is intended in the main for the middle forms of grammar schools. It is written in the belief that every British boy and girl should know something of the broad outlines of the national story, and that the best form of text-book for this purpose is a continuous narrative displaying the main figures, forces and events in a roughly chronological sequence. In the other volumes of the series a larger part of the narrative will be devoted to the social and economic side; here, in *Britain under the Tudors and Stuarts*, I have thought it right to place the main emphasis on the great political and religious developments which above all distinguish that period.

Political and religious changes—and for that matter economic ones—can all too easily bore or bewilder the youthful student. In an attempt to make highly complex matters reasonably interesting and clear, the story is told here in some detail—for the opposite course of generalization usually leaves only the vaguest of impressions. Detail, however, has its own dangers. This book will be at its most effective if teachers offer it to their pupils in short instalments—for which reason the longer chapters are subdivided—and if the emphasis in preparation is on reading and understanding rather than on memorizing. To those key points which should be remembered, the side-notes and charts, it is hoped, will provide a useful guide.

I should like to acknowledge my indebtedness to three friends for their help: to Mr. J. W. Hunt for his comments on my first draft; to Mr. Martin Holmes, of the London Museum, for some very valuable suggestions in the way of illustrations; and to Mrs. Pamela

Johnson for her patience and skill in typing an almost criminally difficult manuscript. I must also express my thanks to my thirteen-year-old daughter Caroline, who read the whole work in typescript to test its suitability for her age-group, and pronounced it—after due attention to her suggestions—to be of an appropriate level.

October, 1957   D.R.

CONTENTS

MAPS AND DIAGRAMS

THE TUDORS

Edmund Tudor, Earl of Richmond, m. Margaret Beaufort, daughter of Duke of Somerset

1485   **HENRY VII**   1509

m. Elizabeth of York, daughter of Edward IV

Arthur

1509   **HENRY VIII**   1547

Margaret
m. James IV
(Stuart)
of Scots

Mary
m. (1) Louis XII
(2) Duke of Suffolk

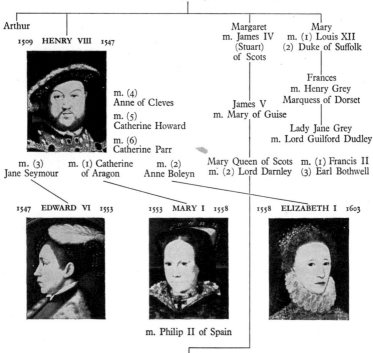

m. (4)
Anne of Cleves

m. (5)
Catherine Howard

m. (6)
Catherine Parr

James V
m. Mary of Guise

Frances
m. Henry Grey
Marquess of Dorset

Lady Jane Grey
m. Lord Guilford Dudley

m. (3)
Jane Seymour

m. (1) Catherine
of Aragon

m. (2)
Anne Boleyn

Mary Queen of Scots
m. (2) Lord Darnley

m. (1) Francis II
(3) Earl Bothwell

1547   **EDWARD VI**   1553

1553   **MARY I**   1558

1558   **ELIZABETH I**   1603

m. Philip II of Spain

James VI of Scotland and I of England

STUART LINE

↓

THE STUARTS

Mary Stuart, Queen of Scots, m. (2) Henry, Lord Darnley

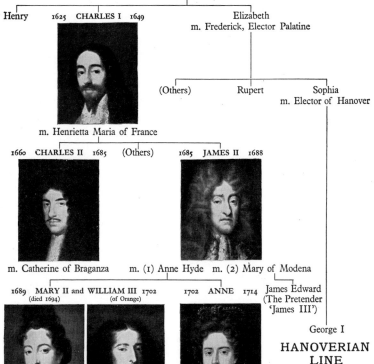

1603   JAMES I   1625

m. Anne of Denmark

Henry   1625   CHARLES I   1649

Elizabeth
m. Frederick, Elector Palatine

(Others)   Rupert   Sophia
m. Elector of Hanover

m. Henrietta Maria of France

1660   CHARLES II   1685   (Others)   1685   JAMES II   1688

m. Catherine of Braganza   m. (1) Anne Hyde   m. (2) Mary of Modena

1689   MARY II and WILLIAM III   1702   1702   ANNE   1714   James Edward
(died 1694)   (of Orange)   (The Pretender
                                                                       'James III')

George I

HANOVERIAN
LINE
↓

m. George of Denmark

ACKNOWLEDGMENTS

Illustrations on pp. 34, 44, 105 and 213 are reproduced by gracious permission of H.M. the Queen.

For permission to reproduce other illustrations we are indebted to the following:

The Duke of Bedford for p. 86 (the picture can be seen at Woburn Abbey during the summer); the Bibliothèque Nationale for p. 103; the Bodleian Library for pp. 187 and 216; Country Life Ltd. for pp. 174 and 220; the Dean and Chapter of Westminster for p. 19; the Controller, H.M. Stationery Office for p. 335 (Crown Copyright Reserved); A. F. Kersting for p. 207; the London Museum for p. 285; Magdalene College, Cambridge for p. 283; Mansell Collection for p. 253; Commander M. Minshall for p. 170; the National Portrait Gallery for pp. 31, 51, 72 and 338 (top left, bottom left and right); the Public Record Office for pp. 16 and 165; the Rijksmuseum, Amsterdam for p. 292; the Royal Society for p. 338 (top right); Lord Torpichon for p. 102; Dr. G. M. Trevelyan for p. 251; The Marquis of Salisbury for p. 113 (photograph by Photo-Precision); the Victoria and Albert Museum for pp. 167, 171, 263, 370, 373 and 376 (these photographs are Crown Copyright Reserved); the Walker Art Gallery, Liverpool for p. 45; the University Library, Utrecht for p. 191.

Illustrations on pp. 5, 11, 22, 37, 56, 62, 67, 68, 74, 79, 91, 93, 129, 133, 149, 154, 168, 169, 199, 203, 205, 215, 224, 227, 232, 240, 255, 258, 262, 276, 295, 298, 304, 306, 307, 312, 317, 320, 329, 371, 375, and 379 are reproduced from subjects in the British Museum, and illustration on p. 287 from a book in the Cambridge University Library.

The portraits included in the charts on pp. xii and xiii, are details of larger pictures and are reproduced by permission of the following:

The Victoria and Albert Museum, for Henry VII; the Walker Art Gallery, Liverpool, for Henry VIII; the Metropolitan Museum of Art, New York, for Edward VI; the Society of Antiquaries, for Mary I, and the National Portrait Gallery, for Elizabeth I and the seven portraits on p. xiii.

The map on p. 132 is adapted from A. L. Rowse; *The Expansion of Elizabethan England*, by permission of Messrs. Macmillan & Co. Ltd.

CHAPTER ONE

'MODERN TIMES'

'**M**ODERN' is a curious word. Like the angler's fish that got away, it may be stretched almost indefinitely. When applied to a car or a wireless-set, it means something produced within the last twelve months or so; but when applied to the history of Europe, it covers several centuries.

Though some historians doubt the value of the practice, history is usually divided into three great periods— ancient, medieval, and modern. Ancient history, it is generally agreed, ends during the 5th century A.D. with the collapse of the Roman Empire in the West. About the dividing line between the medieval and the modern, however, opinions differ. Nowadays some historians think that the growth of scientific interests and the scientific outlook in the later 17th century marks the true beginning of the modern era; but most still accept the traditional division, and regard the Middle Ages as ending round about 1500. *Historical periods*

There are many good reasons for this older view. As the Middle Ages wore on, the barbarian tribes settled down, trade and civilization grew, and a fairly orderly Europe emerged. By 1500 one of the most characteristic features of the Middle Ages—the feudal system of giving service to a lord in order to hold land and receive protection—had served its turn. Men were beginning to look beyond their own district and its local lord, and to feel loyalty to something bigger. In England and France this larger group which claimed men's loyalties was by 1500 already the *nation*. People in England had become conscious of being Englishmen as well as citizens of London or York; people in France were aware of being *End of the Middle Ages marked by:* *(a) Decline of feudalism* *(b) Growth of nationalism*

Frenchmen as well as citizens of Paris or Rouen. And with this great change came a decline in the power of (c) Increase in royal power the local leader—the baron—and an increase in the power of the national leader—the king.

This growth of nationalism and royal power in turn brought to an end another great feature of the Middle Ages—the existence of a single Church covering the whole of Western Christendom and controlled from Rome by the Pope. As the great civilizing influence in early medieval times, the Church had won immense influence over men's minds, and through this had been able to claim obedience from kings no less than from (d) Decline in authority of Church and Pope peasants. Many medieval kings had not exactly relished this power that the Pope, by his control over the Church, wielded within their realms; but they could not do much about it. Kings who could rely on the loyalty of a whole nation, however, were in a better position to alter the situation. They had greater resources; and their subjects, being more aware of their nationality, would be more resentful of any outside authority.

The rise of strong kings and of national feeling was not the only thing which weakened the papacy in the 15th century. For many years, or even centuries, a The Renaissance movement known as the *Renaissance*, or the revived study of the art and writings of ancient Greece and Rome, had been gathering force.[1] Besides introducing many more scholars direct to the texts of the classical philosophers, where they often found ideas opposed to those of the Church, this bred a spirit of inquiry and criticism. Coupled with the growth of national feeling and the existence of many grave abuses within the Church, it led to the movement known as the *Reforma-* The Reformation *tion*, in the course of which several countries, England included, broke away from Rome.

[1] Renaissance = literally 'rebirth'—i.e. the rebirth of classical art and learning.

Together then, Nationalism, Renaissance, and Reformation brought the Middle Ages to a close. The force of these movements, however, would not have been so great without certain inventions. The first of these was *gunpowder*. The introduction of this regrettable substance Gunpowder into Europe in the 12th century, and the slow but sure development of weapons in which it could be employed, was another nail in the coffin of the medieval baron: as a rule only the king had cannon, and against cannon defiance in the baronial castle ceased to be either popular or profitable. Secondly, the invention in the 15th century of *printing* with movable metal type enabled Printing many more scholars to study the classical texts, encouraged men to express their opinions in books, and speeded on the increasing ferment of ideas. In so doing, it helped to undermine the authority of the Church. Thirdly, the development of the *mariner's compass* (which Mariner's compass had been used in Europe from the 12th century and, like gunpowder, had been known for many centuries before that to the Chinese) helped to bring about the great trans-oceanic voyages of Columbus and others, the opening up of fresh continents, and a drastic change in ideas of world geography.

So there are still good grounds for regarding modern times as beginning round about the close of the 15th century, when the Renaissance was at its height, the Reformation was about to take place, the first great voyages of discovery had already been made, and in many parts of Europe loosely grouped feudal territories were being welded into strong national states. At about this time, an age which had looked to religion as the whole source of civilization gave place to a new age, in which religion would still be extremely important, but in which subjects like politics and economics, art and science, would come to have a kind of independent life of their own. In each country of Western Europe a

GROWTH OF NATIONAL
FEELING AND ROYAL POWER: DECLINE OF FEUDALISM

THE RENAISSANCE

EUROPE, 1600

THE REFORMATION: THE CHURCH DIVIDED

THREE GREAT INVENTIONS WIDELY ADOPTED

DISCOVERY: THE NEW WORLD

A NEW AGE BEGINS

different date, round about the same general time, may be chosen as the dividing line between the medieval and the modern. In England the best date would probably be 1529, which marks the beginning of the break with Rome. It is usual, however, to select the year 1485; for in that year the first king of a dynasty which soon became far more powerful than any that had gone before—the Tudors—ascended the throne. The work of Henry VII in the years following 1485 turned his victory at Bosworth Field into a decisive one, brought to an end the Wars of the Roses, and made that unhappy conflict the last grand fling of the English barons. And it was not long before his son Henry VIII was at grips with the other great obstacle to royal and national power— the papacy. With the first of the new Tudor line, then, we approach Modern English History.

The beginning of modern times in England

Music for a King

From a wood-cut in Holinshed's *Historie of Scotland*. It shows the Tudor habit of performing round a table on which the players or singers rested their parts or instruments. (This and the following Holinshed woodcuts were used many times over in Holinshed's histories, which were first published in 1577–78 under the collective title of *Chronicles of England, Scotland and Ireland*. The woodcuts were probably made much earlier, originally for other purposes. The 'Chronicles' were Shakespeare's source book for the themes of *Macbeth, King Lear* and most of his historical plays.)

CHAPTER TWO

HENRY VII AND THE ENGLAND OF
1485

HENRY VII became king by conquest. He had, of course, a claim to the throne by birth; but others had a better. What gained him his crown was his victory over Richard III at Bosworth.

For many years England's monarchs had been insecurely perched on their throne. In 1399 Henry, Duke of Lancaster, had usurped the throne from Richard II and become king as Henry IV; but the long minority and later weakness of his grandson, Henry VI, had Wars of the given rival claimants their chance. In the Wars of the Roses Roses the Dukes of York, who had a stronger title to the throne by descent from Edward III, strove to displace the House of Lancaster. Eventually Edward, Duke of York, had established himself in power as Edward IV and had managed to restore some of the waning strength of the monarchy—only to die while his sons were still youths. This proved too great a temptation for the Protector, or Regent, Richard, Duke of Gloucester, the uncle of these two unfortunate boys. He quickly had them declared illegitimate, clapped them into the Tower (where they were afterwards murdered), and mounted the throne himself as Richard III. But in ridding himself of his nephews and their supporters, Richard made Conspiracy many enemies. The result was a conspiracy, in which against Richard III several leading Yorkists joined, to bring in an exiled Lancastrian leader, the twenty-seven-year-old Henry Tudor, Earl of Richmond.

Landing with a small force at Milford Haven in 1485

Henry at once gathered supporters—for on his father's side he had Welsh blood. With 5,000 men he struck into England; and at Market Bosworth, in Leicestershire, his forces clashed with the King's. The plan of campaign had been carefully prepared and it worked. As soon as the battle began, Richard was deserted by his most powerful supporters. Fighting like a wild animal he was finally borne down by weight of numbers. Bosworth, 1485

With an army behind him and his opponent dead, the victor was soon able to have himself crowned king as Henry VII. What sort of a kingdom had he won?

The England of 1485 was a country with a very small population of between three and four million. It had one really big town (London), a large number of small towns (of which Norwich and York were the most important), and a fertile countryside on which worked nine-tenths of the people. It was a country with almost a dividing line at the River Trent—south of which was comparatively wealthy, highly developed, and well controlled, and north of which was much poorer, wilder, and nearer to nature. And it was a country which over the last century and a half had seen not only much warfare (foreign and civil) but also plague, weakened government, great social changes, and declining prosperity. England in 1485

Many of these things were closely connected. Plague, for instance, speeded on some of the greatest changes in the country manors. Beginning with the terrible Black Death of 1349, the plague struck so hard that soon there was not enough labour to work all the ground normally tilled. As a result, many serfs took the opportunity to escape to other manors where the lords would now employ them for money as free men. Shortage of labour following attacks of the plague also forced lords to let out more land and to accept money rents instead of labour service from their tenants. So everywhere in the Breakdown of manorial feudalism late 14th and 15th centuries plague helped to break down the old village relationships based on service, and to set up instead new relationships based on money.

This was only one of the big changes which the country had recently seen, and was still seeing. Another Decreased prosperity of towns was the harder times in many of the towns as a result of the Hundred Years War, the Wars of the Roses, and, in some cases, the competition of the German merchants of the Hanse. The chief trade to suffer was the greatest, the old-established export trade in wool, controlled almost entirely by the Merchants of the Staple at Calais —which was still an English possession. Also held in check was the rising export trade in cloth, handled for the most part by the Merchant Adventurers of London. However, thanks to the work of Edward IV in concluding peace with France and establishing more settled conditions at home, trade was already beginning to recover from its long set-back when Henry VII came to the throne.

Much the most serious of the troubles which had afflicted England in the 15th century—for it caused Weakness of central government many of the others—had been the weakness of the government. England was a country which for the times had a very well developed system of law and administration, from the king and his council down to the judges of assize, the sheriffs, and the justices of the peace. The system even included the occasional summoning of the great lords and representatives of the Commons to a parliament—sometimes when the king wanted to give special force to a law, and always when he wanted to impose fresh direct taxes. How well all this machinery of government worked, however, depended on the man at the top. If the king ruled justly and was strong enough to make his own free choice of counsellors, then the result was firm direction from above, and law and order in the shires. But if the king lacked these qualities, then powerful groups of barons soon dominated his council and caused confusion with their squabbles, so that local lords were left unchecked to tyrannize over the countryside. This was what had happened in the long reign of Henry VI; and though Edward IV had pulled things together, his early death and the actions of Richard III had once more brought the authority of the Crown to a very low ebb.

A strong, just king could still restore this lost authority, Special privileges and so give the country better order. Not even the most powerful monarch, however, could normally hope to do much about the special privileges, or 'franchises', granted earlier by the Crown. The Church, for instance, The Church had long ago established its right to try clerical offenders; by successfully pleading 'benefit of clergy', the accused could stop proceedings against him in the ordinary courts, and come instead within the scope of the Church courts, which could not inflict loss of life or limb. As there were many thousands of lesser clergy, and thousands of laymen who knew enough Latin to pass for lesser clergy, this meant that large numbers of men could escape the king's justice. In the same way, a criminal had only to take sanctuary within a church or churchyard, and the king's officers could not touch him. Many boroughs and many gilds, too, held privileges Boroughs and gilds which were no longer in the interests of the nation, yet which could not be cancelled by the Crown. And all such privileges had of course greatly multiplied during the long years of government weakness.

The most remarkable privileges, apart from those of the Church, were those enjoyed in the 'Marches'—the The Marches districts bordering Wales and Scotland. The distance of these Marches from London, and their special importance for defence, had enabled their local lords to remain extremely independent. In such parts ordinary county institutions did not exist—the whole county of

Durham, for instance, was one vast sanctuary, for the king's writ had no force and his courts did not sit. Instead the local lords held their own courts, had their own ideas about taxation, and could easily raise an army from their own tenants. All this—combined with frequent raiding and counter-raiding across the borders—made the Marches the worst centres of lawlessness in the whole of the country.

Wales   The Marches in the west covered not only large areas of present-day England, but also about half of what we now know as Wales. Beyond them lay the Principality of Wales, the coastal counties on which Edward I had imposed shire organization. But a few sheriffs and their officers and courts could not alter the fact that this was Welsh Wales—a land with a language of its own where English laws and wishes counted for nothing compared with Welsh loyalties and habits. Like the Marches, the Principality of Wales was wild, backward and lawless. It formed a single kingdom with England, but the two countries had little else in common. Fortunately for Henry VII his Welsh blood simplified the problem of control.

Ireland   Still more unruly was another part of the royal dominions—Ireland. Of this, the English monarch was not king but 'Lord', for in theory he held it as a grant from the papacy. In actual fact, however, he hardly held it at all. He held a coastal strip running north from Dublin known as the Pale, and some of the southern ports. In these places there was direct English rule. Elsewhere, he could only try to make his claim a reality by ruling through the local Irish chiefs—which meant hardly ruling at all. For here again was a wild land with a strange tongue—a land of hills and bogs, minstrels and monks, banshees and blood-feuds, where ancient tribal customs and loyalties meant everything, the link with the English Crown nothing.

Scotland, of course, was no part of the dominions of Scotland the king of England. It was a separate and usually hostile kingdom under a ruling family of its own—the Stuarts. The Lowlands were as far in advance of the

A Fifteenth Century Angler

From a woodcut illustrating a treatise on fishing. It comes from *The Book of St. Albans*, a work printed at Westminster in 1496 by Wynkyn de Worde, the disciple and successor of William Caxton. Gothic type—of great beauty as used here—was very fashionable at the time, especially for Bibles and official documents.

Highlands as the south of England was of the north; but even the Lowlands were very backward compared with southern England. Clan loyalties and feuds, and the murderous rivalry of contending noble factions, paralysed Scottish government and combined with the poverty of the soil to keep the whole country poor. All the same its vigorous sons, swift to anger and ever ready to pour over the border into England, were a standing danger to their southern neighbours. Whether he had to reckon only with raiding or with full-scale war by the Scots in alliance with France, no king of England could forget that in the north lay danger.

Henry's tasks

From this brief glance at the territories with which the new king was most closely concerned, it may be seen what were the main tasks before Henry. They were to restore good order and prosperity in England; to bring the Marches and Ireland more under royal control; and to parry any danger from traditional enemies such as France and Scotland. First and foremost, however, he had to make sure of staying king of England. Rebellion had long been the order of the day, and at any time discontented Yorkists might rally round Edward IV's relatives—notably Elizabeth, his daughter, or the Earl of Warwick, his nephew—and attempt to recover the throne. All the odds were that Bosworth would prove to be, not the end of the Wars of the Roses, but only one more stage in the conflict.

Henry strengthens his position

This situation governed the early years of Henry's reign. To ward off the danger, Henry soon took three important steps: he got parliament to recognize his title, imprisoned Warwick (who was only ten years old) in the Tower, and married Elizabeth. This last action, which honoured a pledge already made before he set out for England, united the Houses of Lancaster and York. It took more than acts of parliament and marriages, however, to control some of the English nobles, and several times Henry had to face rebellion.

Lambert Simnel

The first rising he broke very swiftly. In 1487 Lambert Simnel, an able youth of humble birth who had been carefully coached for the part, set up to be the Earl of Warwick and claimed the throne. Behind the figurehead

Simnel stood some leading Yorkists, who between them won over most of Ireland. Henry answered Simnel's claim by producing Warwick from the Tower—the plotters were surprised to find him still alive—and parading him round London. More important, Henry sought out the conspirators' forces after they had landed from Ireland and shattered them in a single battle at Stoke. To Simnel he extended mercy—and work in the royal kitchens. Stoke, 1487

The next affair was still more dangerous, since it involved foreign powers. A young Belgian adventurer named Perkin Warbeck claimed to be Edward IV's son Richard—the younger of the two princes murdered in the Tower. He was put up to this by Yorkists in Ireland, and was soon enjoying support from, among others, England's old enemies France and Scotland. Flitting about between Ireland, Scotland and the Continent, Perkin gave Henry immense trouble: twice he attempted invasion, and it was six years before he was finally rounded up and confined to the Tower. Even then, he tried to plot with Warwick—or so the government said—with the result that they were both executed. Warwick died by the axe, Perkin by the much less gentlemanly rope. Perkin Warbeck, 1491–1499

All the earlier half of Henry's reign, then, Yorkists were struggling to reverse the verdict of Bosworth. To survive, Henry had clearly to reduce the power of certain sections of the nobility, and in so doing increase, or restore, that of the king. How he did so, we shall shortly see.

CHAPTER THREE

THE ESTABLISHMENT OF TUDOR RULE
(1485–1509)

Factors
favouring
Henry

IN trying to make the king once again the real ruler of the country, Henry could rely on the help of at least two facts. Many of the most ambitious nobles had already been killed or executed in the Wars of the Roses; and the country, tired of being fought over by rival groups of barons, would welcome stronger royal power in the interests of peace and prosperity.

Weakening
the nobility

To tame unruly and 'over-mighty' elements among the nobility, Henry struck at the roots of their power—

Measures
against
livery and
maintenance

their control over their own districts. He strengthened, for example, the laws forbidding landowners to keep private armies of 'retainers': livery—provision of uniform and food—must be given only to genuine household servants. Forbidden, too, was the practice of 'maintenance', by which a lord intervened in court cases to maintain or uphold the cause of his supporters— an intervention often marked by threats against the jury! Such measures as these helped to stop ambitious lords dominating their own districts by force of arms.

With the same object in view, Henry caused many more cases to be referred direct to his own council, which met for this purpose in open session in the room in Westminster Palace known as the Star Chamber. In

Star
Chamber

this, Henry's councillors dealt, among other things, with charges arising from breaches of the peace and of the laws against livery and maintenance: and here people could safely air complaints against high-born offenders. Later, under the Stuarts, the Court of Star

Chamber (as it became by the time of Henry VIII) was to be attacked because its freedom from the normal legal procedure favoured the power of the king. Under the Tudors it was popular for its quick decisions and was a useful safeguard against too much power on the part of the nobles.

By other means, too, Henry strengthened his position. He selected few from the old noble families for his council and instead preferred men of middle birth, who owed everything to him. A bishop like Cardinal Morton, a lawyer like Richard Empson or Edmund Dudley, could be relied upon to act as the king's servant without trying to become his rival. Henry was by no means the first king to see this; but he was the first king for some time to secure a free choice of advisers. <i>Councillors of middle birth</i>

Quite rightly, Henry saw in money the key to the whole situation. Of set purpose he began to build up a large fortune. He made justice a richer source of revenue than ever before—notably by imposing heavy fines in the Star Chamber for offences which other kings would have punished by death. In addition, he compelled wealthy nobles to pay the feudal dues on their land which many of them had long escaped; and he also forced them to lend him money, or make the special contributions known as benevolences. By these means, together with closer personal control over the collection of revenue, economy in expenditure, and some profitable dealings in the wool trade, he was soon in a very strong financial position. And it was typical of Henry that his foreign policy helped towards the same end. Peace, which he carefully preserved for most of his reign, was cheaper than war—and even his wars made money. <i>Finance</i>

By all these methods Henry at last established himself firmly in power and gave to the country what it so badly needed—peace and order. He managed this despite the fact that he had no standing army beyond a few yeomen of the guard, only a very small navy of half <i>Lack of military power</i>

a dozen ships, and no civil service beyond the officials of the royal household. So long, however, as his policy was popular and his purse well filled, he could be sure of hiring soldiers when need arose—as it many times did.

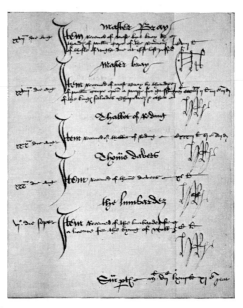

Accounts checked by Henry VII

This is a page from a book of receipts of the Treasurer of the King's Chamber. Each item was checked by Henry, who added a sign which was changed from time to time. On this page it changes after the first item.

Parliament

One of the advantages of Henry's financial success was that it avoided any trouble with parliament. As already mentioned, parliament met only when the king desired, and usually only when he needed fresh taxation. This he was not supposed to require very often, for in normal times the monarch was still expected to 'live of his own'—on the revenue from his lands and courts of justice, the customs duties granted him for life in his first parliament, and the various 'feudal dues' payable by his tenants-in-chief. The peaceful and economical Henry, being soon better off than his Lancastrian predecessors, had less reason than they to summon parliament—which in the second half of his reign met only once.

Henry could not have maintained peace and order in England if he had not also been able to keep in check his outside enemies. Among these he had to reckon the Irish. Because the Irish lords, of whom the greatest was the Earl of Kildare, gave constant trouble by supporting opponents such as Simnel and Warbeck, Henry resolved to bring Ireland much more fully and closely under English rule. He dismissed Kildare from office, and sent over as his Lord Deputy a very able Englishman, Sir Edward Poynings. Though he failed in an attempt to conquer Ulster—the wildest part of the country—he did succeed in extending royal control by two important measures which he put through a specially summoned Irish Parliament. The first, usually called Poynings' Law, and intended to control future Lord Deputies as much as anyone else, stated that no bill should be introduced into parliament at Dublin unless it had first been approved by the king's council at Westminster. The second applied English laws in general to Ireland. After two years, however, Henry tired of the cost of Poynings' campaigns, recalled him, and reinstated Kildare— which meant abandoning the struggle. In fact, it was impossible to enforce royal control over the whole of Ireland without far greater resources than the Tudors enjoyed—yet no Tudor could leave Ireland to itself, for if he did it would certainly become the base for a foreign invasion of England.

As for Scotland, Henry could only go to work in his own patient and far-seeing way. He built up his power

Ireland

Poynings

Scotland

until King James IV (who at one time invaded England
with Warbeck, offering £1,000 for Henry's head, only
to be beaten back within a week) agreed to marry
Henry's daughter Margaret. The eventual result of
this match, a century later, was the union of the Scottish and English thrones—a deferred but outstanding
triumph for Henry's statesmanship.

The behaviour of Scotland largely depended on that
of France. When France was fighting England, Scotland
could rarely resist the temptation to invade her neigh-
bour. Throughout the greater part of his reign Henry
therefore tried to keep peace with France. He strongly
resisted, however, a French attempt to annex the Duchy
of Brittany. In fact, he went so far as to ally with Spain,
and to lead an expedition across the Channel. By that
time the French king had not only secured a hold on
Brittany by marrying the duchess, but was also set on
invading Italy. So he was only too glad to buy Henry VII
off. At the Peace of Etaples Henry agreed to depart
from French soil on conditions which included the payment of his expenses and of large arrears of money due
under a treaty exacted by Edward III. His coffers filled
by this profitable little venture, Henry returned home.

The alliance with the rising power of Spain—which
could put pressure on France and so on Scotland—was
a leading feature of Henry's policy. From the beginning
he worked for this, and his crowning success came with
the marriage of his eldest son Arthur to Catherine of
Aragon, the fifteen-year-old daughter of King Ferdinand
and Queen Isabella. Five months later Arthur died, but
so keen were both sides on the match that they arranged
for Arthur's brother Henry to become engaged to the
widow. Since marriage with a deceased husband's
brother was not allowed by the Church, the Pope was
persuaded to give special permission. Of all this, a great
deal more was to be heard later, in the next reign.

James IV
marries
Margaret
Tudor

France

Henry
invades
France

Peace of
Etaples,
1492

Spain

Arthur
marries
Catherine of
Aragon, 1501

Betrothal of
Prince
Henry and
Catherine

Henry VII's Chapel, Westminster Abbey

This beautiful chapel, commissioned by Henry VII, was designed to be the resting place for the bodies of himself and his wife (who are commemorated in a tomb with splendid effigies carved by the Florentine sculptor Pietro Torrigiano) and for that of Henry VI (which however was never moved from Windsor). Note the 'perpendicular' windows and the lovely fan vaulting of the roof with its elaborate pendants. The chapel, begun in 1504 and finished under Henry VIII, is one of the last great pieces of Gothic architecture in England.

Trade

With an astute but peaceful foreign policy Henry combined constant care for English trading interests. He refused to allow foreigners to trade with England unless they would give England trading privileges in return, and he secured for English merchants the right to trade with Spain, Denmark, Danzig and the Levant. He also twice obtained favourable trading treaties with the Netherlands by stopping the export of unfinished cloth to that country—a ruse which succeeded because the Netherlands had a highly developed industry of their own for smoothing and dyeing fabrics, but depended on England for the unfinished material. As part of his policy of encouraging foreign trade, and because ships were useful in war as well as peace, Henry also did his best to build up a powerful merchant fleet. All this, combined with his restoration of order, helped the country towards greater prosperity.

Merchant
shipping

Henry's
character
and
achievement

Henry was perhaps not an inspiring figure, especially in his later years when he encouraged his ministers to exact every penny they could from the purses of wealthy subjects. But he was clever, wise, devout and cultured—a man who, despite a close check on his expenditure, kept great state and knew how to play the part of a king. An able linguist, a great lover of music, devoted to the chase and to sports like archery and tennis as well as to the less energetic pastimes of chess and cards, he was much more of a personality than the colourless skinflint the history books have sometimes made him. A patron of architecture, he left, in the lady chapel at Westminster Abbey begun in his reign, one of the most glorious of late Gothic buildings. A man of some vision, he encouraged the Genoese mariners John and Sebastian Cabot and so speeded on the discovery of Newfoundland and the north-east American coast—though he rejected the plans of a still greater Genoese, Christopher Columbus. A financial genius who had much of the revenue

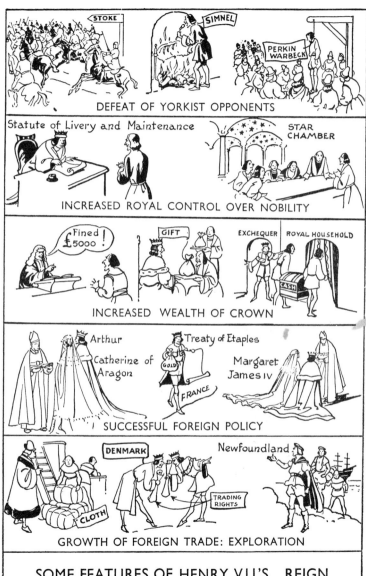

SOME FEATURES OF HENRY VII'S REIGN

paid direct into a department of the royal household instead of into the exchequer, he left the royal finances in a more healthy state than they had ever been before or were ever—until the king lost power—to be again.

All told, though little that he did was entirely new, Henry VII accomplished a great work. He restored order, kept the peace, built up the royal power, tamed the unruly nobility, and gave his country nearly a quarter of a century of the good government it so much needed. He laid, in other words, the foundations of that great Tudor monarchy which under his son Henry was to defy the Pope and under his granddaughter Elizabeth to humble the might of Spain and bring a new glory to the name of England.

A Wrestling Match

A favourite sport in most parts of the British Isles in Tudor times. From Holinshed's *Historie of Scotland*.

CHAPTER FOUR

EUROPE AT THE END OF THE FIFTEENTH CENTURY

To understand developments in England under the Tudors, we must first glance at the Europe of 1500. By that date the work of Henry VII was having its effect, and England was rapidly gaining in strength. Patriotic feeling, too, was intense—for the English nation had now been united for some centuries. Nevertheless, England remained a small country with a small population, and one recently weakened by civil war—so her king had to be very careful in dealing with larger states such as France and Spain.

France, an enemy of long standing, was at first the France greater danger. By 1500 her kings had just completed the process of turning all the old separate provinces into one united kingdom. Calais alone remained in English hands, and with the big exception of the Rhineland territory France covered roughly the area we know today. A state of this size might prove a grave threat to England; but fortunately the French kings now had French ambitions in Netherlands, Burgundy and Italy ambitions in two other directions. They were determined to capture not only the Netherlands and the Free County of Burgundy (which by marriage had passed to the Habsburg family of Austria), but also two states in Italy (one of which, Naples, was ruled by a Spaniard). France's ambitions, then, were bound to bring her into conflict with Austria and Spain—a situation in which England would weigh up the merits of joining in the fray or staying on the touchline.

Like France, Spain was only just becoming united— Spain

the biggest steps having followed the marriage of Ferdinand of Aragon and Isabella of Castile. Already, however, Spanish power extended overseas—to Southern Italy, and to that most exciting of discoveries 'the New World'.

Columbus and the New World   In 1492 Christopher Columbus of Genoa, having sounded many of the courts of Europe in vain, had at last found a patron in Queen Isabella. The old routes to Asia through the Mediterranean and overland were by then at the mercy of the Turks, and it was Columbus's belief that he could discover a new route to the East by sailing west. In this he was following a different line from the great Portuguese navigators, who were bent on finding a route to Asia by way of Africa, and whose first omen of success came when Bartholomew Diaz rounded the Cape of Good Hope in 1488. With Spanish support Columbus set off, sailing far beyond the Portuguese discoveries of the Azores and the Canaries, and eventually struck some islands which he took to be the outposts of Asia—and which were therefore called the West Indies. A year later he returned and discovered many more islands; and in 1498, on his third voyage, he reached the mainland of South America— which he still imagined to be the eastern shores of Asia. Within a few years explorers of kindred spirit had traced the whole eastern coastline of the Americas; and Spain and Portugal had come to an agreement, confirmed by the Pope, by which a line midway between the Azores and the West Indies was taken as the boundary between their areas of discovery and colonization. Portugal was to have all rights to the east, Spain all rights to the west. From these new dominions the Spaniards soon began to exact vast quantities of treasure. Strong in this unexpected wealth, strong in her fierce, tough infantry, and Spanish strength   strong in her deep religious faith, Spain now faced the dawn of her greatest age.

By 1500, Spain, France and England were all more The Italian states or less united countries. Not so Italy. Here the very wealth and artistic splendour of the small states had kept them apart: they had too much sense of their own importance to merge peaceably with others. In the north there were several independent states, including Venice, which had an overseas empire now being lost to the Turks. Farther south, in the centre of Italy, the Pope held sway over a group of four states—in 1500 a pope who had bribed his way to the papacy, openly boasted a large family of illegitimate children, and was not above instigating murder. South again of these states of the Church lay Naples and Sicily, the latter ruled by Ferdinand of Aragon, the former by one of his relations. Italy was thus simply a geographical term covering a number of small states. Because of this its riches and glories now lay at the mercy of its stronger and more united neighbours, France, Spain and Austria.

North-east of Italy lay the vast, powerless mass of the The Holy Roman Empire Holy Roman Empire. This was a loosely organized group of some three hundred and fifty states, mostly in the area now covered by Germany. The Emperor was chosen by the rulers of the seven most important states; but by 1500 the archdukes of Austria were beginning to establish a regular claim to the office. The imperial power, however, was very small; for any decisions taken by the Imperial Diet, or parliament, could only be carried out by the local rulers, who usually acted exactly as they chose. Germany—whose towns were also highly civilized and prosperous—was thus split into even more fragments than Italy. One of the fragments, however, was quite strong. The Habsburg ruler of Austria Austria, who now also controlled the Free County of Burgundy and the Netherlands, and was cornering the imperial title, was a power to be reckoned with.

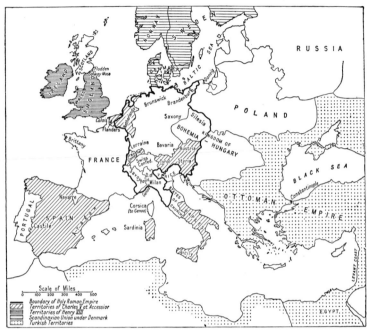

Europe at the Accession of Charles V, 1519

South-east Europe

The countries directly east of the Holy Roman Empire had only slight contacts with Western Europe. The eyes of Europe were much more fixed on events to the south-east, where the Ottoman Turks were still pursuing their career of conquest. Constantinople had fallen in 1453; the whole Balkan peninsula, as well as Asia Minor and Egypt, was now in Turkish hands; and by 1500 only the kingdom of Hungary still stood guard, for a brief while, between the Turks and Austria.

France and Spain the main dangers

These, then, were the chief countries with which Tudor foreign policy was concerned. Italy and Germany presented no trouble; but danger might well spring from France or Spain. And if—as soon happened—the

deaths and marriages of a few princes and princesses
brought the dominions of Spain and Austria into the
same pair of hands, the peril would be greater still.
Fortunately, however, it seemed that there would be at
least two strong powers on the Continent. The danger
to England, as we have seen many times since then, is
always greatest when one power on the Continent is so
strong that it has no real rivals.

One other thing must be noticed about this Europe *The Renaissance in Italy*
of 1500. It was the Europe of the Renaissance, of the
rebirth of classical learning. In Italy, where there was
the ever-present example of ancient Roman architecture, and where the works of the old Roman authors
were more readily available, the ferment had already
been strong for several generations. Through studying
the old Latin texts, the scholars of Italy had been led to
those of the ancient Greeks, the models of the Romans.
The result had been a great outcrop of philosophical
inquiry, literature and art. Most of this was inspired
not by the old medieval desire to serve God but by a
passion to acquire knowledge and discover the truth.
This had many consequences that were good, but not
a few that were bad. It ended, for instance, much
ignorant superstition; but in breaking free from old
beliefs, many people also abandoned old standards of
right and wrong. The result was that while the Italian
Renaissance produced many brilliant and versatile
artists and scholars—men like Michelangelo and Leon-
ardo da Vinci, who were at once painters, sculptors,
poets, architects and engineers—it also produced many
very clever men like Benvenuto Cellini, whose lives
were as remarkable for their vices as for their talents.

Outside Italy the Renaissance took a somewhat dif- *The Renaissance in Northern Europe*
ferent form. It developed more slowly: by 1500 the
study of Greek in France and England was only just
beginning. Above all, the Renaissance in Northern

Europe was at first not so much literary or artistic as religious. In the Netherlands it produced the great scholar and writer Erasmus who, although a priest, desired to suppress monasteries, reduce the power of the clergy, and end the many abuses in the Church (such as bribery at papal elections). Typical of Erasmus's work was his edition of the New Testament in Greek—with a Latin translation which showed up the errors of the Vulgate, the traditional Latin version used by the Church. In Germany, where the invention of metal type had already done much to spread the study of religious writings, the Renaissance produced a much more violent figure in Martin Luther, whose attacks on scandals within the Church soon led to attacks against the whole authority of the Pope. And in England the Renaissance begot first, men like Dean Colet, the founder of St. Paul's School, and Sir Thomas More—ardent religious reformers who began the study of Greek in this country but like Erasmus remained true to the old religion—and then men like Cranmer, who went much further.

The Reformation: Luther and Cranmer

This, then, was the broad picture in 1500: the 'great powers' of France, Spain and Austria just emerging, and the ferment of the Renaissance about to give birth to the Reformation. Such was the scene when, in 1509, two new actors strode upon the European stage—Henry VIII and Thomas Wolsey.

CHAPTER FIVE

KING, CARDINAL, AND CHURCH
(1509–1517)

THE prince who succeeded to the English throne in 1509 was not quite eighteen years of age. "His Majesty", wrote an observer a little later, "is the handsomest potentate I ever set eyes on; above the usual height, with an extremely fine calf to his leg; his complexion fair and bright, with auburn hair combed straight and short in the French fashion, and a round face so beautiful that it would become a pretty woman. . . . He speaks French, English, Latin and a little Italian; plays well on the lute and harpsichord, sings from the book at sight, draws the bow with greater strength than any man in England, and jousts marvellously."

To this it must be added that his eyes were unpleasantly small and 'piggy'; that he was a notable wrestler and player of tennis; that he also spoke Spanish; and that his musical talents included playing the organ and composing. Indeed, he was so fond of music that he would listen to organ recitals for four hours on end. It is also on record that he was good-humoured and a fine scholar with a gift for engineering and a taste for theology. His personal bravery was shown by his love of tournaments and the chase. He was, too, sincerely religious, and heard, according to the Venetian ambassador, "three masses a day when he hunts, and sometimes five on other days". But with all this he combined other less agreeable qualities which emerged as the reign proceeded. Among these were extreme selfishness and a ruthlessness bordering on brutality.

The young king

Marriage
with
Catherine of
Aragon

One of Henry's first actions on coming to the throne was to marry his betrothed, Catherine of Aragon. Catherine, it will be remembered, was the widow of his brother Arthur, and the match with Henry had required, and received, the special permission of the Pope. The marriage at first strengthened the friendship with Spain and for a time pleased Henry. His bride, however, was six years older than himself, and since the details of public business failed to interest him, Henry's affections soon wandered. He became much given over, in the words of one report, to "girls and hunting", gambled heavily and wasted his father's painfully acquired treasure. Among other extravagances he spent huge sums on dress. But though pageantry and pleasure were the keynotes of the first years of his reign, the brilliant young king still retained full command of the situation. It suited him that the dull and laborious routine of government should rest in the hands of the able and energetic Wolsey, who if things went wrong could always be dismissed—or worse.

Thomas
Wolsey

The rise of Thomas Wolsey to fame and fortune was swift. The son of a well-to-do Ipswich cattle-dealer and butcher, Wolsey had entered what was then the one great avenue of promotion for those of middle or lowly birth—the Church. After appointments as tutor and chaplain he had passed into the service of Henry VII, where his outstanding talents and personality soon made their mark. Then Henry VIII became king and, to win popularity, promptly executed his father's over-grasping ministers Empson and Dudley. This cleared the field for new men—including Thomas Wolsey.

Henry's first
war against
France: the
'Holy
League'

Wolsey's first great tasks arose from war with France. True to the Spanish connection and a loyal son of the Church, Henry in 1511 joined a 'Holy League' (which included Spain, the Papacy and the Empire) to drive the French out of Italy, which they had again invaded.

For his part Henry agreed to revive the English claim to the French throne and send a force across to France—

CARDINAL   WOLSEY

Cardinal Wolsey

A contemporary picture by an unknown artist Note the spelling of the surname. Spelling was still very variable and remained so until the 18th century; possibly the record is held by John Shakespeare (father of William) whose name appears in the Council Book of Stratford in sixteen different forms.

though this would almost certainly bring the Scots down on England. Deserted by the Spaniards, Henry's first expedition was unsuccessful: but a second, organized by Wolsey with great skill, fared much better the

English expeditions to France, 1512–1513

Battle of
Spurs

following year. After winning the Battle of Spurs—so-called from the speed with which the enemy retreated—it went on to capture Tournai. Meanwhile the Scots tried to invade England. They were cut off in Northumberland by a force under the Earl of Surrey and utterly routed on the field of Flodden. King James IV, the flower of his nobility, and some 10,000 Scottish soldiers all perished.

Scottish
invasion of
England:
Flodden.
1513

As the invading French armies had also been driven out of Italy, France was by this time ready for peace. So too was Henry, who had now been abandoned by the Empire as well as Spain. Thanks to Wolsey, who conducted the negotiations, England secured excellent terms, including Tournai, increased annual payments, and an alliance with the late enemy. As a pledge of this new friendship Henry's sister Mary was married to the old and decrepit French king, Louis XII. Henry's first great foreign venture was thus safely over. It had ended with England showing Spain and the Empire that she, too, could keep a foot in either camp.

Peace with
France, 1514

Rise of
Wolsey

For his services during this war Wolsey received swift promotion from both King and Pope. Inside two years he became bishop of two great sees, Archbishop of York, and Abbot of St. Albans. All these great offices, with their huge revenues, piled up in his hands without his so much as visiting any of the places concerned. A year later the Pope made him a cardinal, and soon afterwards Henry appointed him Lord Chancellor—the most important post in the kingdom. By 1518, he was also papal legate in England and exercising in this country virtually the powers of the Pope himself.

Wolsey's
character

All this time and for many years afterwards Henry's confidence in Wolsey was complete.

All state affairs [wrote the Venetian ambassador] are managed by him, let their nature be what it may. He is thoughtful, and has the reputation of being extremely just; he favours the people exceedingly, and especially the poor, hearing their suits and seeking to despatch them instantly. He also makes the lawyers plead gratis for all poor suitors. He is in very great repute, seven times more so than if he were Pope.

Elsewhere, however, the same witness points out the dangerous growth of Wolsey's pride. At first, he explains, Wolsey would say "His Majesty will do so-and-so". Later he began to use the phrase "We shall do so-and-so". By 1519 he had reached the point of saying "I shall do so-and-so".

Wolsey held all the great clerical offices mentioned above, and several more, at one and the same time. For this he received special permission from the Pope. His pomp Soon his income was second only to that of the King, and his unique position in the state was marked by a vast outward show. His household numbered several hundred people, and included, according to George Cavendish (his gentleman usher), sixteen "singing men", sixteen chaplains, twelve "singing children", four counsellors "learned in the laws of the realm", and four minstrels. Like many rich men with a love of pomp and ceremony, he built huge and costly residences, of which York House (the later Whitehall Palace) and Hampton Court (which he tactfully presented to the King, while continuing to live there himself) are the best known.

Even Wolsey's movements through the streets were a daily scene of pageantry.

He ... would issue out [wrote Cavendish] ... apparelled all in red, in the habit of a cardinal; which was either of fine scarlet, or else of crimson satin ... holding in his hand a very fair orange, whereof the meat or substance within was taken out, and filled up again with the part of a sponge, wherein was vinegar and other confections against the pestilent airs; to the which he most commonly smelt unto, passing among the press, or else when he was

The Great Hall at Hampton Court

This magnificent hall was built by Henry VIII as soon as he took over the Palace from Wolsey. He was so anxious to have it finished that the work was done by candlelight as well as by day. Note the screens and gallery, the 16th century tapestries on the walls, the perpendicular windows, and the fine wooden 'hammer beams' and mouldings of the roof—also the elaborate pendants in the form of lanterns. On these appear the badges and initials of Anne Boleyn—but by the time the hall was finished she was beheaded and Jane Seymour occupied her place as Queen.

pestered with many suitors. There was also borne before him first, the great seal of England, and then his cardinal's hat, by a nobleman or some worthy gentleman, right solemnly, bare-headed . . . thus passing forth with two great crosses of silver borne before him; with also two great pillars of silver, and his pursuivant at arms with a great mace of silver-gilt. Then his gentlemen ushers cried and said "On, my lords and masters; make way for my Lord's Grace!" Thus he passed down from his chambers through the hall: and when he came to the hall door there was attendant for him, his mule, trapped all together in crimson velvet, and gilt stirrups. When he was mounted, with his Cross bearers, and pillar bearers, also upon great horses trapped with red scarlet, then marched he forward, with his train and furniture in manner as I have declared, having about him four foot-men, with gilt poleaxes in their hands; and thus he went until he came to Westminster Hall door.

This able and magnificent cleric was thus a pluralist (a man who held several appointments at the same time) and an absentee—the sole visit he made to one of his great offices was to York, in the last year of his life. Against all Church law he kept an unofficial 'wife'; and for the son who was born of this union he secured a parish at the age of ten and important offices in eight cathedrals before the boy had reached sixteen. Wolsey, then, besides being clever and hard-working, was rich, haughty, worldly, immoral, devoted to pomp and ceremony and absorbed in affairs of state as opposed to those of religion. Though a great churchman, he broke the most elementary teachings of the Church. And it was because Wolsey was far from alone in doing this that the Church, as a whole, was now coming under heavy fire. *His worldliness*

There were, however, other things besides wealth, worldliness and immorality for which would-be re-formers were now attacking the Church. One was the *Church customs under attack* resented privilege of 'benefit of clergy', by which many guilty parties were escaping without punishment. Another was the Church's power in matters of inheritance, and the heavy charges made for the probate of wills. Many thoughtful men were also disturbed by what they considered purely superstitious practices, including the undue reverence paid to often far from genuine 'relics'—garments and bones of the apostles, parts of the 'true cross' and the like. Such reverence was encouraged partly from reasons of piety, but also because round these relics had grown up a vast money-making business based on pilgrimages.

Doctrinal doubts Besides all this, there were bound to be doubts about important matters of doctrine—doubts sometimes expressed in an earlier generation by Wyclif and his Lollards. How much power, for instance, was—or should be—possessed by the priest, and how much by the greatest priest of all, the Pope? And should the supreme authority in the Church in fact be not the Pope but a General Council, if and when it could meet? Questions of this last sort were sharpened by the memory of the so-called 'Babylonish captivity' of the 14th **Position of the papacy**century, when the popes were at Avignon practically under the control of the king of France, and by the Great Schism (or split) which followed, when two, and at one time three, rival popes struggled for recognition. All told, what with doubts about doctrine, the zeal of the reformers, the growth of national feeling (which was bound to tell against an international organization like the Church) and the growth of criticism springing from the Renaissance, the Church's path in the 16th century was likely to be far from smooth.

Wolsey and Church reform To the need for reform in the Church Wolsey was quite alive. It was largely on the plea of carrying out reforms that he had managed to concentrate so much clerical authority in his own hands. Having obtained the power, however, Wolsey used it to enrich himself; and since he was the Pope's legate, this drew unpopularity on the papacy. His only notable reform was to dissolve some twenty of the most corrupt small monasteries, and to apply their revenues to purposes of education. It was typical of Wolsey that these included endowing his own old school at Ipswich and founding a new institution at Oxford to be known as Cardinal College. Posterity—and Henry VIII—however, proved unkind to his ambition: Cardinal College soon became known as Christ Church, and its founder is commemorated not in the name of the College but in that of 'Great Tom'—its biggest and loudest bell.

Drowning a Witch

From Holinshed's *Historie of Scotland*. The convicted witch is trussed up in a sack and thrown in a river.

CHAPTER SIX

MARTIN LUTHER,
THE STRUGGLE IN EUROPE,
AND THE FALL OF WOLSEY
(1517–1529)

COMPLAINTS against abuses in the Church in the early 16th century were not, of course, confined to England. They rang loudly throughout Europe. And it was not in England but in Germany The that words first gave place to actions—the actions that Reformation ushered in the Reformation.

The sale of indulgences

The crisis in Germany developed after 1514, when that country witnessed a widespread sale of indulgences. An indulgence was a withholding of punishment; and these particular indulgences were grants by the Pope, made for the living or the recently dead, professing to shorten the time spent by the erring soul in Purgatory before entering Paradise. Originally, a living person receiving an indulgence had been required not only to make an offering but also to undertake some severe form of penance or pilgrimage; but now the indulgences were frankly sold outright—or rather, if a penance was imposed, it took the form of a further cash payment. Such at least was the practice of the friar Tetzel, who in the course of a money-raising campaign was entrusted with the sale of indulgences in Germany.

Martin Luther

This gross abuse of spiritual power was attacked by many churchmen, and in 1517 Martin Luther, a monk of humble birth who taught in the university of Wittenberg in Saxony, made a courageous protest. He nailed to the door of All Saints' Church, in Wittenberg, ninety-

five 'theses', or arguments, against the sale of indul- Luther's
gences—arguments which he was prepared to uphold in ninety-five
theses, 1517
debate. A controversy then followed in which the
question soon shifted from indulgences to the whole
nature of the Pope's authority, and Luther was finally
driven into making statements which were violently
heretical, such as that the Pope was Antichrist. In
1520 the Pope therefore excommunicated him—placed Luther ex-
him, in other words, beyond the ministrations of the communicated, 1520
Church.

A frequent sequel of excommunication was the
burning of the heretic by the government, since the
Church itself could not inflict loss of life or limb. In this
case events of a very different kind occurred. When the
papal bull, or order, excommunicating him was re- Luther
ceived, Luther cast it into the flames of a ceremonial burns the
bull of ex-
bonfire at the gates of Wittenberg before a large crowd communi-
cation
of students—and with it went copies of documents used
to prove the supremacy of the Pope. Luther could do
this, and survive, only because the Elector of Saxony,
his ruling prince, disliked the flow of money from his
state to Rome and sympathized with Luther's views.

Luther's action in defying the Pope split German
opinion in twain. Many of the princes and their peoples
warmly supported his stand, but others as fiercely condemned it. By this time the controversy covered an
extremely wide field. The essence of the matter, however, from Luther's point of view lay in his newly Lutheran
proclaimed belief that the sole key to eternal life was beliefs:
(a) 'Justifi-
the individual's personal faith in God. Compared with cation
by Faith'
this vital personal conviction, he regarded all the good
works recommended by the priest—pilgrimages, candle-
burning, bead-telling and the like—as of much less
importance. This greatly reduced the part to be played
by the priest in acting between man and God. And
since man must have some final authority on this earth

(b) The authority of the Bible

to look to, he tended to substitute the authority of the Bible (which he soon translated into German) for that of priest and Pope.

Luther and the Emperor

Since his own prince favoured and sheltered him, Luther could only be suppressed by that prince's superior, the head of the Holy Roman Empire. And this superior, the Emperor Charles V, was now a ruler with an unequalled collection of territory. From one set of grandparents (Ferdinand and Isabella) he had inherited Spain, the Spanish possessions in the New World, Naples and Sicily; from his other set of grandparents (the Emperor Maximilian I and Mary of Burgundy) Austria and the other hereditary Habsburg lands nearby, the Free County of Burgundy, the Netherlands, and his claim to be elected head of the Holy Roman Empire. So huge a concentration of power in one pair of hands boded ill for France, and perhaps for England. It also promised little good to Martin Luther.

Charles V

Charles V had no sympathy with heresy, and soon resolved to crush Luther and his growing body of supporters. The Emperor, however, had many duties; Spain rather than Germany was the centre of his power —for he had quickly given over control of Austria and its associated lands to his younger brother Ferdinand— and his most pressing tasks were defence against the Turks and the struggle against France's new young king, Francis I, for the control of Italy. In both matters he needed the support of a united Germany, and so hesitated to take steps which would cause a German civil war. More than once, after favourable turns in his conflict with France, Charles got the Lutherans condemned by the majority of the German princes in the Imperial Diet—a decision against which in 1529 the minority issued a protest and so gave birth to the new term 'Protestant'. But because of his constant struggles against the French

Charles's many tasks —wars against Turks and French

and the Turks, it was not until the 1540s that Charles felt free to take actual military measures against the Lutheran princes. By that time Lutheranism was too strong to be crushed, and the only result was some years of warfare from which Germany emerged more or less permanently divided between Catholic and Protestant.

Meanwhile in Zurich another and more extreme reformer, the pastor Ulrich Zwingli, had plunged the Swiss Federation into similar discord. Going beyond Luther, Zwingli denounced not merely the supremacy of Rome, the ban on clerical marriage, the monastic vows, the use of Latin in the services, and other things to which the German had objected, but also the basic Catholic belief that Christ is miraculously and bodily present in the consecrated bread and wine at the celebration of the Lord's Supper. For Zwingli this celebration became simply a very holy service of commemoration, but for Luther (although he departed somewhat from the strict Catholic view) it remained a miracle. This difference of opinion prevented the two great reformers ever reaching agreement, and their movements continued in separate directions. By 1531, when Lutheran reform was well established in about half the states of Germany and was spreading through Scandinavia, Zwingli's agitation had brought the Swiss cantons to the point of civil war. In that year Zwingli himself fell in battle; and from the struggle Switzerland, like Germany, emerged divided in faith. Here again Charles V could not intervene in time to nip the reforming movement in the bud.

Charles powerless to suppress Protestantism

Germany split between Catholic and Protestant

Zwingli and Switzerland

*   *   *   *   *

The wars between Francis I and Charles V thus helped to save Protestantism at birth. Meanwhile, where did England stand in the conflict between the two young monarchs?

Henry VIII
supports
Charles V
against
Francis I
At first, Henry VIII and Wolsey supported Charles—though only with money. Their reasons were fairly clear. Charles not only controlled the Netherlands (the great foreign market for English wool), but was also the nephew of Catherine of Aragon and had promised to help Wolsey become Pope; France on the other hand was England's traditional enemy. Nevertheless when a new phase of the conflict was opening, Henry and Wolsey were not above negotiating with France—possibly to bring home to Charles that he must pay a high price for England's friendship. So came about the

Negotiation
with France
—Field of
Cloth of
Gold, 1520
famous ceremonial visit of Henry and Wolsey to Francis in 1520—the Field of Cloth of Gold. The festivity, so called from the rich display of this material and the general lavishness of the entertainment, produced several days of feasting; but at the end of it England remained uncommitted to France.

Having made it clear that they were prepared to bargain with his enemy, Henry and Wolsey went on to meet Charles near Calais in a strictly business encounter. They came to terms, and soon afterwards made a full

Alliance with
Charles, 1521
military alliance. By now Henry and Wolsey had yet another point of sympathy with the Emperor—for

Henry's
treatise
against
Luther
Henry and Wolsey both disapproved violently of Luther and about this time Henry completed a treatise ('A Defence of the Seven Sacraments') opposing the German reformer's views. For this the papacy awarded

Henry
'Defender of
the Faith'
Henry the title 'Defender of the Faith'—which continues to be inscribed on our coins even if the faith is no longer that which the Pope had in mind.

Henry's
second war
against
France,
1522-1524
Entry into the renewed fighting between Charles and Francis brought England no gains. Two English expeditions to France were forced to retire; the Scots as usual crossed the border; and despite the deaths of two Popes, Charles made no effort to fulfil his promise to Wolsey. The result was that the enthusiasm of Henry and

Wolsey for Charles soon cooled, and in 1524 England England
withdrew from the conflict. This proved to be just too deserts
Charles, 1524
soon; for the next year Charles's forces utterly defeated
Francis at Pavia, in North Italy, and took him prisoner. Pavia, 1525
By deserting Charles England had lost any claim to
consideration, and the Emperor now stood supreme in
Europe.

This supremacy was soon felt by the Pope, who just
before the fatal battle of Pavia had changed sides and
joined France. In 1527 a starving and unpaid section
of Charles's troops entered Rome and sacked it with Sack of
Rome, 1527
brutal ferocity. From then on the Pope was as good as a
prisoner—and a more and more compliant one—in the
Emperor's hands.

All this had a big effect on events in England. Among Effects on
England of
other things the war led to taxes which cost Henry some Charles's
of his popularity and added to the feeling against success
Wolsey. Far and away the main result of Charles's
success, however, was that it dashed to the ground
Henry's hopes of freeing himself from Catherine of
Aragon.

For some time now Henry had been convinced that Henry's
desire
he must marry again. The reason for this was not mere for a son
desire for a change of partners—which he could have
had (and did) outside marriage. The deciding fact was
that Henry had no male heir, for though Catherine had
borne him many children, none had survived birth
except one girl—Mary. But no queen had ever yet Princess
ruled in England, with the single exception of the Mary
attempt by Henry I's daughter, Matilda; and the long
years of civil war which then occurred only went to
show that a female ruler usually meant disorder.[1]

[1] This was partly because a very strong hand was needed to control
the many violent characters of the times: partly because a female ruler
must either remain unmarried (which probably meant a disputed succession), or else take unto herself a husband who would have the usual
views of the time about the dominance of the male, etc. etc.

Henry VIII Embarking at Dover

From a picture at Hampton Court by an unknown artist. It gives an excellent idea of the warships of the time. The King,

Henry VIII in Middle Life

This picture is one of many versions painted after an original by the famous German artist Hans Holbein the Younger (who spent long periods in England—and died there—during the latter part of Henry VIII's reign). It gives an unforgettable study of an immensely powerful and dominating figure. The effect is heightened by the built-out shoulders, a fashion in men's clothes at the time.

Henry was quite determined to avoid the evils of a disputed succession; his only means of doing so, however, was to leave behind him a son—and a son born within the bounds of matrimony. He had been thinking on these lines for many years, and convincing himself that the death of his children was a divine proof that he should never have been allowed to marry Catherine. By 1526 Catherine was over forty years of age and unlikely to bear further offspring. Henry resolved to wait

Henry seeks annulment of marriage with Catherine

no longer. Through Wolsey he asked the Pope to declare that the permission given earlier was invalid, and that in the eyes of the Church he had never married. This the Pope, Clement VII, would willingly have done—it was usual to gratify royalty in these matters—but by 1527 Clement was no longer a free agent. As a virtual prisoner of Charles V he had to do what he was told; and Charles, unwilling to see his aunt (and Spanish in-

Charles V forbids annulment

fluence in London) set aside, and Wolsey's influence established at Rome, had forbidden the annulment.

For two years, however, the door was not quite shut in Henry's face. The Pope resented the power of Charles; and Henry had always been a loyal son of the Church. With the idea of freeing Clement from his

English alliance with France, 1528

dependence on the Emperor, in 1528 Wolsey allied England with France. This kept Henry's request alive, by enabling the Pope to play for time until he saw whether the French could now beat Charles. Clement even

Campeggio and Wolsey to try the case in England

went so far as to allow a legate, Cardinal Campeggio, to proceed to England—though in leisurely fashion —to try Henry's case with Wolsey. But by the time the case opened, the French army in Italy, as Clement had shrewdly anticipated, was shattered: Charles was

Defeat of French by forces of Charles V in Italy, 1529

stronger than ever, and the Pope must bow to his wishes. On papal orders the hearing in London was adjourned. Soon afterwards the Pope summoned Henry and Catherine to appear before him in Rome. Of all monarchs, Henry VIII was not the man to obey this order; nor did Clement expect him to. It was merely a way of saying that the Pope did not see his way free to annul the marriage. Case recalled to Rome

The alliance with France had been fruitless, and Wolsey now had to pay the price of failure. His foreign policy, successful at first, had ended by allowing Charles to become too strong; Charles had forbidden the annulment; and Henry was out for blood. A few weeks after the case was recalled to Rome, Wolsey was stripped of most of his offices. Departing from the Court he resolved to visit his long-neglected diocese of York. There he proved unable to resist the temptation of again negotiating with France. In 1530 he was accused of treason and summoned south. Only his death on the way at Leicester—repenting, if legend is true, that he had not expended his zeal in the service of God rather than the king—saved him from a still more dramatic and painful end in London. Failure and disgrace of Wolsey His death, 1530

CHAPTER SEVEN

THE BREAK WITH ROME
(1529–1536)

Reformation
Parliament,
1529–1536

WITHIN a few days of hearing that his case was summoned to Rome Henry decided to call a parliament. Usually known as the Reformation Parliament, it lasted far longer (in and out of session) than any previous parliament in English history. When its members first gathered together, England was still a fully Catholic country. When they separated for the last time, every link with Rome was broken.

Henry's reasons for calling parliament

The decision to call parliament showed Henry's skill as a ruler. Parliaments were usually summoned because the king wanted money; but on this occasion Henry had a different motive. What he now needed above all was support. For if he could range behind him the full force of the dislike which many of his subjects bore to foreigners and priests, he might perhaps compel the Pope after all to annul the marriage with Catherine.

First reforms

With this in mind, Henry first encouraged parliament to pass Acts against recognized scandals in the Church, including clerical non-residence, plural livings, and the very high fees charged for funerals and the probate of wills. Having attracted popular support and shown the clergy which way the wind was blowing, the king then waited while his agents consulted the universities of Europe about the validity of his marriage with Catherine. This move had been suggested by Thomas Cranmer, a cleric who in his early days had been one of a group of young reformers around Erasmus at Cam-

The universities consulted

Cranmer

(48)

bridge, and who was now marked out for the King's favour. It turned out that the universities, however, held differing opinions about the case—which was scarcely surprising.

Disappointed in this, Henry then took stronger measures. First he bullied the clergy into paying a large fine for alleged misuse of their authority in Church courts. He also forced them to recognize royal control over all Church law-making. Then—with the bishops in the House of Lords well subdued—he put through parliament the Act of Annates. This drastically reduced the annates or 'first fruits' payable to the Pope when a bishop or abbot was appointed to his post: instead of the whole of the first year's income, only five per cent of it was to go to Rome. The Act was not to come into force for a year. The Pope, in other words, was given the choice of dissolving the marriage with Catherine or losing much of his revenue from England. *Act of Annates, 1532*

Pope Clement, however, was still in the power of Charles V. So he ignored the threat, and the deadlock continued. It was broken by a new and critical development. For three or four years Henry had been passionately in love with Anne Boleyn, a lady of his court. Towards the end of 1532 she became pregnant, and Henry resolved that he must wed her with all speed in order that the child—their child—should be born within the bounds of marriage. For if only he and Anne were legally husband and wife, this infant might prove the longed-for heir to the English throne. *The Pope unmoved* *Anne Boleyn*

There was no time to lose. If the Pope would not set aside the marriage with Catherine, Henry must achieve the same result in some other way—though one which his subjects would accept. And a way was now open. The old Archbishop of Canterbury had died and the place was vacant for the compliant Cranmer—if the Pope would agree. The Pope, anxious not to offend

Henry more than was necessary, did agree. Meantime, Henry secretly married Anne. This done, there were but two steps more to take. In April 1533 there was passed through parliament an Act forbidding appeals in Church cases to be taken to Rome. This left the way clear for the King's case against Catherine to be heard by his new archbishop. In May, Cranmer duly reopened the proceedings in England, declared the marriage with Catherine null and void, and recognized the union with Anne Boleyn. On June 1st, in Westminster Abbey, he anointed and crowned Anne Queen of England.

Cranmer archbishop: Henry marries Anne

Act restraining appeals, 1533

Cranmer grants annulment

Henry need not have hurried. The child, born in September, turned out to be only another girl—if such a phrase may be used of someone who later became Queen Elizabeth I. There was still the prospect, however, that the disappointed parents would later have a boy. Meanwhile it was only too obvious that Henry had burnt his boats. Declaring the proceedings under Cranmer completely invalid, the Pope excommunicated both King and Archbishop.

Birth of Elizabeth, 1533

Henry and Cranmer excommunicated

This did not halt Henry, who plunged ahead along his chosen path. By a series of swift measures in 1534 he soon completed the process of breaking with Rome and of making himself, instead of the Pope, the master of the English Church. The change was summed up in a final Act of Supremacy declaring Henry the "only Supreme Head on earth of the Church of England".

Act of Supremacy, 1534: Henry 'Supreme Head' of the Church

All these measures went through parliament with very little opposition. This was partly because they were known to be the will of a ruthless monarch, and partly because they reflected the feelings of the Commons and most of the lay Lords. But it was also because parliament was handled with supreme skill by Thomas Cromwell, a layman who after travelling widely as a merchant and lawyer had taken service with Wolsey and was now the King's secretary. From 1532 onwards

Thomas Cromwell

Cromwell's hand had shaped all the big measures put through parliament. Convinced that the interests of England demanded a strong central authority free from foreign interference and supreme over the Church

Thomas Cromwell

This portrait, a copy of one by Holbein, shows us the hard eyes, tight lips and firm jaw of a man of great ruthlessness and power. The gown and cap are those of a Doctor of Law. The handsome volume on the table, with the jewelled binding and clasps, is presumably a Bible—the translation of which Cromwell did much to encourage.

as well as all else, he saw that this could be built up only by the Crown acting in co-operation with parliament. Apart from the 'popular' aspect of parliament, parliamentary statutes alone could give the force of law to the many great changes required, and parliamentary

statutes alone could lay down penalties—death and
dismemberment—fierce enough to silence opponents.
This co-operation on the part of parliament Cromwell
secured not only by giving the Commons work after
their own heart, like the laws against Rome, but also
by sitting himself as a Member of the House and by
seeing that 'reliable' persons were elected to fill
vacancies.

Though the great majority of England's leading
men, including the bishops, accepted all these changes
quietly enough, some proved ready to defend the old
order even at the cost of their lives. In 1535 the heads of
two great monasteries, together with two other monks,
were hanged, drawn and quartered (the usual punishment for high treason) for denying the King his new
title of Supreme Head of the Church. All four were
executed in their monastic dress—an unheard-of action.
A few weeks later the scaffold claimed two victims
of greater fame—John Fisher, the aged Bishop of
Rochester, and Sir Thomas More, who had reluctantly
accepted the Chancellorship on the fall of Wolsey but
soon resigned. Both had championed Catherine; both
had refused to take an oath to an Act which (in fixing
the succession on Anne Boleyn's children) denied the
Pope's supremacy and declared that the marriage with
Catherine had been null and void from the start.

The death of these two men scandalized Europe.
Fisher was a man of saintly character and a cardinal—
an honour rashly conferred on him by the Pope during
his imprisonment (it so angered Henry that he vowed
to send Fisher's head to Rome to save the Pope sending
the cardinal's hat to England). More, the author of the
famous book *Utopia* describing an imaginary island with
a 'perfect' social system, was perhaps the most remarkable combination of saint, scholar, family man and wit
ever known in England. So keen was his sense of

*The first
Catholic
martyrs*

*John Fisher
Sir Thomas
More*

humour that it lasted to the very moment of his death.
The executioner was about to strike when More sig-
nalled for a brief delay while he moved aside his beard.
"Pity that should be cut," he murmured, "that has
not committed treason." "With which strange words",
comments the historian Froude, "the strangest, perhaps,
ever uttered at such a time, the lips most famous through
Europe for eloquence and wisdom closed for ever."

*   *   *   *   *

Thus far Henry had set up his own authority over the
English Church in place of the Pope's and had taken
for the Crown far more clerical money than had ever
gone to Rome. He had not, however, otherwise interfered with the religious life of the nation. Now, prompted
by Cromwell, he was to strike a blow which would be
felt throughout the land. His new object of attack was
nothing less than the monasteries, which with their
agriculture and their almsgiving were closely bound up
with the life of the people. *Next object of attack— the monasteries*

There were three main ideas behind the attack on the
monasteries. In the first place, monasteries were nearly
all exempt from control by the local bishop and owed
their allegiance either to the head of their order in
England or else direct to Rome. This meant that their
old habits of obedience to the Pope might persist.
Secondly—and most important—they were in many
cases very wealthy and a tempting subject for plunder.
Thirdly, monasticism was no longer the great force it
had been in the Middle Ages; many monks were idle
or worldly, and in a few monasteries there was serious
vice and corruption. This last fact had been noted by
many people before Henry and Cromwell. But now, of
course, it became the official excuse for all that followed. *Henry's motives*

In 1535, Cromwell, who had become Vicar-General
or deputy for the king in religious affairs, appointed *Investi- gation of monasteries*

commissioners to look into conditions in the smaller monasteries. These men knew what was wanted of them. At the end of four months (a time so short as to rule out all possibility of careful investigation) they declared their work done. Acting on their reports, which painted life in the monasteries in the blackest colours, in 1536 Cromwell put through parliament an Act which dissolved nearly four hundred of the smaller monasteries and declared their property forfeit to the Crown. Within three years the larger monasteries were to follow the same way.

Dissolution.
1536-1539

The dissolution of the monasteries was carried through with great ruthlessness. Those heads of houses who tried to oppose the King's policy received short shrift—the abbot of Glastonbury, for example, was hanged within sight of his own monastery. There was also much senseless destruction. Not only was plate and jewellery instantly seized, but buildings were torn down (usually by some local purchaser) for the sake of their stone or the valuable lead on their roofs, and priceless manuscripts were trodden underfoot or burnt by peasants ignorant of their worth. On the other hand, the monks who submitted quietly—all except a handful —were given pensions, and many were appointed to other positions in the Church. So passed away, amid scenes of plunder and terror, one of the most characteristic features of medieval England.

Resistance

Though the monks themselves could offer little resistance, their cause was taken up outside the monastery walls. During 1536 the North of England—where the King's power was weakest—became aflame with a movement known as the Pilgrimage of Grace. Many causes entered in, such as the people's dislike of enclosures—the fencing-in by wealthy landlords of parts of the old open fields and commons—and the North's resentment at increasing control from London. In the

Pilgrimage
of Grace,
1536

main, however, this was a protest against recent religious changes and especially against the dissolution of the monasteries.

The main leader of the movement was Robert Aske, Robert Aske a brave and able Yorkshire country gentleman and lawyer. Inspired by him and bearing crosses, the pilgrims, as they called themselves, took possession of York, Hull, Lancaster and several other towns. No rebel by nature, Aske avoided a clash with the nearest royal troops, even though these were at first heavily out-numbered, and contented himself instead with securing favourable promises from the King's general. The pilgrims then dispersed, whereupon the King began to garrison the North, with the result that in 1537 some of the more rash disregarded Aske's advice and took up arms again. This enabled the King to crush the rebels Revival of and repudiate previous promises with a good conscience. movement, The affair then ended with the seizure and execution of Aske and several other leaders, including the abbot of Execution Jervaulx, together with some two hundred of the rank of Aske and file. The dissolution of the remaining monasteries followed as a matter of course.

With the collapse of the Pilgrimage of Grace there ended the one serious challenge to Henry's policy. He had proved himself strong enough not only to break off the Church's allegiance to Rome and plunder the monasteries but also to ride out the storm which followed. The union with Anne Boleyn, however, failed to give him what he so badly wanted. Two more children were born after Elizabeth, but both too pre-maturely to live. By the end of 1535 Henry was plainly tired of Anne and equally plainly in love with Jane Jane Seymour, a lady of royal descent who had been care- Seymour fully drilled by her relatives to permit no approaches by the King short of marriage.

The death of Catherine in 1536 and the premature

Men Hanged from a Cart

A frequent method of execution: the cart drove away and the men were left swinging. From Holinshed's *Historie of Scotland*.

A Flogging through the Streets

Note the execution in the distance, the heavily cobbled street, the whip of several knotted thongs, and the very pleased expression of the prosperous looking gentleman on the extreme right. From Holinshed's *Historie of Scotland*.

SOME CAUSES OF THE REFORMATION IN ENGLAND

birth of Anne's third child on the day of Catherine's funeral sealed Anne's fate: if Anne as well as Catherine were dead there could be no questioning the legality of a new marriage. Within a few weeks Anne found herself on trial for her life. The charge was adultery, which, when the injured husband was the king, ranked as high treason. The evidence would not have convinced a modern British jury, but Anne's arrogant behaviour had made her unpopular, and the court of peers knew what Henry wanted. Unanimously they declared the Queen—and her five alleged lovers—guilty. On Tower Green Anne then showed that if there were faults in her life, at least she knew how to die.

Execution of Anne Boleyn, 1536

The day after Anne's execution Henry became betrothed to Jane Seymour and before the month was out they were married. A little over a year later Henry's longing for a son was at last gratified. The boy, christened Edward, soon proved to be far from strong, and within two or three weeks of his birth his mother died. But at least there was now an heir to the throne; and since the death of Jane had left Henry free to marry yet again, further princes might still be born in the royal line. Henry might rest at last for the moment content. He had what he wanted, a son and successor. Not in vain had he severed the links with Rome.

Marriage with Jane Seymour

Birth of Edward, death of Queen Jane, 1537

CHAPTER EIGHT

THE PROBLEMS OF
HENRY VIII'S LAST YEARS

(1537–1547)

ONCE he had a male heir (and firm control over the Church) Henry's greatest worry was ended. But he had still to face many problems. Among these were how to check the growth of Protestant doctrine, how to preserve his realm against Charles V and Francis I, and how to make ends meet in a time of rising prices.

Henry's objects, 1537–1547

In religious doctrine Henry had never wanted change. He disliked the ideas of Luther and it was not from any religious reasons that he had broken away from Rome. Having done so, he desired to keep England Catholic, so to speak, without the Pope. But at the same time, he would have to allow alterations to please those who now disbelieved in parts of the Catholic faith—for such men would prove his strongest supporters against Rome.

These alterations, which were made on the advice of Cromwell and Cranmer, mostly took the form of a greater use of the native tongue. This would naturally be popular at a time, as this was, of growing national feeling; but it would be supported more by those who wanted people to think afresh for themselves than by those who wanted people to accept without question the old authority of priest and Church. Those of Reforming or Protestant sympathies would press for a Bible and a service in English; those who put their faith

Concessions to Reformers

in traditional authority would strive to retain the Latin.[1]

In this matter Henry was prepared to approve change. Between 1537 and 1544 he permitted the intro-

An English Bible and English prayers duction of English prayers for part of the service, the printing of a Bible in English, and the setting up of a Great Bible (so called from the size of the page) in every church. Readings aloud and sermons in English were also encouraged. This, however, and a readiness to

Removal of relics remove sacred relics and images—particularly if they were valuable ones—was about as far as Henry was prepared to go.

Act of Six Articles, 1539 In 1539, in an attempt to stop the growing split into two religious parties, Henry came down heavily in favour of the traditionalists. The Act of Six Articles, passed against the wishes of Cranmer and Cromwell, listed six points of doctrine which all were required to accept. Among these were that priests must remain unmarried (Cranmer, who had taken a wife, was compelled to put her away): that all must attend confession: and that in the celebration of the Lord's Supper the substance of the bread and wine became miraculously changed into that of the body and blood of Christ.[2] This last belief—known as the *Real Presence* of Christ in the sacrament—was at the very heart of the Catholic creed; for it implies that the priest can achieve things impossible to ordinary men, and so supports the

Death for denying doctrine of Real Presence whole idea of a priestly authority. And by the Act of Six Articles the punishment for denying this doctrine was death at the stake.

---

[1] The term Protestant did not come into popular use in England until the reign of Edward VI. In the time of Henry VIII those whom we now think of as Protestants would have been known, according to circumstances, as Reformers, Lutherans, Men of the New Learning, or heretics.

[2] This occurred, according to the medieval philosophers, through *transubstantiation*, i.e. a change in the essential substance, or nature, of the bread and wine, but not in their outward properties.

Though Henry was in general anxious to preserve the old beliefs he was sometimes forced to look for support to the Reformers. This also applied in foreign affairs. In 1538 Charles V and Francis concluded a truce, which meant that either or both of them might be tempted to settle scores with England. To meet this danger Cromwell urged Henry to ally with a league of German princes, mostly Protestant, which had been formed to resist the Emperor. The outward sign of this alliance, Cromwell suggested, should be a marriage between Henry and the Princess Anne of Cleves (a small state in North Germany). Henry, who preferred to choose his brides personally, objected, but his reluctance was overcome after special messengers, possibly anxious to please Cromwell, had reported favourably on Anne's beauty. A portrait by Holbein also proved reasonably pleasing, and the match was arranged. *Truce between Charles V and Francis I, 1538*

Henry allies with German princes and marries Anne of Cleves, 1539

When Anne arrived in England Henry took an instant dislike to her appearance. He went through the ceremony, but he was soon wondering how he could get rid of a bride whom he likened to a "Flanders mare". His anxiety was sharpened still further when he fell in love with the youthful Catherine Howard, niece of the Duke of Norfolk. Since Norfolk was a leader of the strict Catholic party and one of Cromwell's main opponents, Cromwell did not move very swiftly to secure yet a third annulment for Henry. This soon aroused his master's wrath. Hated by the Church, by the old nobility, and by his fellow-members of the council, Cromwell, for all his services and ability, was one of the most unpopular men in the country. All that Henry had to do was to toss him, so to speak, to his enemies, who quickly passed through parliament an Act declaring him guilty of heresy and treason. *Failure of marriage.*

Execution of Cromwell

The day that witnessed Cromwell's death also saw Henry married for the fifth time—to Catherine Howard. *Henry marries Catherine Howard*

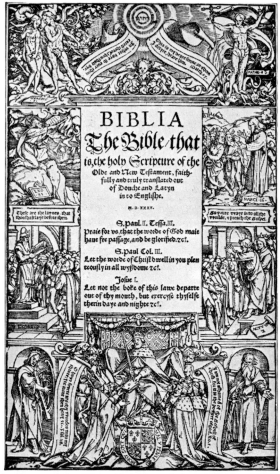

Title Page of the First Complete Printed Bible in English

This shows the finely engraved title page of Miles Coverdale's translation published in 1535. Scenes from the Old Testament appear on the left and from the New Testament on the right. At the bottom, between David on the left and St. Peter on the right, the King presents the Bible to his bishops and peers (though this version was never adopted officially). Coverdale was one of the Cambridge group who became extreme Protestants: he fled abroad in the later years of Henry VIII, became a bishop under Edward VI, went into exile again under Mary and returned once more under Elizabeth.

A week or so earlier Anne of Cleves, accepting her situation with good sense, had agreed that her marriage should be declared void, and had retired to the country generously pensioned off. All this Henry could do because Charles and Francis had already shown signs of falling out.

To ward off the danger from these two great rivals, Henry had meanwhile been creating a strong Royal Navy.[1] His interest in naval affairs dated back many years. Already as a young man he had designed ships, encouraged the planting of timber, made the Navy a permanent force and given it a proper organization under a Navy Board, founded Trinity House for the training and organization of pilots and the maintenance of navigation lights, and built new dockyards at Deptford and Woolwich. His enthusiasm in the early years of his reign may be seen from a description by a French envoy, who records how the whole English court went to see the launching of a new ship, and how Henry himself "acted as pilot and wore a sailor's coat and trousers, made of cloth of gold, and a gold chain with the inscription 'Dieu est mon droit', to which was suspended a whistle, which he blew nearly as loud as a trumpet".

Above all, Henry had early realized that the future lay with warships built for sails and artillery, not with warships built for oars and grappling. This idea he had already embodied in vessels armed with light guns in the built-up castles fore and aft. During his struggle with the Pope, he had paid less attention to naval affairs; but now, with the danger of war against Charles or Francis looming ahead, he again gave close thought to the defences of his country. New and slimmer ships appeared, armed with *heavy* guns peering from portholes in the sides of the hull, and so able to fire deadly *broadsides*

Henry and the Royal Navy

Measures for defence

[1] He inherited half a dozen warships and left about ninety.

into the enemy. Coastal forts, too, were built—some from the stones of dissolved monasteries—and many other measures taken against possible invasion.

*   *   *   *   *

In 1542 the situation eased when Charles and Francis once more began fighting. This prompted Henry to attack Scotland—for since Flodden Scottish power had revived, and the king, James V, refused to give up his alliance with France. The English expedition, however, had to turn back with little accomplished. Encouraged by this, a large but very disunited Scottish army then invaded England, only to suffer a crushing disaster in the western border country at Solway Moss. For the loss of seven English soldiers, hundreds of Scots were taken prisoner. The news proved fatal to James V, who died a few days afterwards, leaving as his successor, Mary, Queen of Scots—a child one week old.

This great victory then tempted Henry to continue the war until the Scots should agree to betroth their infant Queen to his young son Edward, and to accept the English king in due course as their ruler. The result was a long and indecisive struggle in the course of which Henry also declared war against Scotland's ally, France. During this, Henry's fleet showed its worth by defeating the French in the Channel after they had landed a small force in the Isle of Wight.

These wars cost an immense sum by the standards of the day. Apart from wastefulness, prices were rising sharply, and during his closing years Henry had to go to great lengths to raise funds. In the last seven years of his reign he required parliament to vote more in direct taxation than in the first thirty. Also the Crown began selling the newly acquired monastic lands—at no very high price, since they came on to the market in large quantities. The sale, however, had another result doubtless intended

Charles and
Francis at
war again:
English
attack
Scotland

Solway Moss,
1542

Mary, Queen
of Scots

Henry's
third war
against
France

Henry's
financial
worries

Taxes from
parliament

Sale of
monastic
lands

by Henry—the new owners would certainly support him against any attempt to re-establish the monasteries!

To these ways of recouping the royal fortunes Henry added a third—the debasement of the coinage. The coinage was not at that date a 'token' one, as it is today; it was a coinage in which the value of the gold or silver used was supposed almost to equal the face value of the coin. Already Wolsey had slightly reduced the weight of the silver coins; and now, in the last five years of the reign, Henry's government introduced a high proportion of base metal—more than fifty per cent— into a large part of the silver coinage. The immediate gain was twofold: the government created more money to spend and also kept some of the silver. In the long run, however, the debasement caused more problems than it solved. Above all, it quickly led to a great increase in prices—for when money itself is less valuable, people selling goods demand more of it, i.e. a higher price, for their wares. Very soon, then, the Crown was harder up than ever, as the increased prices sent Henry's expenditure soaring far beyond his normal revenue. *(Debasement of coinage)* *(Leads to higher prices)*

This bad effect was felt not only by the King but by many of his people. Everywhere those earning low wages or depending on fixed rents found themselves hard hit by the rise in prices. Landlords, for instance, found that to keep their old standard of living they had to raise rents and increase inheritance payments— where the law permitted—and work their own demesne in more profitable ways than before. In the corn-growing Midlands, in particular, the landlord's answer to his difficulties often took the form of enclosing some of his plough-land and turning it into pasture for sheep farming. This cost him less in labour, yet at the same time brought him good prices from the sale of wool—for the cloth trade, particularly to the Netherlands, was now flourishing as never before. *(Effects of price rise: (a) Increased rents, etc. (b) More enclosure for sheep farming (c) Boom in cloth trade)*

The boom in the cloth trade and the growth of enclosures for sheep farming threw many rural workers out of employment. In thousands of cases it also cost them their homes, either for lack of work or because some landlords did not scruple to enclose groups of cottages with the rest of the sheep run. In the worst affected area, the Midlands—where perhaps almost a third of the old open cornfields were enclosed during the Tudor period—many scores of villages disappeared entirely, leaving the unfortunate inhabitants to roam the countryside in search of food or work. A number of separate but closely related things—the debasement, the rise in prices and rents, the growth of the cloth trade, the enclosure of estates for sheep farming—thus produced, besides their better results, a great amount of distress. Together with the dismissal of retainers and monastic servants, all these things helped to create the vagrants known at the time as 'sturdy beggars'. These were sturdy because they were not afflicted by old age or infirmity; they were beggars because there was as yet no system of poor relief or of finding work for the unemployed.

Besides these far-reaching social changes, the reign of Henry VIII (which is usually remembered for the King's religious—and matrimonial—changes) also saw important advances towards the unification of the British Isles. In Ireland, English control increased— and Henry assumed the title of king. Much more important was Henry's treatment of Wales. He abolished the privileged and troublesome lordships in the Marches, and from 1536 extended English laws, justice and county organization to cover all Wales. From the same date, Welsh counties and county boroughs began to send representatives to parliament at Westminster. As regards institutions, if not habits and feeling, England and Wales were now fused into one country.

(d) Rural unemployment

Sturdy beggars

Ireland and Wales

Meanwhile the monarch himself became less and less
attractive as the years went on. His body grew bloated
and diseased. A perpetual ulcer in his leg gave him
dreadful pain. The blood of another Queen stained his

Henry VIII Towards the End of his Reign

From an engraving by Cornelius Matsys. Showing the
King in all his hard, calculating ruthlessness, this was
published just after Henry's death.

hands: Catherine Howard was beheaded on charges
similar to those made against Anne Boleyn. All the
tact and charm of her successor, the twice-widowed
Catherine Parr, were needed to make the final total of
royal wives no more than six.

Picts and Irish hunting the Stag

A favourite pastime among the English as well! From a wood-cut in Holinshed's
Historie of Scotland.

Eating in Camp

From Holinshed's *Historie of Scotland.* Female camp-followers cook for the soldiers.

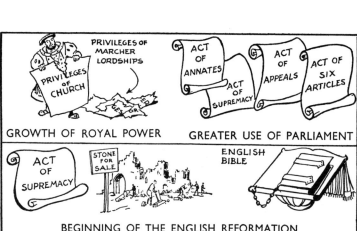

GROWTH OF ROYAL POWER   GREATER USE OF PARLIAMENT

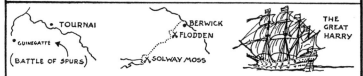

BEGINNING OF THE ENGLISH REFORMATION

WARS WITH FRANCE AND SCOTLAND DEVELOPMENT OF NAVY

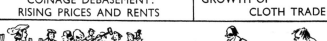

COINAGE DEBASEMENT: GROWTH OF
RISING PRICES AND RENTS   CLOTH TRADE

SPREAD OF ENCLOSURE AND VAGRANCY

SOME FEATURES OF HENRY VIII'S REIGN

Whatever the defects in Henry's character and whatever the merits of his action in breaking with Rome, there can be no doubt that his reign bears the stamp of greatness. The building up of the royal power, including the establishment of royal control over the Church and the Marches: the attempt to bring Scotland, Ireland and Wales within the English system: the use of parliament and the care taken to preserve good relations between Crown and Commons: the creation of a big Navy and the wresting of control over the Channel from foreign hands—all these were developments of vital importance for the future. It is notable, too, that in a reign of nearly forty years teeming with changes of every kind there should have been no popular attempt to overthrow the monarch, and only one serious attempt to challenge his policy. Though his military resources were slender, Henry not only held his throne secure but also greatly increased the strength and fame of his country. With all his faults, and despite all the religious upheaval of his reign, he gave to England what she most needed at the time—a government powerful enough to be respected by every class of citizen in every corner of the land.

Henry's achievements

CHAPTER NINE

EDWARD VI AND THE GROWTH OF PROTESTANTISM

(1547–1553)

1. *Protector Somerset*

EDWARD VI was only nine years old when he came to the throne. By the terms of his father's will, government was entrusted to a council. But one of Edward's uncles—a brother of Jane Seymour—soon managed to become Lord Protector, or Regent, and to overshadow his fellow-councillors. Until his fall two years later this nobleman, now created Duke of Somer- set, was king in all but name.

Somerset Protector

Though vain and ambitious, the Lord Protector was also brave, attractive, humane, and well-meaning. Unlike many of his fellow landowners, he was sincerely anxious to limit the hardships inflicted in some parts of the country by enclosure. In religion he favoured Protestantism, but had no desire to persecute opponents.

One of the first incidents of Somerset's rule was a further clash with Scotland. Somerset decided to enforce Henry VIII's demand, accepted by the Scots but not carried out, that the young Scottish Queen, Mary, should be married to Edward. Leading an expedition into Scotland he won an overwhelming victory at Pinkie, in Midlothian. His force, however, was not strong enough to make the enemy come to terms; all it could do was to pillage the countryside and make the Scots more determined than ever to resist English rule. The result was that they soon made a

Scotland

Pinkie, 1547

treaty with the French instead: Mary was to marry the Dauphin and the thrones of France and Scotland were to be united. A French ship then picked up Mary from the west coast of Scotland and the young Scottish queen was beyond England's reach.

Scottish alliance with France

Mary Queen of Scots in France

Edward VI at the age of Nine

This is a trick-perspective picture from the National Portrait Gallery. Viewed squarely from the front, the face is distorted sideways right across the picture. Viewed from a peephole in the frame on the right hand side, it appears in perfect perspective.

Changes in religion

Back in London, Somerset soon took steps in the Protestant direction. He had already ordered the removal of statues and pictures of saints and prophets from the churches, on the ground that many people worshipped them and so fell into idolatry. Now he caused parliament to repeal the old laws against heresy, the Act of Six Articles, and all restrictions on the printing and use of the scriptures. With a few exceptions, too, he suppressed chantries (bodies founded to sing masses for the dead) and took over their lands and endowments for the Crown. Any

Removal of images of saints

Repeal of heresy laws and Act of Six Articles

Suppression of chantries

endowments held by gilds and colleges for masses for the dead were confiscated at the same time.

Not content with these great changes, Somerset Marriage of allowed priests to marry, and laymen to take the wine priests as well as the bread at Communion. Then, for a while, he permitted the Latin Mass and a new Communion service partly in English to exist side by side—priests could use the Latin when by themselves. Finally, after all England was in an uproar from these changes, he allowed Cranmer to introduce a new order of service First Prayer entirely in English—the First Prayer Book. An Act of Book in English and Uniformity enforced this on the clergy; but no law was Act of Uniformity,1549 passed to make laymen attend the service.

The first result of the new service was a rebellion in The Western the west of England. Incidents grew until large numbers Rebellion, 1549 in Devon and Cornwall were taking up arms in defence of the religion of their forefathers.

> We will have [ran their petition] the sacrament hung over The rebels' the high altar, and thus be worshipped as it was wont to demands be, and they which will not thereto consent, we will have them die like heretics. . . . We will have . . . images to be set up in every church. . . . We will not receive the new service, because it is but like a Christmas game. . . . We will have the Bible, and all books of scripture in English, called in again, for we be informed that otherwise the clergy shall not of long time confound the heretics. . . .

To all this the rebels added the demand that one-half of the monastery and chantry lands should be restored. But they were stronger in spirit and numbers than in military resources. They besieged Exeter, but the city held out until relieved by government troops. These included Italian and German mercenaries, who Defeat of rapidly cut the rebel force to pieces. rebels

Meanwhile another popular movement was in pro- The riots in gress in Norfolk. To Somerset's embarrassment it had Norfolk aims which he himself approved. The Norfolk rioters

were not aggrieved about the new prayer book—
which they used in their camp—but about changes
The rioters' grievances which affected their standard of living. They resented
the rising prices, the rising rents and inheritance fines,
the rising fortunes and luxury of the upper classes.
Above all, they resented the fact that so many land-

The Courtyard of Old Somerset House

This is from an 18th century print (complete with 18th century figures and
vehicles). It shows one side of the house built for Protector Somerset in the
Strand, and pulled down in 1776. The rounded arches of the arcade and the
general simplicity of the design show the influence of classical architecture,
and the building is one of the first examples in England of the Renaissance style.

lords, tempted by the high prices obtainable for cloth,
were folding their sheep on common land (which they
often tried to enclose), or else were enclosing plough-
land and turning it into sheep runs, so depriving many
rural workers of their employment.

As Somerset had set up a Commission to combat
precisely this sort of enclosure, the rebels, when they
began to flatten down palings, fill up ditches, and break
up new enclosures, merely claimed to be carrying out

the policy of the government. They denied that they were rebels at all; and they were orderly enough in their great camp at Mousehold Heath, outside Norwich, until the sympathetic Somerset, through a herald, offered a pardon to all who would lay down their arms and disperse. But neither they nor their leader, a prosperous tanner and landowner named Robert Ket, would accept the idea of pardon, for it implied that they had committed an offence. The herald then proclaimed Ket a traitor, and within a few hours the indignant countrymen marched into and occupied Norwich. In the end, however, they were heavily defeated by a force including German mercenaries under the Earl of Warwick. About three hundred victims, including Ket himself, were afterwards selected for execution. *Mousehold Heath* *Robert Ket* *Defeat of rebels: execution of Ket*

Though these revolts and others were all quelled, they proved fatal to Somerset's authority. The great land-owners, most of whom wanted to be free to carry out enclosure, regarded Somerset as directly responsible for the unrest, for he had many times publicly rebuked enclosing landlords. Their opinion of him was not im-proved by the fact that he had assumed vast powers, and that he had feathered his own nest in the dissolution of the chantries. So the Lords of the Council, led by Warwick, united against him. In vain Somerset summoned the Commons of England to rise in his defence—the call merely cost him the support of the generals who had put down the rising in the West. Surrendering to the Council, he was deposed from the Protectorate and imprisoned in the Tower. *Opposition to Somerset in Council* *Fall of Somerset, 1549*

2. *The Duke of Northumberland*

After the fall of Somerset power passed very largely to Warwick. This unscrupulous man (whose father, Dudley, had been the highly unpopular minister of Henry VII) had no sincere religious beliefs; but he was *Warwick (later North-umberland)* well aware that Protestantism held out opportunities which Catholicism did not. There were churches which, on the plea of stopping abuses and superstition, could be stripped of their precious possessions; and there was the fact that the boy-king Edward, for all his tender years, was already an ardent believer in the need for Reform. Warwick, in brief, resolved to press on with the Reformation for unworthy reasons. He thought the tide was running that way; and in Protestantism he saw a means of enriching himself and gaining a hold over the young king.

His religious policy

Within a few weeks Warwick induced parliament to decree the removal of all religious images—whether in paintings, sculpture, or stained-glass windows—which still survived in the churches. At the same time all the old manuals of prayer and ceremony were to be suppressed, and the whole service was to be found from the new prayer book. But though these measures passed parliament with the approval of Cranmer and the enthusiastic support of extreme reformers like Bishop Ridley and the great preacher Bishop Latimer, they by no means pleased all the Church leaders. However, the foremost opponents of the Reformation—Bishops Gardiner and Bonner—were in no position to lead resistance, for they were already in prison.

'Reforming' measures

Ridley and Latimer

Gardiner and Bonner

Side by side with these actions Warwick took pains to strengthen the government against possible revolts. Many new forms of treason were created—including breaking down an enclosure—and even to agitate for lower rents became a crime. In addition a new official known as the lord lieutenant was appointed in each county to be responsible for its armed forces. To ensure the support of the landowners Somerset's Enclosure Commission was allowed to lapse, and in certain cases landlords were even encouraged to enclose commons.

Strengthening governmental authority

New treason laws

Lords lieutenant

Enclosure Commission dropped

Most of these measures pleased the nobility, but they

were little comfort to the thousands of peasants who had been turned out of their holdings or were unable to pay increased rents. So Warwick soon found himself very unpopular among the lower classes, who continued to regard Somerset as their champion. The ex-Protector had by now been readmitted to the Council; but while he lived he was a threat to Warwick's power. In 1551 a sudden grant of honours to Warwick's main supporters —Warwick himself became Duke of Northumberland— gave warning that Somerset was in danger. Within a few days he was arrested on charges of plotting to kill Northumberland and raise a revolt. Three months later he was executed amid demonstrations of sympathy by a large crowd, many of whom strove to dip their handkerchiefs in his blood.

Warwick becomes Northumberland

Execution of Somerset, 1551

During 1551 the Council began to pay some attention to Bishop Latimer and others who were calling for action against the growing luxury and immorality of the age. The charges were unfortunately all too true. The mockery poured on practices once held sacred, the dissolution of the monasteries and the stripping of the churches had shaken the religious faith of the people and at the same time opened up new possibilities of getting rich quick. And where the Crown and the nobility had shown the way, others had not been slow to follow.

The spirit of the age

Recognizing, then, that some example of rightful dealing should be set up by the government—even a government headed by Northumberland—the Council during 1551 attempted to mend matters in two directions. It set aside a part of the confiscated endowments from the chantries to support new schools—the King Edward VI grammar schools (most of which, however, sprang from earlier chantry schools). And it began to take the road back towards an honest currency by declaring that the silver coins should be worth only one-half of their face value. The result of this second

King Edward VI grammar schools

Currency reform

action, however, was not all good; for by halting the fall in the value of the English coinage, it put up the price of English goods to foreigners (who had to give more of their own currency to make up the required One result— sum in English money). This caused a slump in the English cloth trade, and so further sharpened the general distress.[1]

One result—
slump in
cloth trade

Meanwhile changes in religion proceeded apace. Many foreign Protestants, including some who had fled from the Netherlands to escape persecution by Charles V, had now arrived in England.[2] The influence of these men, of the Frenchman Calvin (who had followed Zwingli as the leader of the Swiss Reformation and set up an extreme form of Protestantism at Geneva) and of Calvin's Scottish disciple, John Knox, all tended towards further alterations. Ridley, too, was already demanding the abolition of the altar—which he regarded as a relic of pre-Christian sacrificial religions and a means of magnifying the importance of the priest. He urged that instead of an altar set back from the congregation, there should be a table in the body of the church. Round this table those who intended to take the Communion would then gather on terms of far greater equality with the minister.

Further
religious
changes

Jean Calvin

John Knox

The altar
controversy

With all this Edward VI himself was in complete agreement. Almost everything connected with the old services, and certainly everything which would fill the

[1] The decline in the export of cloth to Flanders led to efforts to open up markets elsewhere. It was this which prompted Chancellor and Willoughby, in the closing months of the reign, to seek a north-east passage to Asia (see page 116).

[2] "Women who have fallen into heresy", ran Charles's orders in the Netherlands "shall be buried alive, and men shall lose their heads, even if they desist from their errors; if they continue obstinate, they shall be burnt; and whichever be their punishment, their goods shall be forfeited . . . if a man or woman be suspected of heresy, no one shall aid, protect or shelter him or her; they shall be denounced to the nearest inquisition."

pockets of Northumberland and his fellow councillors, was therefore stripped from the churches. Rich vestments, gold and silver plate, even the church bells and organs, all went the same way. The genuine Reformers were not, however, content with purely destructive actions. At their desire the government also decided to

The churches despoiled

Pages from a Treatise by Edward VI

These two pages are from a treatise (now in the British Museum) on the Sacrament of the Body and Blood of Christ, written in French by Edward VI at the age of twelve. Already an ardent Protestant, he is here arguing against the doctrine of transubstantiation. The corrections are by his tutor.

introduce a revision of Cranmer's prayer book, undertaken by the Archbishop himself.

This revised prayer book was much more advanced than the original version of 1549. The word 'priest', for instance, was replaced by the word 'minister'. Above all, there were vital differences in the order for the Communion. The 1549 prayer book had still retained the Catholic belief that Christ was really present in the bread and wine; but the 1552 book now discarded this

The Second Prayer Book, 1552

doctrine, with all that it implies in the matter of the priestly power. To match this change, the 'altar' duly became a 'table' in the choir or chancel of the church.[1]

The Second Act of Uniformity, 1552 To enforce this Second Prayer Book there was passed another Act of Uniformity. By this, those who attended any other service could be imprisoned. A little later, the doctrine of the Church was officially defined in

Forty-two articles forty-two articles of religion. These were much the same as the thirty-nine articles approved later by Elizabeth I and retained to this day. All candidates for the ministry had to accept them before being admitted to holy orders.

So Protestantism was pushed on, far faster than the country as a whole desired. But it was now more important than ever for Northumberland to stand well with

Illness of the King his royal master: for the days of the young king were numbered, and the Duke had resolved on a desperate scheme to prolong his influence into the next reign. Edward, never strong, was by the spring of 1553 in the grip of consumption. By the terms of Henry VIII's will, if Edward died without children the throne would pass to his elder half-sister, Mary. And Mary, daughter of Catherine of Aragon, had remained true to the Catholic

The Reformation— and Northumberland— in danger faith. The whole Protestant Reformation, in which Edward so firmly believed, was in mortal danger—to say nothing of the life of the Duke of Northumberland.

Edward alters the succession Northumberland had no difficulty in persuading Edward in his last weeks of life to alter the succession. If Henry VIII could do so by will, Edward might do so too—or so at least Edward readily believed, though Henry VIII's decisions had been confirmed by Act of Parliament. The gist of the new arrangement was that

[1] To emphasize their view that the body and blood of Christ were *not* present, some Reformers were anxious that the communicants should sit, not kneel, when they received the bread and wine. Cranmer, however, was unwilling to go so far as this.

Mary and her half-sister Elizabeth, being illegitimate according to Acts of Parliament (passed at various times to oblige Henry VIII), were to be barred from the succession. So, too, was Mary Queen of Scots, the child of Henry VIII's elder sister. Instead the title was to be traced through Henry VIII's younger sister to Edward's cousin, the sixteen-year-old Lady Jane Grey. From Edward's point of view the all-important thing was that Jane was a Protestant. From Northumberland's it was that he had just secured Jane in marriage for one of his sons. Jane Grey to succeed

In July 1553, Edward died, but the fact was not at once announced. Four days later, after the news had leaked out, the Council proclaimed Lady Jane as Queen. She disliked accepting the position, but could do nothing else in face of the pressure put upon her. Meanwhile Northumberland had bungled at a vital point, or rather had been outmatched by the vigour and daring of a Tudor princess. For Jane to succeed quietly it was essential that the heir approved by parliament, Mary, should be under lock and key. It was to gain time for this that Northumberland had postponed announcing Edward's death. But Mary, summoned to London from Hunsdon while Edward lay dying, had sensed danger. Warned by supporters she set off instead on a hundred-mile ride, night and day without halt, into Norfolk, there to take shelter with powerful Catholic supporters. When two of Northumberland's sons arrived to capture her at Hunsdon the morning after Edward's death they found their quarry departed. Death of Edward, 1553 Proclamation of Jane Mary escapes capture

On her journey Mary proclaimed herself Queen. So strong was the belief that she was the rightful heir, and so widespread the dislike of Northumberland's actions, that crowds soon flocked to her support. Northumberland's sons sought her out, only for their Popular support for Mary troops to turn round and join her escort. Risings broke

Mutinies out on her behalf; the Fleet declared for her; and when Northumberland himself set off to bring her to London, his soldiers mutinied. Meanwhile in the archplotter's absence from the capital, his opponents brought the

The Council proclaim Mary Council to the point of disowning Jane and proclaiming Mary. There was then nothing for Northumberland to do but accept the Council's decision and himself declare for Mary. The ten-day reign of Queen Jane was over.

There remained the question of punishment for the rebels. Mary herself would have forgiven even North-

Jane imprisoned umberland, but her advisers had other views. Jane and her husband and Bishop Ridley were lodged in the Tower; and seven ringleaders were condemned to

Execution of Northumber- land death. Only three, however—Northumberland and two others—were actually executed. All seven condemned men while in prison forswore Protestantism and embraced the full Catholic faith, so showing themselves traitors not only to their monarch but also to their recently professed religion. If Protestantism could find no worthier champions than these, England might well turn with relief to the rule of a Catholic.

CHAPTER TEN

MARY AND THE CATHOLIC REACTION
(1553-1558)

1. *The Return to Rome*

THE princess who now took her rightful place upon the throne had shown herself honourable, brave and merciful. As a person she was probably the most admirable of all the Tudors. As a ruler she was certainly the least successful. Character of Mary

Thirty-seven years of age and not more than moderately good-looking, Mary had for long been starved of affection. Her happy childhood had suddenly given place, when Henry decided to rid himself of Catherine of Aragon, to a long period of harsh treatment. Separated from her mother, disinherited and declared illegitimate, she had found consolation only in religion —the religion of Catherine. And to the Catholic faith she had remained constant, despite all changes ordered by the government. Her zeal for Catholicism

One of Mary's first acts as Queen was therefore to release the imprisoned Catholic leaders, including Bishops Gardiner and Bonner, and make them her chief advisers. At the same time she gave the leading Protestants a chance — which many took — to flee abroad. Among those who stayed, Cranmer and Latimer were soon lodged in prison to await trial. With Catholics again in most of the offices of Church and State, Mary then set about her sacred task—first to restore the old services and doctrine, and then to bring the English Church once more under the control of Rome. Mary's policy

(83)

The first part of this plan was popular enough. For most people, Northumberland had gone much too fast and too far. So parliament quickly agreed to repeal all the laws concerning religion passed since the death of Henry. The prayer book service was dropped, and the old Latin services revived. At the same time parliament cancelled the divorce of Catherine of Aragon. It also petitioned the Queen to marry—but not a foreigner.

Repeal of religious measures passed since 1547

A foreign husband, however, was exactly what Mary had in mind. There was no really suitable English candidate for her hand; but Prince Philip of Spain, the son of Charles V, seemed to be everything Mary desired. He was Spanish and Catholic, like her mother; his father was the most powerful monarch in Europe; and in due course he would inherit Spain, the Netherlands, part of Italy, and the Spanish territories in the New World. Moreover, his portraits showed a prince of good appearance, and reports—from Spain—told of his splendid character. The fact that he was nearly eleven years younger than Mary weighed little with either side. Charles V and Philip wanted an ally against France; Mary wanted a suitable husband.

Mary's marriage

Philip of Spain

Mary's counsellors, however, were well aware of the dangers of the marriage. England might become a mere province of the Spanish Empire; and the ordinary Englishman would certainly resent a foreign king. They therefore insisted that Philip must cease to be king when Mary died, and that no foreigners should occupy English official positions. To these conditions Charles V agreed, and the marriage treaty was duly signed—when parliament was not in session to protest.

Conditions of marriage

Within a week a group of noblemen, including Lady Jane Grey's father, rose in revolt. The one who came nearest to success was Sir Thomas Wyatt, a notable diplomat, scholar, sportsman and lover, who quickly gained control of Kent. His aim was not merely to

Wyatt's rebellion, 1554

prevent the Spanish marriage but to depose Mary and bring Elizabeth to the throne. Rapidly he marched on London, only to find that the spirited Mary had by her own efforts (including a stirring speech in the Guildhall) rallied the citizens to her defence. After retiring westwards and forcing a passage of the Thames at Kingston, Wyatt then attacked the City from the west, but his tiny band were repulsed at Ludgate. Turning back, the rebel leader battled his way with a handful of companions down the length of Fleet Street before he was finally overwhelmed at Temple Bar.

Wyatt paid for his rashness with his head, and so did over a hundred of his supporters. Among those executed was Lady Jane Grey, though she had no share in her father's guilt. She met her end with that same sweet temper and serene courage which she had shown through all her misfortunes. Meanwhile Elizabeth, though cleared by Wyatt on the scaffold from any knowledge of his intentions, came under deep suspicion from Mary and was committed to the Tower, where she was held for two months. *Execution of Wyatt— and of Jane Grey*

Imprisonment of Elizabeth

Rebellion was nearly always regarded by the bulk of the country with horror, and the effect of Wyatt's action was only to rally the nation behind the Queen. Mary's second parliament, meeting soon afterwards, approved the marriage treaty with Spain. However, it was not yet prepared to follow all her wishes. Above all, it resolutely refused to exclude Elizabeth from the succession, as Mary now desired. *Parliament refuses to exclude Elizabeth*

In the summer of 1554 Philip at last arrived to claim his bride. It says much for the reception he expected that he wore a coat of mail beneath his shirt, chose trained soldiers for his personal attendants, and brought his own cook for fear of poisoning. All, however, went well. A suitable husband safely acquired, Mary then turned to the great task of bringing the English Church *Arrival of King Philip, 1554*

King Philip and Queen Mary I
From a picture at Woburn Abbey by Antonio More.

back to obedience to Rome. In this she was aided by many, including Gardiner, who had helped to repudiate the authority of the Pope under Henry VIII; for the growth of extreme Protestantism under Edward VI had convinced these men, and Mary too, that separation from Rome meant opening the gates to all sorts of undesirable heresies.

The Latin service had already been restored. The next step was to dismiss all those clergy of Protestant tendencies and especially those who had married and refused to put aside their wives. This was done in the autumn of 1554, over a quarter of the clergy losing their livings. Meanwhile the Pope had appointed as his legate to receive England's submission the Englishman Cardinal Pole—a cousin of Henry VIII's who had fallen out with Henry over the break from Rome and had been in exile for over twenty years. Pole was burning with eagerness to return home on his mission, but could not set foot in England until an Act of Attainder condemning him had been reversed. This the Lords refused to do until the Pope had accepted their terms— that they should keep the Church lands which had come into their hands from the dissolution of the monasteries and chantries. All the changes of doctrine the English lords were prepared to accept. They drew the line only at a change which would have touched their pockets. Steps in the return to Rome Cardinal Pole Bargain about Church lands

The Pope having reluctantly agreed to this bargain, the Lords reversed the attainder against Pole. The legate (who was also to succeed Cranmer as archbishop) at once sailed for England. Then followed a series of dramatic scenes. First came an address from Pole to the Lords and Commons at Whitehall Palace in the presence of the King and Queen. The next day parliament voted for return to Rome—the Commons with only two members disagreeing, the Lords with none. The day Arrival of Pole The return to Rome, 1554 after that the two Houses, again meeting at Whitehall, petitioned the King and Queen to undo the anti-papal laws and to intercede with the legate for the return of the kingdom "into the bosom and unity of Christ's Church". The King and Queen duly interceded; then Pole rose, and while Philip and Mary and all else present knelt, and the Queen sobbed with emotion, he pronounced the words of absolution. England was forgiven. The faith of Englishmen was once more that of their forefathers.

Mary's hopes of a child

The Queen's cup of happiness was by this time full to overflowing, for in addition she now thought that she was going to have a child. She would thus be succeeded by a true Catholic instead of the untrustworthy Elizabeth, who seemed to attend Mass more from caution than conviction. With the church bells ringing out to celebrate this news as well as the return to Rome,

She determines to stamp out heresy

Mary looked forward to completing her work. She had brought England back to Rome. She must now stamp out heresy.

2. *The Persecution of the Protestants*

Mary's advisers

In resolving to persecute heretics Mary was urged forward by Pole and Gardiner. The latter believed that if a few examples were made of leading Protestants the rank and file would quickly come to their senses. No blame rests on Philip who, though a fierce persecutor in the Netherlands, preferred to avoid stirring up strife in England and so weakening a useful ally against France.

Before the Queen could proceed with her intention the clock had to be set back still further. This was not difficult, for since the bargain with the Pope about Church lands, parliament had become much more

Repeal of religious measures passed since 1529

pliable. At the end of 1554 Mary's third parliament approved proposals which her first had rejected. It abolished all the religious measures of Henry VIII

from the year 1529 onwards—except the confiscation
of Church lands—and restored certain powers to the
Church courts. In addition, it revived the laws of Repeal of
heresy laws
Henry IV and Henry V, abolished under Somerset, by
which the punishment for heresy was death at the
stake. Probably it imagined that these laws would be
used in much the same infrequent way as before—a
bad mistake.

Thus armed, Pole gave orders that all, clergymen and
laymen alike, should individually declare that they
submitted to the Church. Any who refused were to be Persecution
of Protes-
proceeded against with the utmost severity of the law. tants begins
1555
Within a few days the campaign against the Protestants
was in full swing. Of those who, before the reign was
out, chose death rather than submission, about one- The
Protestant
third were clergy and almost a fifth women. Outside martyrs,
1555-1558
the clergy, all came from the middle or lower ranks of
society. A third of the burnings took place in East
Anglia and the Home Counties, and nearly a half in
London under Bishop Bonner. These were the districts,
the most highly developed and the most closely in
touch with the Continent, where Protestantism had
gained its greatest hold.

At first the burnings were attended by the public
rather in the holiday spirit of any other public execution of the time. But when it became clear how harshly
the government intended to act, and how most of the
condemned were ready to die bravely for their beliefs,
the atmosphere changed. The victims were encouraged Change in
public
by the crowd, even beseeched by members of their own opinion
families, to stand firm; and each successive martyrdom
became a triumph, not for the government and
Catholicism, but for the common people of South-east
England and Protestantism. Other governments had
persecuted heretics before, and other governments
were to do so afterwards—hardly anyone yet believed

it right or safe to tolerate different religious opinions—
but never before or since in England did religious
persecution on anything like this scale take place. Over
the whole one hundred and fifty years before Mary came
to the throne an average of perhaps one heretic had
been executed each year; for the three and a half years
of persecution under Mary the average of burnings was
nearly two a week.

This violence defeated its own end not only at the
time but for centuries afterwards. The executions of
those Protestant leaders who had scorned to flee,
recounted as they were within a year of Mary's death in
Bishop Foxe's "Book of Martyrs", engraved themselves
on the nation's memory, and helped to create in this
country a bitterness against Roman Catholics which
lasted well on into the 19th century. Moreover, in the
fires of Smithfield and Oxford, Norwich and Canterbury, Protestantism proved itself not the mere excuse
for self-enrichment that it had seemed under Northumberland but a creed as enduring as Catholicism itself.
"Be of good comfort, Master Ridley!" cried Latimer to
his companion at the stake in Oxford as the flames came
crackling about them: "Play the man: we shall this day
light such a candle by God's Grace in England as I trust
shall never be put out."

Latimer and Ridley never faltered in their chosen
course. Not so the deposed archbishop, Cranmer. Less
robust by nature, the kindly, scholarly Cranmer was
driven by fear and sustained pressure into recanting all
his Protestant opinions. He was led to hope—for this
was the usual practice—that if he acknowledged his
errors he would be spared his life. By degrees he not
only accepted every article of Catholic doctrine, but
finally agreed to describe himself as a blasphemer, a
persecutor, and a sinner who by abolishing Masses for
the departed had robbed even the souls of the dead.

And when he had thus humiliated himself to the depths, he was told that, after all, he was to die. One privilege He recants, but is to die only would be allowed him. He might deliver a speech, so that the citizens of Oxford could hear from his own lips of his sins and his repentance.

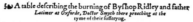
A table deſcribing the burning of Byſhop Ridley and father Latimer at Oxforde, Doctor Smyth there preaching at the tyme of their ſuffering.

The Burning of Ridley and Latimer at Oxford

This print is taken from John Foxe's famous book published in 1563 *The Actes and Memorials of these latter and perillous Dayes, touching matters of the Church* (etc. . . . seven lines more of title, and hence always referred to by its popular name of " The Book of Martyrs "). Note Cranmer praying for the two bishops on top of his prison tower on the right. A firm Protestant and an early believer in toleration, Foxe fled abroad under Mary and returned under Elizabeth.

In this the government badly miscalculated. Having stripped Cranmer of his self-respect they should have let him live, an object of general contempt. Instead, in their passion for revenge they gave him a chance to redeem himself. He grasped it nobly. On account of heavy rain his farewell speech was given in St. Mary's, His last speech

Oxford, and not at the stake outside Balliol. After first praying for himself as a great sinner, he beseeched his hearers to love God, to obey the King and Queen, to live together in brotherly affection, and to show charity to the poor. Then he came to the matter which, as he said, troubled his conscience more than any other thing in his life. At this stage the congregation expected him to refer to his work in spreading Protestantism. Instead he went on to say that he had recently signed a number of papers—his various recantations—which did not represent his true opinions: "and for as much as my hand offended in writing contrary to my heart, my hand therefore shall first be punished; for if I may come to the fire, it shall be the first burnt. As for the Pope, I utterly refuse him . . ." This much, and a few words more, Cranmer managed to say before the astonished officials hustled him from the church and bore him off to his death.

His final gesture

At the stake Cranmer, so far as we can gather, was as good as his word.

> For when the fire was put to him, [runs a contemporary account] and pretty while before the fire came to any other part, he stretched out his right hand, and thrusted it into the flames, where it was seen of everyone sensibly [clearly] burning, crying with a loud voice, "This hand hath offended".

With that superb action Cranmer more than atoned for all his moments of weakness and hesitation. From it, as from the deaths of all the other martyrs, the whole cause of Protestantism drew fresh strength.

Failure and grief of Mary

The persecution of the Protestants brought Mary no happiness, for it showed only too clearly that their ideas were not to be stamped out by a few burnings. In every other respect, too, her reign ended in failure. The child to whose birth she so passionately looked forward was never more than imaginary: in fact the

Queen proved to be suffering from an incurable internal disease. The husband for whom she had longed failed to return her love; he left England after little more than a year, succeeded his father as King of Spain when Charles V abdicated in 1556 and, apart from one brief visit the next year, never saw Mary again. And even that visit brought the Queen further grief; for its

Looting a Village

From Holinshed's *Historie of Scotland.* A scene which frequently occurred during the Wars of the Roses and during raiding over the Border.

object was to persuade Mary to ally England with Spain in war against France, and its result (when Mary pressed her Council into agreeing) was the loss of England's most treasured possession—Calais.

By 1558 then, failure everywhere stared Mary in the face. Especially galling was the suspicion that her successor's religious opinions differed from her own. Elizabeth was heir by law; and the daughter of Anne Boleyn could hardly be a true Catholic. Moreover, parliament would certainly not now agree to exclude Elizabeth; while the Catholic with the best claim, Mary Queen of Scots, was now married to the Dauphin of

[margin notes:] Philip, King of Spain, 1556

England supports Spain against France: loss of Calais

Elizabeth still the heir

France and so on the side of Philip's enemies! For this reason, Philip, in his wife's last months, beseeched her to smooth Elizabeth's path to the throne, and so dealt yet one more blow to the tragic figure from whom life was ebbing away. "Childless after all, [writes a great historian] hated by her people, slighted by her husband whose favour was already turning towards the sister who must survive and succeed her, fearful that Elizabeth would quickly ruin her work for God, the most honest and ill-advised of the Tudors turned away to die." [1]

[1] G. M. Trevelyan: *A History of England.*

CHAPTER ELEVEN

THE ELIZABETHAN RELIGIOUS SETTLEMENT AND THE STORY OF MARY STUART

(1558-1569)

1. *The Religious Settlement*

ELIZABETH was twenty-five years of age when amid general rejoicing she succeeded her half-sister. Tall, good-looking and of fine presence, she was a true daughter of the Renaissance, for she was highly educated and intelligent, devoted to studies, skilled in foreign languages (including Latin and Greek) and a brilliant performer on the virginals. Also, like many Renaissance rulers, she was interested in religion less for itself than for its effect on the strength and loyalty of her kingdom. *Personality of Elizabeth*

Although impulsive by nature—she was not above boxing a favourite's ears and once threw beer in the face of an offending courtier—Elizabeth had learnt in youth the value of caution and pretence. Under Henry VIII her mother had been executed and she herself declared illegitimate. Under Edward VI she had attracted the attentions of Somerset's brother, who had suffered death for his ambition. Under Mary she had been the unwitting centre of several plots, had seen the inside of the Tower, and had come through safely only by conforming to the Catholic religion—yet not so whole-heartedly as to lose herself the support of Protestants. To pick her way so warily through such dangers she had needed not only a stout heart but a cool head. Both were to serve her in good stead in the still greater perils of the years to come.

Elizabeth's first actions

Elizabeth was not long in showing her wisdom. She chose as her chief adviser the able, honest and moderate **William Cecil** Sir William Cecil; called in the debased coins issued by her predecessors; and made peace with France. Still **No immediate change in religion** more wisely she gave orders that no immediate change should be made in religion, with the result that she was firmly in power before the Catholics became fully aware of her true feelings.

Difficulties in way of religious settlement

Her most pressing problem was, of course, to settle religious affairs in a way acceptable to the nation. This was a task of the greatest difficulty. Clearly the Queen could not hope to please everybody. On the one hand the great trading areas of London and the south-east, together with many of the most thriving towns in the **The Protestants** south-west, had become strongly Protestant. The Protestants, moreover, were the Queen's keenest supporters; while she herself, as the daughter of Anne Boleyn and the pupil of Protestant tutors, was a living emblem of Henry VIII's break with Rome. On the other hand **The Catholics** the Catholics, and those who were Catholic in all except obedience to the Pope, probably made up at least two-thirds of the nation; all the most powerful monarchs of Europe—whose enmity England seemed too weak to risk—were Catholic; and the English Protestants now included many who had returned from the Continent with views much more extreme than those they carried into exile.

Extreme Protestants: The Calvinists or Presbyterians

Among this last class were some whose Protestantism followed the pattern not of Luther but of Calvin. From Geneva, Calvin had proclaimed his ideas of a church rigidly based on what was set forth in the scriptures and on the practices of the early Christians in the first three centuries A.D. Control of this church would rest neither with pope nor king nor bishops, but with *presbyters*, or elders. For each congregation in Calvin's system (which became known as *presbyterianism*) there was to be a minister to conduct the services, and a group of elders to organize the affairs of the parish. Both minister and elders would be *elected* by the congregation. At higher levels—for larger districts or the Church as a whole—the principle of election and of mixed clerical and lay control would also apply. Obviously such a system was much too democratic to appeal to 16th-century kings—or queens.

Neither Catholicism nor advanced Protestantism thus offered a satisfactory choice to the Queen. But at least it was clear that, to ensure control for herself and satisfy her strongest supporters, she must again sever the connection with Rome. When she set about doing this, however, she found that she had to go still further; for her first House of Commons showed itself very Protestant, and Elizabeth had to take some notice of its wishes. Yet at the same time she had to avoid offending the Catholics, the greater part of her subjects, more than was absolutely necessary. So besides breaking with Rome again, she eventually agreed to have a Church Service in English, as the Protestants desired— though one which would embody a great deal of Catholic doctrine and tradition. The point she now aimed at was like that reached after the introduction of the First Prayer Book but before Protestantism had gone to great lengths. By a midway position of this kind she could not only resume royal control over the Church but also hope in time to win the support of the great majority of the nation.

Broadly speaking, this was the sort of settlement that by the Acts of Supremacy and Uniformity in 1559 Elizabeth put into effect. But owing to continued pressure from the Commons and the Protestant leaders, the new prayer book was mainly based not on the First

The Queen's views

Pressure of Protestant Commons

The New
(third)
Prayer Book
1559

Prayer Book of 1549 (as Elizabeth had intended) but on the much more Protestant Second Prayer Book of 1552. In certain respects, however, the Queen's wishes prevailed and the earlier book was followed. As for the Holy Communion, the vital phrases were taken consecutively from each book. The words to be said in giving the bread were: "The body of our Lord Jesus Christ, which was given for thee, preserve thy body unto everlasting life. Take this, and feed on Him in thy heart by faith with thanksgiving." The first of these two sentences comes from the 1549 Prayer Book and implies the Real Presence of Christ in the consecrated Bread; the second comes from the 1552 Prayer Book and implies only a Spiritual Presence. This was an obvious attempt, within a clearly Protestant settlement, to satisfy as many points of view as possible.

Act of
Uniformity,
1559

The new prayer book was enforced by an Act of Uniformity. All those who stayed away from Sunday service without reasonable excuse were to be fined 'twelvepence' for each absence—a moderate sum which many Catholics could well afford. There was no penalty for attending any other service; none could be held publicly, but Catholics would be able to attend Mass in private houses. All this, which was very tolerant compared with arrangements elsewhere in Europe,

Act of
Supremacy,
1559

followed the all-important Act of Supremacy which once again placed the English monarch, instead of the Pope, in control of the English Church.[1]

The Thirty-
Nine Articles

The Elizabethan religious settlement, which took further shape later with the Thirty-nine Articles defining the doctrine of the Church of England, was only partly successful. It succeeded in that the Church of England which it set up has held together as the national

---

[1] As a woman, however, Elizabeth no longer claimed Henry VIII's title of 'Supreme Head of the Church': she became instead 'Supreme Governor in . . . all things spiritual'.

church throughout four centuries, and has attracted the loyalty and devotion of many generations; but it failed in that its attempt to cover the whole English people soon broke down. For a few years there was some hope that this great aim would be achieved. Then the attacks of the Catholics on the one hand, and the extreme Protestants or Puritans on the other, destroyed any chance that the Church would eventually win the support of the entire nation.

Success and failure of settlement

2. *Elizabeth's Diplomacy and the Story of Mary Stuart*

For a short time all seemed to be going well. The new religious settlement, though bitterly opposed by the existing bishops (who were nearly all dismissed), was received quietly by the lower clergy and the people; and as there was no persecution beyond the weekly fines for non-attendance, the country enjoyed greater harmony than for many years past.

The settlement received quietly

Elizabeth's reluctance to persecute Catholics also served another good purpose. It encouraged Philip II of Spain and the Pope to believe that the Queen might be won over to Catholicism, and so made them hesitate to use force against her. Philip, in fact, tried to win Elizabeth for Catholicism (and England for himself) by the weapon of marriage. He proposed almost as soon as Mary was dead. But Elizabeth, waiting only till she was properly established on the throne, quickly put paid to Philip's hopes. She did so partly because one of Philip's conditions was that she should declare herself a Catholic, partly because she knew that her subjects would detest another alliance with Spain. Everything in her character revolted at the idea that England should again become, as under Mary, a pawn to be moved on Spanish orders. While turning down Philip

Attitude of Pope and Phillip II

Negotiations for the Queen's marriage

Philip II

she was careful, however, not to offend another suitor, a cousin of Philip's, whom Philip favoured almost as much as himself—the Archduke Charles of Austria.[1]

Archduke
Charles

Elizabeth kept the Archduke Charles in play, so to speak, for the better part of eight years. Other suitors who also paid court at various times included members of the French, Scottish and Swedish royal houses. By constantly keeping open the possibility of marriage Elizabeth made likely enemies think in terms of matrimony instead of war, and so gained priceless time for strengthening her realm. She also caused Spain and France, at different times, to alter their policy for fear that Elizabeth would marry into the rival camp.

Other suitors

The Queen's
policy

One man—an Englishman—Elizabeth might well have married in other circumstances. Early in her reign she became dangerously fond of the handsome and ambitious Robert Dudley, later Earl of Leicester—a son of the ill-fated Northumberland. But Dudley was already married; and worse still, just when rumours were spreading that he intended to rid himself of his wife, that neglected and unfortunate woman was found dead at the foot of a staircase in her home. The verdict at the inquest was accidental death, but the possibility of suicide could not be ruled out and many tongues were eager to suggest foul play. In any case the scandal was so great that the Queen could have married Dudley only with grave danger to her throne. This, for all her infatuation, she was wise enough to see. Henceforth Dudley was a close friend and adviser, but not a possible husband.

Leicester

The question of Elizabeth's marriage was so important because on it turned not only the balance of power

The
succession

[1] The Archduke Charles was the younger son of the Emperor Ferdinand, who had succeeded his brother Charles V as Emperor when the latter retired into a monastery. Charles V had wanted Philip to become Emperor as well as inheriting the rest of his dominions, but he failed to secure his son's election.

in Europe but also the succession to the English throne. If Elizabeth had no children the best claim to the The strongest claimant —Mary Queen of Scots throne by descent would rest with the young Mary Stuart, Queen of Scots. And Mary Stuart, to the Protestant majority in the House of Commons, was doubly dangerous in that she was both a Catholic and allied by marriage with France. No wonder that parliament was soon imploring Elizabeth to marry; and no wonder that, when the Queen continued her successful policy of encouraging many suitors but accepting none, hard words were sometimes exchanged between Monarch and Commons.

The key to some of these problems lay in the hands of Mary Stuart. It will be remembered that the Scots had betrothed Mary to the Dauphin and sent her to France. Mary Stuart's youth There she had spent her 'teens, while her French mother, Mary of Guise, acted as Regent in Scotland. Mary of Guise During these years the influence of the Reformation began to be felt in that country and there grew up a Protestant party known as the Congregation, strongly Protestantism in Scotland— the Congregation opposed to the Regent and Catholicism.

In 1559 the growing Protestant opposition in Scotland blazed up into outbreaks of violence. Fired by the return of the great preacher John Knox—an ardent John Knox reformer who in exile had come under the spell of Calvin—the Scottish Protestants began an orgy of Religious riots image-breaking. Against this the Regent tried to take a firm stand backed by French troops, with the result that the Congregation declared her deposed. But meanwhile Mary Stuart's husband had just become king in France Mary Stuart Queen of France as Francis II, and was certain to send the Regent in Scotland all the forces she needed to suppress the Congregation. The question therefore arose—would Elizabeth intervene to save the Scottish Protestants from defeat?

Elizabeth hated war, bitterly resented its cost, and

detested all rebels. But on this occasion facts proved
too strong for these feelings. With Mary Stuart Queen of
France as well as Scotland the Franco-Scottish connection was altogether too close for England's safety. So
Elizabeth agreed, though with much shifting and

John Knox

The dominating nose shows something of the
strength of character of Scotland's great Reformer.
Likewise, perhaps, the extreme length of beard.

Elizabeth
helps the
Congrega-
tion

evasion, to send aid to the Congregation. Before long
English money, munitions, ships and soldiers were
helping the Protestant rebels towards victory.

Treaty of
Edinburgh,
1560

The Treaty of Edinburgh then laid down that all
French troops should leave Scotland and that the
Scottish government would recognize Elizabeth as
Queen of England. Nothing was said about religion;

but the departure of the French gave the Congregation their chance. Under the inspiration of John Knox, Catholic services were swept away, the link with Rome severed, and a thorough-going Presbyterian system established. Such was the situation when, after less than Presbyterianism in Scotland

Mary Stuart, Queen of Scots

From a drawing by the great French painter François Clouet. It shows Mary as a young widow shortly before her return from France to Scotland.

a year on the French throne, Francis II died, leaving Mary an attractive and adventurous widow of eighteen. Death of Francis II

There was now no reason why Mary should remain away from her native land. In 1561 she returned to Scotland to take over her throne. She soon won many hearts by her charm, her vivacity and her daring feats Return of Mary Stuart to Scotland, 1561 as a horsewoman; and at first, though strongly Catholic herself, she was careful not to disturb the recent arrangements establishing Protestantism. Her spirited character, however, soon led her into trying to strengthen her title to the English throne—for use whenever possible.

For this purpose (and because she had fallen in love with his looks and failed to perceive his vices) in 1565 she married her young cousin Henry Stuart, Lord Darnley. He was a Catholic, an English subject, and, like herself, a descendant of Margaret Tudor. Mary, in other words, was uniting Darnley's claim with her own and so bidding hard for the support of Elizabeth's Catholic subjects.

The marriage with Darnley proved Mary's undoing. She soon discovered his worthlessness, allowed his title of king to remain unsanctioned by the Scottish parliament, and began to shun his company. Her confidence, possibly her affection, she gave instead to her secretary, an Italian named David Riccio. At this the neglected and spiteful Darnley began to conspire with the leading Protestant lords, whom Mary had by now driven from the Council, promising to reinstate them if they would act with him against Riccio and induce parliament to recognize him as king. The Protestant nobles were the more ready to do this as besides being eager for power they suspected the upstart Riccio of advising the Queen how to restore Catholicism. The result was that one night in the spring of 1566 some of the foremost Protestant lords were admitted by Darnley to the Queen's boudoir, where they seized Riccio and bore him off to a violent death outside.

This wicked deed, doubly brutal in that Mary was soon to give birth to a child, the Queen did not forgive. She pretended to be reconciled to Darnley and when he caught smallpox a few months later she even nursed him during his convalescence. Her affections, however,

Darnley and his Younger Brother

This picture by Hans Eworth was painted two years before Darnley's marriage to his cousin Mary Stuart. Note the fine panelling of the Elizabethan hall—also the ceiling beams and the classical pediments above the leaded windows.

had meanwhile turned in a very different direction. Early in 1567 she persuaded the still sick Darnley to move to a place named Kirk o' Field, on the outskirts of Edinburgh. A few days after his arrival she left at midnight to attend a festivity at Holyrood Palace. Less than two hours later there was a loud explosion and Kirk o' Field was blown sky high. The lifeless body of Darnley was found nearby in a garden. By some additional touch of mystery, it was not the gun-powder that had killed him. He had been strangled.

There was, of course, at first no proof that Mary had any share in this dark action. Very strong evidence, however, pointed to the guilt of her latest admirer, the reckless, brutal and unscrupulous Earl of Bothwell. So it was essential for Mary, if she hoped to retain the goodwill of the Scottish people, to dissociate herself from the reputed murderer. But far from bringing Bothwell to book, she first allowed his followers to overawe the court of investigation, then let him kidnap her. Pleading that her honour demanded immediate marriage with her captor, she then helped to arrange a divorce between Bothwell (who was a Protestant) and his wife, and a few days later herself married Bothwell. This outraged all parties in Scotland except a small number of Mary's personal supporters. The Lords of the Congregation took the field, outmanoeuvred the Queen's few thousand men at Carberry Hill, and persuaded Mary to surrender to save Bothwell. The latter, thus shielded, escaped from the field and eventually took refuge in Denmark, where he ended his career some years later as a lunatic chained to a pillar in a dungeon.

The Scottish lords now tried to make Mary renounce Bothwell. This she refused to do. So they imprisoned her in Lochleven Castle, in the middle of a lake, and forced her to abdicate in favour of her (and Darnley's)

Side notes:

Murder of Darnley, 1567

Bothwell

Marriage of Mary and Bothwell, 1567

Carberry Hill, 1567

Imprisonment and forced abdication of Mary: proclamation of James VI, 1567 baby son, who was declared King as James VI. But Mary was nothing if not resourceful. Within a few months she escaped and raised a small force of Catholic adherents, only to be defeated by the Protestant Regent—her half-brother the Earl of Murray. From the battlefield at Langside an almost non-stop ride of ninety miles carried the fugitive Queen into England. There she threw herself on Elizabeth's generosity and begged for help in regaining her throne. When aid was not at once forthcoming, she asked at least to be allowed to leave England for France.

Mary's escape into England, 1568

The Queen of Scots, however, was much too dangerous a rival and valuable a hostage for Elizabeth to let slip in this fashion. For good or ill, fate had delivered Mary into the hands of her calculating cousin. Elizabeth prudently decided that Mary should be held in honourable captivity until the question of her responsibility for Darnley's murder could be investigated. And though the inquiry was soon held and produced a non-committal verdict, in honourable captivity Mary remained for the next nineteen years.

Elizabeth retains Mary in captivity

Mary captive, however, was scarcely less mettlesome and dangerous than Mary free. From the moment the former Queen of Scots set foot on English soil the perils surrounding Elizabeth grew thick and fast. They were not to be dispersed until Mary was dead and the invasion fleets of Philip of Spain, her would-be heir and avenger, overwhelmingly defeated.

THE STORY OF MARY STUART, QUEEN OF SCOTS

THE COUNTER-REFORMATION IN EUROPE AND THE OPENING OF THE CATHOLIC CAMPAIGN AGAINST ELIZABETH

(c. 1560–1572)

WHILE the tragedy of Mary Stuart was being played out in Scotland, events equally dramatic had been taking place on the Continent.

After the attacks of Luther, Calvin and others, the Roman Catholic Church had to choose between concessions to the rebels or a fight against them. At the Council of Trent, which met on and off from 1542 to 1563, the Popes ruled out any idea of giving way over doctrine; Catholic beliefs were defined in terms impossible for Lutherans or Calvinists to accept. At the same time, however, the Council took action against the corruption which had first angered the Reformers. By setting their house in order in this way the Catholics gained the strength not only to survive the onslaught of their opponents but also before very long to pass over to the offensive. *Council of Trent*

Catholic reforms

In its struggle, the Roman Catholic Church was now to have the help of a new religious order—the Society of Jesus. Founded by a Spanish officer called Ignatius Loyola, this was distinguished by an almost military organization and a very strict oath of obedience not only to immediate superiors but to the Pope. "If the Church defines anything", wrote Loyola, "that seems to us white to be black, we must at once assert that it is *The Jesuits (founded 1536)* black." The 'Jesuits', as the members were soon called, regarded themselves as soldiers of Christ under papal orders. Their fervour and iron discipline soon attracted many fine spirits and before long the order had establishments as far afield as China and Japan. In this devoted body the Pope had a powerful weapon both for the foreign mission field and for the fight against Protestantism.

Soon, too, the papacy had another weapon. Inquiry, or inquisition, into religious beliefs in areas suspected of heresy had been a feature of the medieval Church. In Rome the organization responsible for this had lapsed by the 15th century, but in Spain the practice had been carried much further by Ferdinand and Isabella. Under these monarchs over two thousand Spaniards were burned in a single diocese within twelve months. The Spanish Inquisition surpassed in horror anything known elsewhere, but its success was too striking to be ignored. In the mid-16th century one of the Popes reintroduced the Inquisition at Rome by setting up a Holy Office, or committee, to supervise inquiry. Burnings increased, and it was not long before a later Pope descended to the level of ordinary monarchs by permitting torture during the investigations.

The Inquisition

In Italy, as in Spain, all this succeeded well enough— the few Protestants were completely crushed. In Northern Europe, however, the Inquisition aroused such opposition that its activities did the Catholic cause more harm than good.

The Index

As part of the fight against heresy the papacy at about this time also started to issue a 'black list' (known as the *Index Librorum Prohibitorum*) of books and authors not to be read by the faithful. This, like the extension of the Inquisition, the foundation of the Society of Jesus, and the work of the Council of Trent, was a step in the great Catholic movement known as the Counter-

Reformation. We must now see how this movement fared in France and the Netherlands before turning again to England.

Despite severe persecution Protestant doctrines— France mainly those of Calvin—had gained a foothold in France. By 1563 the French Protestants or Huguenots (from a German word meaning 'sworn companions') numbered less than ten per cent of the nation, but they enjoyed powerful support from part of the nobility. In that year, after many atrocities, civil war broke out between the two parties. Under the name of the French Wars of Religion, it was to continue on and off Wars of Religion for thirty years—with the Catholics appealing for help mainly to Spain, the Huguenots to (among others) England.

Meanwhile a bitter struggle had also begun in the Netherlands Netherlands. This territory, covering roughly the modern Holland and Belgium, was the most prosperous and privileged part of the whole Spanish Empire. In its go-ahead commercial atmosphere, however, Protestantism had soon gained a hold. Charles V did his best to suppress it; but his attempt to introduce the Spanish Inquisition aroused violent opposition. After perhaps as many as thirty thousand men and women had been put to death he eventually had the sense not to insist on his laws being obeyed. His son Philip II, however, was determined to stamp out heresy at all costs. "Rather than suffer the least thing in pre- Philip II's resolve judice of religion", he wrote, "I will lose my states and a hundred lives: for I will not live to be a king of heretics. . . ."

In 1567 Philip took the decisive step. To this group of provinces he sent an army under his foremost soldier, the Duke of Alva. The Duke's orders were to Alva enforce not only the Inquisition, but also the Decrees of the Council of Trent, with many of which the Catholics of Northern Europe disagreed. With ruthless zeal, and by numerous executions, Alva carried out his master's policy, but only at the price of arousing the hostility of the greater part of the population, Catholic as well as Protestant. He aroused, too, the undying enmity of Prince William of Orange (William the Silent), who raised troops and challenged him by force. The flame of resistance, valiantly kept alive by William, was soon fanned to fury by the atrocious behaviour and cruelty of the ill-paid Spanish troops; and like the Huguenots in France, the rebels in the Netherlands began to look to England for help. Such was the Continental background to the events in England which followed the arrival of Mary Stuart.

Netherlands revolt: William the Silent

Mary had not been long in England when there occurred the biggest move in her favour. Some of the great nobles of the Catholic North plotted with the Duke of Norfolk: Mary was to marry Norfolk, and Elizabeth be forced to restore Mary in Scotland and acknowledge her as the rightful heir in England. Mary herself wanted to go even further, and secretly avowed that, if Philip would help, she would be "Queen of England in three months" and Mass would be "said all over the country". But Philip was busy with other opponents and still reluctant to come out into the open against Elizabeth. When Cecil got wind of the conspiracy and arrested Norfolk, Philip therefore did nothing. The remaining conspirators were the Earls of Northumberland and Westmorland, whose word counted for far more in the North than that of any monarch. Defying a summons to London, they took up arms, and a rebel force tried to fight its way south to rescue Mary. Elizabeth's commanders, however, were soon able to move north and stamp out the revolt. By way of punishment the already far from wealthy North was then made poorer still by huge fines and confiscations,

England after arrival of Mary Stuart

Conspiracy of the Northern Earls, 1569–1570

Caution of Philip

The revolt in the North

and something like eight hundred rebels were executed. Up to this point the normally merciful Elizabeth in twelve years of rule had not executed a single person for

Elizabeth I

There are many contemporary portraits of Elizabeth, mostly by unknown artists. This one, from Hatfield House, is known as the "Ermine" Portrait, from the little animal—an emblem of royalty—on her arm. Note the fine, artistic, somewhat hard features of the face; the superb lace ruff; and the great magnificence of the jewels on the gown.

political or religious offences, but even she could not tolerate rebellion.

It was just at this moment, far too late to be effective, that the Pope issued a bull declaring Elizabeth excommunicated and deposed. News travelled slowly in

Pope declares Elizabeth excommunicated and deposed, 1570

the 16th century, and in Rome they were aware only that a revolt was intended, not that it had already broken out and failed. The bull, nevertheless, marked a turning-point in the reign. It not merely released Catholics from their allegiance to Elizabeth, but, by threatening dire penalties to those who obeyed her, practically ordered Catholics to become rebels. As a result the religious difference took on a new bitterness, for to the Protestants all Catholics, no matter how honourable or loyal, were now possible traitors.

Increased bitterness

This bitterness was increased still further by a fresh Catholic plot in 1571—to assassinate Elizabeth and set Mary Stuart on the throne—and by the dreadful Massacre of St. Bartholomew in 1572. To free the young French king from Huguenot influence the French Queen-Mother, Catherine de' Medici, prompted an attack on the leading Huguenot nobles (who were gathered in Paris to celebrate the wedding of the Huguenot Prince Henry of Navarre to the king's sister). In the early morning of August 24th, St. Bartholomew's Day, the deed was done. To make the thing appear spontaneous, mobs were also incited, in Paris and elsewhere, to butcher all the Huguenots they could find. Within a few days some eight thousand Huguenots, women and children no less than men, had been done to death.

Catholic plot of 1571 (Riolfi's plot)

France: Massacre of St. Bartholomew, 1572

This fearful crime—which the French government pretended was merely nipping in the bud a Huguenot plot—was greeted with lively satisfaction by Philip and the Pope. The latter ordered a special medal to be struck, Rome to be illuminated for three nights, and a *Te Deum* to be sung in St. Peter's. In England it was of course regarded with horror; and when the Huguenots in the South-west of France rose in revolt, Elizabeth allowed help to be carried to the rebels in their fortified port of La Rochelle. The help remained

Unofficial English help to Huguenots

unofficial however; the English Queen neither desired nor was prepared for war with France.

In case war came, however, she thought it well to be on a more friendly footing with Spain. She had already withdrawn from the Dutch 'sea-beggars' (Netherlands rebels operating against Spanish shipping) a short-lived privilege of using Dover as a base; and she now set out to reach agreement with Philip about other matters. The expulsion of the sea-beggars from English waters, however, drove them to their own country, where in 1572 they seized the port of Brill. Fired by this example, Flushing and other ports along the Dutch coast soon drove out their Spanish garrisons, and before long four of the northern provinces were engaged, under the leadership of William the Silent, in all-out war against Spain. This heroic struggle continued for many years. From the English viewpoint it interfered with trade, but was highly useful in diverting the attentions of Philip.

Elizabeth attempts agreement with Spain

Expulsion of 'sea-beggars' from Dover

Dutch in full revolt, 1572

CHAPTER THIRTEEN

HAWKINS, DRAKE, AND THE
CLASH WITH SPAIN
(1567–1587)

WHILE the Dutch were battling to free themselves from Spanish rule in the Netherlands, a number of Englishmen were trying, quite unofficially, to challenge Spanish supremacy in the New World. The voyages of the Cabots apart, English seamen had entered the great adventure of exploration much later than the Spanish and Portuguese, and they were annoyed to find so much of the new sphere of discovery already closed to them.

The English could, of course, quest in seas remote from Spanish and Portuguese possessions. At the end of Edward VI's reign Northumberland, drawing on the
knowledge of Sebastian Cabot and the young geographer John Dee, had formed a company to discover a route to China round the north of Russia—the 'North-East Passage'. The leaders of the expedition
were Sir Hugh Willoughby, a soldier, and Richard Chancellor, a skilled sea captain. Willoughby with his two ships was forced to winter off Lapland, and none of his company survived the experience. Chancellor, more fortunate, found the entrance to the White Sea—previously unknown to Englishmen—and the port of Archangel. Thence he travelled one thousand five hundred miles to visit the Tsar, Ivan the Terrible, in his capital at Moscow. From this came a useful
trade between England and Muscovy (as Ivan's realm was then called), though Chancellor himself

(116)

was drowned in a storm while returning from a second visit.

Wealth was much easier to come by, however, in the warmer regions already opened up by Spain and Portugal. William Hawkins of Plymouth had carried out some successful trading expeditions to West Africa and Brazil during the 1530s; and others—despite Portuguese protests—had continued to trade with the chiefs of the West African Guinea coast. It was left to William Hawkins' son, however—John Hawkins—to break into the preserves of Spain.

William Hawkins: West Africa

The activities of John Hawkins, and later of his young cousin Francis Drake, led to fighting with Spain in American waters long before war was recognized in Europe. The first big clash came through Hawkins' efforts to sell English goods and black slaves (which he bought or kidnapped on the West African coast) to the Spaniards in the West Indies and on the American mainland. The Queen, Cecil and other courtiers were shareholders in his ventures, and he sailed under the royal standard. Two voyages passed off well, but the third—on which Drake commanded one of the ships— ended in disaster. After a show of force had helped him dispose of his cargo—the Spanish colonists wanted his wares, but were frightened of breaking regulations against foreign traders—storms drove him into San Juan d'Ulloa, in Mexico. While he was there the new Viceroy of Mexico with a large fleet arrived from Spain. Hawkins had control of the port's batteries and could have kept out the fleet; instead, he allowed it in on promises of peaceful behaviour. Three days later, without warning and at dead of night, the Spaniards suddenly set upon his little expedition. Hawkins and Drake both managed to fight their way out, but Hawkins carried so many survivors from the other vessels that he had to put a hundred men ashore, where many

John Hawkins' slave trade

Hawkins' third voyage, 1567

fell into the hands of the Inquisition. Some of these were burned at the stake, others sentenced to two hundred lashes and several years in the galleys. Meanwhile, those who remained in Hawkins' ship, which had been surprised almost without food, suffered all the torments of famine and died by the score. Only fifteen, it is said, still survived when Hawkins reached Mount's Bay: they were so weak that they could not bring the vessel unaided into Plymouth.

From this time on, Drake, who had arrived home five days earlier, resolved to wage war against the Spaniards in the New World. For all practical purposes the English friendship with Spain, which had lasted since the days of Henry VII, was now dead—though some years were to pass before hostilities became official.

Drake's attack on Central America 1572

After some voyages to the West Indies, in 1572 Drake set off for Central America—the Spanish Main, as it was known to the English sailors. His force, probably financed by important figures at Court as well as by Hawkins, consisted of three tiny ships and little over a hundred men. He first struck by night against a port on the Isthmus of Darien (in the modern Panama). Then with a few companions he set out inland and made friends with the local tribesmen. From a tree-top he had his first glimpse of the Pacific and from two Spanish mule-trains a rich store of gold—the silver was too heavy for the invaders to carry away! He regained Plymouth a wealthy man.

Oxenham in the Pacific, 1576

Three years later one of Drake's lieutenants, John Oxenham, returned to Darien, built himself a pinnace and crossed the Isthmus with the help of the tribesmen. He seized two Spanish treasure ships on the Pacific—then he and his little band were overwhelmed, captured and hanged.

Drake's voyage round the world, 1577–1580

All this led up to Drake's most spectacular achievement—his voyage round the world. Financed by the

Queen, Leicester, Hawkins and others, in 1577 Drake sailed from Plymouth in the *Pelican*, a vessel of one hundred tons, in company with four smaller ships. His official object was to find the great Southern continent which was believed to exist; but he also had the Queen's secret permission to strike a blow against Spain. In fact he intended, apart from looking for the Southern continent, to pass through the Strait of Magellan at the tip of South America—a feat only twice before accomplished—and bring his little force into the Pacific. Off Chile and Peru he would find Spanish vessels carrying gold and silver, brought to the coast from the mining areas and *en route* for the great centre of Lima: vessels almost unarmed whose crews would be utterly unprepared for attack.

Having survived a challenge to his authority led by his second-in-command—whom he executed—Drake eventually reached the Strait of Magellan. He had no sooner passed through than the expedition was scattered by a storm. Out of touch with each other all the surviving vessels then turned for home except the *Pelican*, He reaches which passed on into the Pacific. Making his way the Pacific north, Drake first seized a ship and stores at Valparaiso, then, after raiding the port outside Lima, set off in search of a large treasure ship named the *Cacafuego*. The Outdistancing all pursuers he came up with his quarry *Cacafuego* and helped himself to booty which, according to an eye-witness, included "jewels and precious stones, thirteen chests full of reals of plate, four score pound weight of gold, and six and twenty ton of silver".

Content with this and the proceeds of a few minor prizes, Drake next sailed farther north to California, which he declared annexed for the Queen under the name New Albion. Here he repaired his ship (now renamed the *Golden Hind*). Then, after more exploration to the north, he turned west across the Pacific. His intention was now to complete a voyage right round the world—the second in history. After many adventures he made his way through the Spice Islands, passed south of India, rounded the Cape of Good Hope, and in 1580, nearly three years from the time he left home, sailed proudly into Plymouth Sound.

Home via Spice Islands and Cape

Soon the country rang with Drake's exploits. The cautious Cecil—or Lord Burghley as he had become—disapproved, but the Queen was more than content to accept her share of the rich haul brought home by her "little master-thief". The entire fortune was worth about twice her normal annual revenue, and represented a return of about 4,700 per cent on the capital invested. No wonder she sent for Drake, dined with him on board his vessel in the Thames, and caused him to be dubbed a knight—a gesture the meaning of which could not be lost on Philip of Spain.

Drake knighted

*   *   *   *   *

From the time of Drake's voyage relations with Spain grew steadily worse. The temper of Protestant England, too, became thoroughly aroused by the papal campaign to win back the country for Catholicism—for the methods favoured included supporting rebels and encouraging attempts against Elizabeth's life. Groups of priests were also sent secretly into England, many of them coming from a college for Catholic Englishmen set up at Douai, in Flanders. The youths of this college were specially trained for their perilous task: pictures of torture-chambers adorned their rooms, and the whole intention was to produce missionaries prepared to become martyrs. There was no shortage of volunteers and by 1580 over a hundred priests trained at Douai were secretly at work in England.

The papal campaign against Elizabeth

Priests from Douai

On top of this the Pope in 1580 approved the despatch to England of a secret mission by the Jesuits.

Jesuit mission, 1580

Led by Edmund Campion (a lovable and saintly man Campion whose concern was purely to save souls) and Robert Parsons Parsons (who later spent much of his energy in schemes to overthrow the government with foreign help), the mission had great success for a year, until Campion was captured and brutally executed and Parsons forced to flee abroad.

From the Catholic point of view these missions were Increased fully justified, for they checked the gradual drift of penalties against Catholics towards the official Church, and so preserved Catholics a foothold for Catholicism in England. But at the same time they brought severe trials to the English Catholics —against whom the government soon began to pile up penalties. The fine for failure to attend church was increased to £20 a month; attendance at secret Mass became punishable by fine and imprisonment; while to *become* a Catholic (as opposed to being one already) or to convert others to Catholicism became high treason Death for —to be punished by hanging and quartering. Under conversion to Catholic- these laws, each year for the rest of Elizabeth's reign ism about ten Catholics suffered death or died in prison. According to the Catholic viewpoint, they died for their religion. According to Elizabeth's, they died for treason —for strengthening the forces of her declared enemy the Pope.

In this worsening atmosphere fighting broke out War with between England and Spain over the Netherlands. By Spain in Netherlands 1584 Alva's successor, the Prince of Parma, had managed to restore the southern (and more Catholic) provinces to obedience. In that year, too, a Catholic murdered William the Silent. With the French pre- Murder of William the vented from helping by a fresh outbreak of civil war, Silent, 1584 the Dutch were now in desperate straits and Elizabeth at last agreed to come to their aid. She sent over to English Holland an expedition under Leicester. But Leicester expeditions to help was a poor leader and the troops ill-provided, and Dutch, 1585–1586

Zutphen apart from one success at Zutphen (where the poet Sir Philip Sidney was mortally wounded) the English forces did little.

While England and Spain were slipping into war in the Netherlands, the situation on the seas went from bad to worse. Angered at the English activities in the New World and at the negotiations between English Spanish seizure of English ships, 1585 and Dutch, in 1585 Philip suddenly ordered the seizure of all English ships in Spanish ports. Imprisonment and torture became the lot of many of the crews. In reply, Elizabeth allowed dozens of 'privateers' to prey on Drake attacks Vigo, Canaries, San Domingo and Cartagena, 1585–1586 Spanish shipping; and she also sent off Drake—officially to get back the confiscated vessels. But after plundering Vigo Drake sailed on, wrought great damage in the Canary and Cape Verde islands (Portuguese possessions which Philip had now taken over—together with Portugal itself) and then fell with full force on the town of San Domingo, the capital of Hispaniola (Haiti). This he stripped of its guns and held to ransom, burning ships and parts of the city until the Spaniards paid up. These tactics he repeated at the port of Cartagena, the capital of the mainland. The total booty did not quite cover the cost of the expedition—a disappointment to the Queen, who was the main shareholder—but the whole venture was immensely successful in that it forced Philip to divert to the defence of his overseas empire resources he was anxious to employ in Europe.

Philip prepares Armada Events were now moving towards their long-delayed climax. In 1586 Philip began serious preparations for a great naval expedition, or 'armada', against England. Up to this point he had thought it essential to subdue the Netherlands first; and besides, if he overthrew Elizabeth he would be morally bound to set on the Mary Stuart the Catholic claimant throne the recognized Catholic claimant, Mary Stuart —whose ties were not with Spain but with France.

So Philip moved slowly, stung to desperation though he was by England's actions. He could always hope, however, that during an invasion the English would assassinate or execute Mary, and so clear his path to the throne.

From his perplexity in this matter Philip was released by Mary Stuart. In captivity—where until 1585 she was allowed much local freedom—Mary had never ceased to plan, not merely her return to Scotland, but the best means of supplanting Elizabeth in England. Plots and conspiracies in Mary's and the Catholic interest had abounded; and in 1586 there was now revealed a fresh design, known as Babington's plot, to murder Elizabeth and set Mary on the throne. *Catholic plots* *Babington's plot, 1586*

All details of this fresh plot were known to Elizabeth's principal secretary, Sir Francis Walsingham, for he had cunningly made possible a 'secret' channel for letters between Mary and Babington, who had once been her page. Needless to say all such correspondence was read by Walsingham before being passed on; and he was careful not to strike until he had in his hands a letter from Mary to Babington approving the whole scheme. The result was not only the execution of Babington but a general outcry for the death of Mary. Greatly as she disliked the thought of shedding the blood of a cousin and a queen, and much as she feared the reactions of Scotland, France and Spain, Elizabeth was forced to agree that Mary should be put on trial. *Walsingham* *Mary approves the plot*

At the trial there could be only one verdict. Strongly pressed by Parliament, Elizabeth then found herself forced to condemn Mary to death. A little later, after rumours of a further plot, she got as far as signing the warrant for the execution, but still delayed sending it off to the noblemen whose grim duty it would be to supervise the ceremony. At the same time she made it clear to her principal Councillors that, if Mary had to *Trial and condemnation of Mary* *Elizabeth's caution* die, murder by some private hand would be a much more diplomatic method than public execution. Mary's custodians, however, refused to lend themselves to this scheme. Terrified that some ardent Catholic would strike down Elizabeth while she still hesitated, Burghley and his fellow Councillors then took decisive action. Early in February 1587, without consulting the Queen further, they sent off the warrant.

Execution of
Mary, 1587

When it was received at Fotheringay Castle in Northamptonshire where Mary was confined, the noblemen and gentlemen in charge again considered the alternative of murder. They knew that Elizabeth would greatly prefer it, since it would both relieve her of responsibility and avoid the sacrilege of executing an anointed monarch. Nevertheless they decided against it. On the evening of February 7th Mary Stuart was therefore informed that she was to die by the axe the following morning. Nineteen years of constraint had left her prematurely old and white-haired—she was still only forty-four—but her sense of drama and adventure had not deserted her. She declared—quite wrongly—that she was being put to death for her religion, and did all she could to give the final scene the aspect of a martyrdom. She met her end, as she had met every other situation in life, with unfailing spirit and courage. No less true to form, Elizabeth greeted the news of the execution with fury. She declared that the warrant had been despatched by mistake, imprisoned the secretary in the Tower for over a year, ordered a state funeral for Mary, and went into mourning!

In letters written before her death Mary acknowledged her son James VI (who had been brought up a Protestant) as the reigning king of Scotland. Her claim to the English throne, however, she desired should pass to Philip II. That monarch, who already had a distant claim of his own, could now regard himself as the rightful Catholic ruler of England. His determination to overthrow Elizabeth was accordingly strengthened. From the moment of Mary's death a new vigour marked the preparations for the great Spanish Armada.

Philip the Catholic claimant

CHAPTER FOURTEEN

THE DEFEAT OF THE ARMADA
(1586–1588)

The preparations

IT was in 1585 that Philip had finally decided to invade England. In the next twelve months his plans advanced very slowly while he gradually persuaded the Pope to share the cost of the expedition. During the same year the English, well aware of Philip's intentions, made arrangements for training and mustering able-bodied men and for giving general warning by a chain of beacons.

Since there was no professional army, everything depended on meeting and beating the Spaniards at sea. Fortunately the Royal Navy had for some years been growing steadily stronger. In 1577 Elizabeth had appointed John Hawkins as Treasurer of the Navy Board and under his direction much waste and corruption had been stopped, the seamen's pay had been increased, and old vessels had been rebuilt on more up-to-date lines. Bulky vessels with high superstructures fore and aft gave place to slimmer ships of deeper draught which were altogether speedier and more manœuvrable. The new ships were specially designed, in other words, to carry still further the idea, already developed under Henry VIII, of outmanœuvring opponents and pouring cannon-shot into them from a distance. They therefore carried all the artillery they could, and to this end an upper deck—the 'gun-deck'—was added, so that the heavy guns could still fire through portholes yet leave room for storage below. This reliance on the power of the 'broadside' rather than on hand-to-hand fighting

The Royal Navy

(126)

meant that the ship's company could be smaller—
which saved space and so once again made for handier
vessels.

The low-built, readily manœuvrable galleon, heavily
armed, was the type of ship which Hawkins had made
standard in the English Navy by the time of the Armada.
By contrast the Spaniards, who had large numbers of The Spanish
skilled soldiers, still relied to a great extent on an older- vessels
fashioned pattern of vessel. Though they had built many
fine large ships for their Atlantic voyages and now
mounted all the cannon they could, their vessels were
still in general higher-built and much less handy than
the English ones. Elizabeth's Navy might be very small,
but technically it was well in advance of Philip's.

In 1587 the English government decided to strike at Drake's raid
the Spanish preparations. Boldly sailing right into Cadiz on Cadiz, 1587
harbour, Drake burnt, sank or captured some thirty
ships. He also took two forts near Cape St. Vincent,
paralysed shipping in that area for some weeks, and
seized a prize off the Azores containing enough treasure
to pay for the entire expedition twice over. Having
thoroughly "singed the King of Spain's beard", as he
put it, he returned to Plymouth a popular hero—but
officially in disgrace for having gone beyond his orders.

The English sea captains were naturally eager to con- English
tinue this offensive strategy. They longed to seek out and strategy
destroy the great Spanish Armada in its own waters.
But for a number of reasons—including the difficulty of
keeping a large fleet at sea properly supplied, and the
fact that the Spaniards might evade the English fleet
and find the Channel almost undefended—their plans
were for long turned down. So it came about that in The Armada
May 1588, the Armada eventually sailed from Lisbon sails, May 1588
undisturbed.

No less than one hundred and thirty ships set forth The Armada
on the great venture. The spirit was that of a crusade. a crusade

The crews attended Mass before departure and vowed to avoid all coarse language, the expedition was blessed by the Church, the ships wore the crusaders' cross on their masts or sails, and the banner of the whole enterprise bore the words "Rise, O Lord, and Judge Thy Cause". Philip himself, living more like a monk than a king, spent much of his days praying for the success of the expedition. Bitter was his disappointment when, putting into Corunna for supplies, it was scattered and damaged by a great storm.

Armada scattered

At length, in mid-July, after the English fleets had tried to reach Spain but had been stopped by bad weather and victualling difficulties, the great expedition left Corunna. The plan was for the Spanish fleet to sail through the English Channel and link up at the eastern end with Spanish forces from the Netherlands. The Duke of Parma, in fact, was to supply the main body of troops; but as his fleet was in Antwerp blockaded by the Dutch he would be able to get his soldiers to sea only in small vessels and barges. The main job of the Armada was to defeat or hold off the English fleet so that Parma's men could be ferried across to England.

It sails again: July 12th, 1588

Spanish plan

Unfortunately for Philip his military talent was not equal to his religious zeal. He made a number of mistakes which put the Armada at a disadvantage from the start. To master the English fleet, the Armada should have been much more of a purely naval force; as it was, it was hampered by slow-moving transports, not more than thirty-seven of its one hundred and thirty ships were of a size and strength suitable for heavy fighting, and the soldiers aboard outnumbered the sailors by two to one. Moreover there could be no fixed scheme for meeting Parma, as the Dutch revolt had deprived the Spaniards of all the deep-water ports on the Netherlands coast. Finally, though he handled his forces reasonably well when the time came, the Duke of Medina Sidonia

Spanish mistakes and weaknesses

Medina Sidonia

was an inexperienced and reluctant commander who had protested that he "had neither aptitude, ability, health, nor fortune for the expedition".

On the English side the major fighting ships also numbered something less than forty, most—but not all —belonging to the Royal Navy; in addition there were some smaller naval vessels and nearly one hundred and

The English forces

Queen

Queen Eliz: vifiting her Camp at Tilbury being mounted on Horfeback wᵗʰ a Truncheon of an ordinary Captain in her hand

An Elizabethan Playing Card

From a pack depicting scenes of the Armada. Not surprisingly, Elizabeth figures as the Queen of Hearts.

fifty small ships privately owned. The Lord Admiral was a competent nobleman, Lord Howard of Effingham, fully prepared to listen to his brilliant subordinates Drake, Hawkins and Frobisher. The English ships had the advantage in speed and manœuvrability—which meant that their artillery, though not as superior to the enemy's as had been hoped, could still be used to better

Howard of Effingham

effect; but they were handicapped by a weak supply system. On land, the beacons were ready, command of the musters was given to Leicester, and a large camp was set up at Tilbury—a point well chosen to meet a landing either north or south of the Thames.

The camp at Tilbury

A week's voyage brought the Armada across the Bay of Biscay and on July 19th the great force was sighted off the Lizard. It was in crescent formation, and sailing slowly up Channel under a following breeze. The main English fleet under Howard was then in Plymouth, together with a smaller force under Drake, but for safety's sake—and to deal with any move from Parma—a third group had been stationed at the eastern end of the Channel. By July 21st the Armada and the fleets from Plymouth were in action, to begin a running fight up the Channel which lasted on and off for a week. There were stiff encounters off Portland and the Isle of Wight, but for most of the week it was a matter of the English hanging close on the Spanish rear, sailing to within gunshot, opening fire, and breaking off again to avoid the enemy's unexpectedly powerful retaliation. By the end of the week the Spaniards had lost three ships and the English none, and the English vessels had shown superior sailing and fighting qualities. The Armada had nevertheless kept formation and come through the Channel almost intact. As he anchored off Calais on July 27th Medina Sidonia could congratulate himself that he was well on the way to a meeting with Parma.

Armada sighted off Lizard, July 19th, 1588

The battle in the Channel

Armada off Calais, July 27th

By the 28th, a Sunday, Howard had been joined by the squadron at the eastern end of the Channel. With the English forces linked up but short of food and ammunition it was essential to drive the Spaniards from their anchorage and bring on a decisive battle. That night Howard sent eight fire-ships drifting in with the wind towards the enemy. The trick was not new, but it worked to perfection. Terror seized the Spaniards, their

Armada driven from anchorage, July 28th

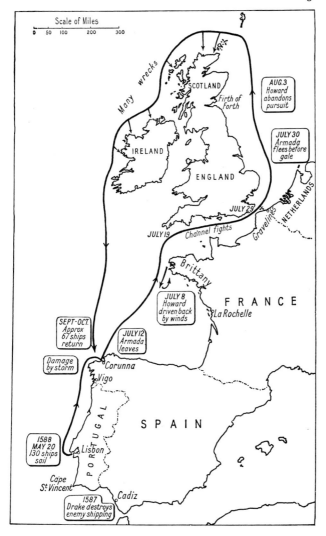

Scale of Miles
0 50 100 200 300

Many wrecks

SCOTLAND

Firth of Forth

AUG. 3 Howard abandons pursuit

JULY 30 Armada flees before gale

IRELAND

ENGLAND

NETHERLANDS

JULY 29

Gravelines

JULY 19 Channel fights

Brittany

JULY 8 Howard driven back by winds

FRANCE

La Rochelle

SEPT-OCT. Approx 67 ships return

JULY 12 Armada leaves

Damage by storm

Corunna

Vigo

P O R T U G A L

S P A I N

1588 MAY 20 130 ships sail

Lisbon

Cape St. Vincent

Cadiz

1587 Drake destroys enemy shipping

The Armada—the Voyage

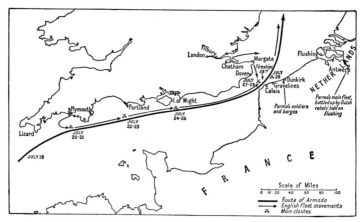

The Armada—the Fight in the Channel

formation was broken, and many of their crews cut loose anchors in their haste to escape.

The fight off Gravelines, July 29th

Escape they did, only to have to face Howard next day off Gravelines. Once again the English proved stronger, but shortage of ammunition stopped them pressing home their full advantage. Towards the end of the

The gale

day a fierce squall sprang up and threatened to drive the Spaniards, caught between the shore and their enemies, right on to the shoals and sandbanks of the Netherlands coast. From this fate they were saved only by an abrupt change of wind which enabled them to stand off from the shore and sail north. Dejected by the English superiority and the grave damage he had already suffered, and despairing of linking up with Parma, Medina Sidonia fled

Armada flees north

before the gale into the North Sea. Watchfully, the greater part of the English fleet followed him up the east coast.

The Spaniards made no attempt to land. When they

English break off chase, August 2nd

had passed the Firth of Forth, Howard (whose supplies were alarmingly short) decided that the danger was over and broke off the chase. In desperate plight, short of food and with the water rotten in their butts, the ships of the Armada sailed on. The most heavily damaged broke up or were wrecked even before they could round the north of Scotland; many more perished off the north and west of Ireland. Those of the enemy who, wrecked or in quest for food, set foot on the soil of the British Isles were slaughtered almost to a man. Of the one hundred _{Spanish casualties}

The Ark Royal

The largest English vessel (800 tons) in commission at the time, the *Ark Royal* was Howard's flag-ship in the struggle against the Armada. Compare it with the earlier ships depicted on page 44, and note how much longer it is in proportion to breadth and how much lower in the water. Note, too, that there are now several sails to each mast, so permitting much greater fineness of trimming.

and thirty ships which left Lisbon not more than nine had been sunk or taken in the Channel, but only half got back to Spain. Of the crews who reached their homeland, nearly all died soon afterwards from the hardships and diseases of the voyage.

So England's triumph was complete. The country had been saved from Spanish rule, the Protestant religion preserved, and both at incredibly little cost—though Elizabeth did not think so, for the war had by now emptied her Treasury and plunged her into debt. In the whole of the fighting only one English ship had been lost and less than a hundred men killed. Many more, it is true, died soon afterwards, of the fevers and scurvy which were the main dangers of the seaman's life; and many were poisoned, it was said, by the rotten beer supplied to the fleet. The sick were landed at Margate, where they lay in their hundreds in the streets, ill and uncared for. At Plymouth Howard and Drake had earlier ordered wine and arrowroot for casualties, but the hardpressed Elizabeth refused to meet any extra charges and the two commanders had to find the cost themselves. In such fashion did Tudor England reward its heroes and saviours.

English casualties

CHAPTER FIFTEEN

THE LAST YEARS OF ELIZABETH I
(1589–1603)

1. *Spain, Ireland and the Earl of Essex*

THE war with Spain did not end with the defeat of the Armada. It dragged on throughout the fifteen years that remained of Elizabeth's reign. The main battlegrounds were the Netherlands, France, Ireland and, of course, the sea. *The war with Spain continues*

In the Netherlands Elizabethan Englishmen helped the Dutch to defy Spain and gain their independence. In France they helped the Huguenot Henry of Navarre, when he became king as Henry IV, to survive the combined attack of Spain and his French opponents. In Ireland Elizabeth repeatedly upset the Spanish plans. But at sea, where the English hoped for their greatest triumph, the war turned out less well than they expected. *The main areas of conflict*

Much of the English fighting at sea took the form of raids. These weakened Spain and helped to end the threat of Spanish rule over Europe, but they were often costly ventures. In 1589, for instance, one hundred and fifty ships were sent off under Drake and Sir John Norris with the double object of destroying Armada shipping and wresting Portugal (or at least the Azores) from Spain. The commanders did much damage at two Spanish ports, but made no serious effort to attack Armada shipping and failed badly in an attempt to take Lisbon. Several of their ships sank in storms, and thousands among the crews became ill and died. The *Drake's raid on Spain and Portugal, 1589* result was that the Queen lost confidence not only in Drake but in all the bolder naval plans.

Grenville and the *Revenge*, 1591 In 1591 there occurred a famous incident in the fighting. A Spanish force surprised off the Azores a small group of English ships lying in wait for the annual Spanish treasure fleet. Most of the English vessels escaped, but either by accident or design the junior commander, Sir Richard Grenville, was slower to leave than his superior and was caught by the whole Spanish force of fifty-three ships. He nevertheless gave combat with his single vessel, the *Revenge*, and fought on until his powder was all spent, his sailors killed or wounded, and the *Revenge* riddled and carrying several feet of water. Mortally wounded, he would then have blown up his ship, had not the survivors among his crew compelled him to surrender.

The *Revenge* was the only galleon of Elizabeth's which the Spaniards were able to capture during the whole of her reign. They did not hold her long. Within a few days a great cyclone hit the Azores. With the *Revenge* it sent to the bottom some seventy Spanish vessels, "not suffering her", as Sir Walter Raleigh later wrote, "to perish alone, for the great honour she achieved in her life-time".

The struggle in Ireland Meanwhile in Ireland a grim struggle had long been going on between the English invaders and the native Irish—who were also always fighting amongst themselves. To stay in Ireland at all, and to keep England safe from invasion, the English soon found it essential to bring most of Ireland under their direct rule. By stern fighting during Elizabeth's reign they had thus far extended their control beyond Leinster and the Pale into Munster. Their only hold over the wild northern territory of Ulster, however, lay in the fact that the most important of the Ulster chiefs, Hugh O'Neill, had recognized English overlordship. A clever and ambitious

man who had been educated in England and held the
English title of Earl of Tyrone, O'Neill in 1595 now Tyrone revolts in Ulster, 1595
confronted Elizabeth's government with one of its great-
est problems. In the hope of creating a Catholic Ireland
united under his own rule, he threw off the English He appeals to Spain
overlordship and appealed for help to Spain. The result
was a fierce struggle which spread to Munster and
caused much outpouring of blood and treasure for the
rest of Elizabeth's reign.

This did not stop England continuing to attack Span- The last voyage of Hawkins and Drake, 1595–1596
ish ships and territory. Individual captains delivered a
multitude of successful pin-pricks and in 1595 Drake
was at last entrusted once more with a command. Together with the veteran Hawkins he set off for the West
Indies. But the expedition turned out unhappily: the
Spanish colonies were now much better defended, little
was accomplished, and both commanders died in the
course of the voyage.

Meanwhile in 1596 Spain had scored a great success
by capturing Calais from France. Anxious to offset this,
Elizabeth unleashed her sea-dogs in full force on a
venture for which preparations were already well advanced. A large expedition including Dutch ships set
off to attack Cadiz—the scene of Drake's famous raid Raid on Cadiz by Essex and Howard, 1596
nine years earlier. The admiral was Lord Howard of
Effingham and the commander-in-chief of the land
forces the Earl of Essex, a brilliant and handsome young
man who was stepson to Leicester and a great favourite
of the Queen. Among the other commanders was
Sir Walter Raleigh. Forcing its way into the harbour
the expedition took two ships and burnt two more—
after which the Spaniards set fire to some fifty others,
including most of their treasure fleet, to save them from
capture. Not content with this, Essex also stormed and
sacked the town, then treated two other ports in similar
fashion on the way home. So great was the damage that

the finances of the hard-pressed Philip were toppled over into bankruptcy—so he repudiated his debts and ruined many of his own subjects.

The second Armada, 1596

This disaster did not stop Philip sending off that autumn a second great Armada—intended no doubt to support Tyrone's rebellion. So determined on revenge was the Spanish king that he drove this fleet to sea, against the protests of his chief naval authority, during the last week in October—a time far too late in the season. The expedition had hardly left Spanish waters when it was caught in a great storm and lost some thirty ships. For the second time, only the broken relic of a mighty armament regained the shores of Spain.

Essex attacks the Azores, 1597

The next year Essex, with Raleigh as one of his squadron commanders, set off to destroy the enemy fleet—for Philip was already building up another—and intercept the annual treasure convoy at the Azores. The expedition misguidedly failed to attack the Spanish warships in Corunna, and concentrated instead on the Azores—where it missed the treasure fleet by three hours.

The third Armada, 1597

A third great Armada, of one hundred and thirty-six ships, was thus able to sail. It put out while Essex was still at sea, and got as far as the entry to the Channel, but once more storms drove back most of the vessels before they came in sight of England.

Death of Philip II

In 1598, death at last removed Philip II from the scene. By this time Spain and France had agreed to make peace, but Essex and other warlike advisers were

Death of Burghley

now in the forefront, the cautious Burghley had died just before Philip, and the war between England and Spain continued.

Essex in Ireland, 1599

In Ireland Tyrone had held out by this time for over four years. Ever thirsting for power and adventure, Essex was now rash enough to seek the task of crushing him. He was appointed Lord Lieutenant of Ireland and given better supplies of money and troops than any previous commander in that country. But fighting in wild and often trackless territory against a hostile population ready for any lengths of savagery was no easy task. After frittering away his strength in minor actions, Essex found himself too weak to deal with the main enemy. Directly against his orders, he failed to attack Tyrone in force, and instead made a truce. His truce with Tyrone

On Elizabeth's furious protests and again contrary to orders, Essex then took ship to England with a company of followers, rode hard for London and, still mud-bespattered from the journey, sought out the Queen. His rivals—among them Robert Cecil, the clever, hunch-backed son of Burghley—were not slow to fan Elizabeth's anger. He was arrested that evening, and held in house custody for many months. Before being released he was deprived of his offices. Then he learnt that he was to lose, too, a royal grant which was his main source of income. His return to England, 1599 · Robert Cecil · Disgrace of Essex

In desperation Essex now set out to turn opinion against Cecil and gather his own followers about him. Clearly he intended to overthrow his rivals at Court by force. So the Council summoned him to explain his conduct. He pleaded illness and instead rode off with a band of supporters from his house in the Strand into the City. Crying out that the succession was sold to Spain and that there was a plot against his life, he tried to stir up a popular demand for the removal of the Queen's "false counsellors". The appeal fell on deaf ears and he attempted to return, only to find his way blocked at Ludgate. A doomed man, he slipped back to his house by water and was promptly arrested. A few days later he and five of his main supporters paid for their follies on the block. Essex's bid for power · His execution, 1601

Meanwhile, in 1600, yet another Spanish Armada—the fourth—had set off from Spain but failed to reach The fourth Armada, 1600

Spanish
landing in
Ireland, 1601

the British Isles. In 1601 a force of four thousand Spaniards at last managed to land at Kinsale, in the south of Ireland, but they were quickly besieged and their help could not save the Irish rebels from defeat.

Mountjoy

By great patience and skill, Lord Mountjoy, the general chosen to succeed Essex, was able to regain a firm hold on Munster and then to strike at the root of the trouble

Surrender of
Tyrone, 1603

in Ulster. By 1603, as the Queen lay dying, Tyrone was on the point of surrender. The English conquest of Ireland was complete, and as the last great Elizabethan achievement an uneasy peace reigned throughout that troubled land.

2. *Puritans, Parliament and the Succession*

Elizabeth's
other
problems

Spain, Ireland and the Earl of Essex were not Elizabeth's only worries in her last years. Among her other problems were religion, finance, parliament, and the widespread distress in the countryside. Another topic which much occupied her ministers, but on which the Queen herself remained obstinately silent, was the question of the succession.

The Puritans

After the defeat of the Armada the chief danger to Elizabeth's religious settlement no longer came from the Catholics but from those who wanted the Elizabethan Church to become still more Protestant. These extreme Protestants had become known as Puritans, since they aimed at a Church 'purified' from the last traces of Catholicism. Some of them objected to the wearing of surplices and other vestments, others disliked set prayers, or organ music during the service, or the use of the ring in marriage, or the burning of candles on the altar. All such things they opposed because they could find no ground for them in the Scriptures—which they regarded as the direct word of God, and therefore as their final authority in religion and life generally.

What Elizabeth disliked most about the Puritans, Puritan however, was that many of them also had strong ideas dislike of on the government of the Church. Such Puritans mostly bishops wanted either to lessen the authority of the bishops or else do away with it altogether. In fact, one important section of the Puritan movement—a section which in Elizabeth's reign was largely confined to the clergy— Presbyterian desired a complete system of Presbyterianism, in which Puritans ministers would be elected by the congregation instead of appointed by a bishop, and in which many other duties of the bishop would be taken over by elected councils of clergy and laymen. As the bishops were chosen by the Crown and were the main means by which the monarch controlled the Church, Elizabeth of course strongly opposed any lessening of their powers.

Another section of the Puritan movement, small in Elizabeth's reign but afterwards to become very important, objected to any general system of Church government and believed instead that each congregation should be independent under its own elected minister. Puritans of this type were known first as Brownists (from Thomas Browne, their leader), then as Brownist or Independents, then—much later, and still in our own Independent day—as Congregationalists. As far as personal conduct Puritans was concerned, all Puritans, of whatever variety, aimed at showing they were the elect or chosen of God. Their ways of doing this included—not always in the same persons!—working very hard, shunning extravagance and expensive pleasures, avoiding theatres (which they thought encouraged vice), wearing very plain clothes, and even—to distinguish themselves from the common herd—using biblical phrases in everyday speech and talking through the nose.[1]

Convinced that these views were a threat to the power

---

[1] This last habit, carried to the New World by emigrants in the following reign, is the origin of the modern 'Yankee' accent.

Elizabeth and Whitgift attack the Puritans, 1583

of the Crown and the unity of the country, Elizabeth in 1583 appointed Whitgift, a great opponent of the Puritans, as Archbishop of Canterbury. He attacked them vigorously by suspending ministers of Puritan opinions—only to be attacked back with equal vigour in anonymous pamphlets. Puritanism was still a movement to reform the Church from within, not to leave it; but besides attending Church, many Puritans were now meeting in private gatherings for prayer, prophecy and discussion. This the government would not allow.

Death for attending unauthorized religious gatherings

By 1593 exile or death became the penalties for those who refused to attend Church or persistently attended unauthorized religious meetings—a measure which struck at Catholics and Puritans alike.

Elizabeth and parliament

Elizabeth's dislike of Puritanism and of any discussion of her religious policy caused some trouble with parliament. So, too, did her refusal to permit discussion of the succession. One Puritan member of the Commons,

Peter Wentworth

Peter Wentworth, boldly defied these bans and went so far as to claim that parliament had the right to discuss all matters of Church and state with complete freedom of speech—but he was not supported by the House, and suffered several spells in the Tower.

The role of parliament

In point of fact parliamentary privileges such as freedom of speech were not at that time understood to apply against the wishes and interests of the Crown. Parliament, though important, still played only an occasional part in government. The Queen and her privy council at the centre, working through royally-appointed officials like the lord lieutenant, the sheriff and the justices of the peace in the shires, still bore the everyday burden of rule. Parliament's power was vague, and the main points clearly recognized were still that laws made in parliament had the highest authority, and that parliament's consent was necessary for fresh direct taxation

New or increased taxes, however, were not yet things to be expected regularly. The ruler was still expected in time of peace to live 'of his own'.[1] Moreover, Elizabeth herself was an expert in living economically. Among other things, she made a practice of setting out on procession in the summer to certain of her royal manors, *Elizabeth's economy* and so was able to enjoy an immense amount of hospitality on the way. Even Elizabeth, however, could not make ends meet when several years of warfare came to cap a general rise in prices caused by the influx of gold *The great price rise* and silver from the New World [2] In the last fourteen years of her reign she had to ask parliament four times *Elizabeth asks for taxes* for extra taxation. This was voted fairly willingly, but the request naturally gave parliament a greater sense *Increased importance of parliament* of power and importance. It is notable that in Elizabeth's reign there occurred the first recorded instance of someone trying to secure a seat in the Commons by bribery!

The growing confidence of parliament, like the growing force of Puritanism, was to be felt much more in the next two reigns. Even so, there were times when only the great personal skill and prestige of the Queen prevented a serious clash. A good example came towards the end of the reign, when trouble arose over the question of monopolies—grants by the Crown to individuals *Conflict over monopolies* or companies of the sole right to make, import, or sell a certain article.

These monopolies were not confined to inventions or specially hazardous ventures, but were being used as a form of payment to Elizabeth's counsellors. This meant not only that the public had to pay more for the article under monopoly but also that the ruler was getting an

---

[1] See pages 16–17.

[2] The precious metals spread through Europe from Spain. By becoming more common, gold and silver were reduced in value. This caused people to ask more of them, i.e. higher prices, in return for their goods.

extra revenue uncontrolled by parliament. In 1601 the
matter came to a head when the Commons broke into
a storm of criticism and one member read out a great
list of monopolies. "Is not bread there?" cried another,
greatly daring. Sensing trouble, the Queen, while not

The Queen's concessions

abandoning the system itself, abolished a number of
monopolies which had been abused. She also made her
concessions so gracefully as to leave Members of Parliament more devoted to her than ever. When a deputation
waited on her to express thanks, her speech to them—

Her last speech

her last public address to any of her subjects—struck a
note at once tactful and deeply felt: "Though God hath
raised me high, yet this I count the glory of my crown,
that I have ruled with your loves. . . ."

In the last three years of Elizabeth's life there occurred
two developments of great importance for the future.
The East India Company was founded, and a new Act
of Parliament completed the framework of a national
system of poor relief.[1] The subject of the greatest concern
to Elizabeth's counsellors, however, was the succession.

The succession: James VI of Scotland

The obvious candidate by birth was James VI of Scotland, son of Mary Stuart; and since the execution of his
mother James had behaved with a shrewd eye to his
own interests. He had protested against the execution,
but not too strongly; he had resisted any temptation to
ally with France; and though he had worked hard to
overthrow the Presbyterian system in Scotland he had
not become Catholic.

Elizabeth to the last made no public announcement—
except, according to Robert Cecil, a sign of consent on
her death-bed. Nevertheless the choice was clear, and
during her closing years Cecil was quietly working to
bring in James as soon as Elizabeth died. When in 1603
the sixty-nine-year-old Queen was smitten by a fatal
illness, arrangements were complete. A few hours after

[1] See pages 151–153.

RELIGIOUS SETTLEMENT CHALLENGED
BY CATHOLICS AND PURITANS

EXPLORATION: GROWTH OF OVERSEAS TRADE

THE STRUGGLE AGAINST SPAIN

GROWTH OF INDUSTRY   DEVELOPMENT OF POOR LAW

INCREASED WEALTH AND COMFORT

LITERATURE: THE THEATRE: MUSIC

SOME FEATURES OF ELIZABETH I'S REIGN

the Queen breathed her last the Privy Council and other leading men approved the proclamation of James, which was then read by Cecil in the streets of the capital. Soon official messengers, already outstripped by unofficial ones, were spurring north with the news for which King James VI of Scotland had long been working and waiting—the news that he was also King James I of England.

James I of England

CHAPTER SIXTEEN

ELIZABETHAN ENGLAND (I)

1. *Population, Agriculture, the Poor Law*

THE achievements of the Elizabethan period be- *Population*
come all the more remarkable when we remember
that England was still a country with a very small
and scattered population. No more than $4\frac{1}{2}$ million
people, it is thought, inhabited England and Wales at
the beginning of the reign, and 5 million at the end. Of
these, some 300,000 lived in London; but the next biggest city, Norwich, had only about 17,000, and probably
no other town more than 10,000. Most people, then,
were still country dwellers; and most still lived in the
more advanced south and east. The western counties,
however, especially Gloucestershire and Devonshire,
were now developing very fast.

Except for a tiny remnant of serfs and villeins still
'bound to the manor', Elizabethan Englishmen were a
race of free men. But though the old differences in men's
legal status had almost passed away, new divisions in
social classes were already growing up instead. The *Gentle and*
main distinction was between 'gentle' and 'simple'. *simple*
Among the gentry (who were below the small class of
nobility, and who were technically distinguished from
the 'simple' by the right to a coat of arms) were to be
found learned clergy, lawyers, university men, and all
those—and their families—who by owning land (or anything else) could live without toil. In the class of 'simple'
came the broad mass who worked for their daily bread,
from the country labourer to the ordinary craftsman in

the towns. Regarded as somewhere between gentle and simple, however, came the 'yeomen' (strictly a term for the smaller owners of freehold land, though loosely used to include also the larger tenant farmers) and the many prosperous merchants and masters in the towns.

This social distinction was sharpened by the fact that no one beneath the ranks of the gentry was appointed to the important office of sheriff or justice of the peace. But though the gentry in this way largely 'ran' the counties, they did not control the most important towns, which usually had charters entitling them to an elected mayor and corporation. Fortunately, too, the gentry, like the nobility, were not a 'closed' caste; for as the eldest son normally inherited the family estate, his younger brothers often entered professions or served apprenticeships in the more select trades and so caused the lower ranks of the gentry to merge into the growing middle class. Moreover a poor townsman might prosper in trade, buy land, and find the humble origins of his family very quickly forgotten—or forgiven. As Burghley wisely remarked, "Gentility is but ancient riches".

'Degree'

On the whole, the idea of *class* counted for very little with the Elizabethans, whose interest in social distinctions was not between class and class, but between person and person. The Elizabethan thought much in terms of *degree*; as God was entitled to more respect than the angels, and the angels to more than man, and man to more than the beasts, so within the race of man a duke should command more respect than an earl, an earl more than a baron, a baron more than a knight, a knight more than an esquire, an esquire more than a gentleman, and a gentleman more than a labourer. Similarly a master was entitled to more respect than an apprentice; and a master in some trades (such as the goldsmiths') to more than a master in others. This meant that social position by no means depended on high birth alone; for if a knight became a baron, or a merchant a landed gentleman, or an apprentice a master, he at once received the respect due to his new status. Every man thus had a more or less clearly understood place in society, in accordance with which he acted, and expected other people to act to him. 'Jack's as good as his master' was an idea very foreign to the Elizabethans.

Haymaking

From a ballad sheet. Everyone—women and children too—joined in for haymaking. It was, as the couple in the background seem to indicate, one of the more enjoyable tasks in the annual round.

By far the greater part of the people—as at any time until the 19th century—still worked on the land. The most highly cultivated areas were the East (apart from the great wastes of the Fens) and the Midlands. Over a good deal of these more fertile stretches, but especially in the Midlands, the old 'open field' system still continued, with the division into strips as in medieval times. *Their main work—agriculture*

Except in times of bad harvests, the countryside grew enough to feed the Elizabethan people very well. The *Food supply* chief crops were wheat (especially in the Midlands and south-east), barley (which was grown very widely for beer) and oats (a common crop in the North). Fruit—including apples, pears, cherries, quinces, apricots and peaches—grew plentifully in orchards and gardens; it was enjoyed by all except those—a fair number—who thought it brought on colic and other internal disorders. Vegetables, too, were produced in fair quantity in the thousands of household plots. Of the different kinds, cabbages, carrots, onions and parsnips were mainly used in soups and stews; the potato, introduced during the reign from North America, remained a luxury; the most popular were probably salads, peas, beans and—more surprisingly to us—lupins. Of produce new in Tudor time, hops, for flavouring beer, were perhaps the most important. They were grown mainly in Kent, a county which had never had the open-field system, and where it was therefore easier to introduce a new crop.

Among livestock, sheep were increasing rapidly, and pigs and poultry were plentiful. But because there was not enough hay or root crops to sustain them during the winter, cattle were mostly still killed and salted down at Martinmas (in November). For at least half the year, only the rich tasted beef that was not salt.

The autumn slaughter

All told, the land was being made to yield more than ever before. No longer did each family or village produce only enough for its own wants. Spurred by the great rise in prices, landlords strove to increase the income from their estates, both by producing more and by putting up rents. Where the kind of tenancy permitted, rents and inheritance fines (paid by the son on succeeding to his father's holding) were often raised very sharply, the intention of the lord of the manor being to drive out tenants who could not pay the increase. The lord could then either relet the land to someone who would pay the higher rent, or else farm it himself and

Increased production and rents

secure a bigger return by using improved methods or perhaps turning it into a sheep run. This taking back of land into direct use by the lord of the manor considerably reduced the number of peasant land-holders—the descendants of the earlier villeins. Most of the land-holding peasantry in fact survived until the 18th century, but already in some parts of the English countryside the landless labourer was becoming common

The landless labourer

In the course of securing a greater income from the land, many lords also took to enclosing and cultivating large stretches of wild or waste. This enclosure of fresh land from the waste was usually regarded quite favourably. So too was the grouping together and enclosure of the land (including land in the open fields) held directly by the lord of the manor, as long as this was still kept under the plough. Two kinds of enclosure, however, already mentioned earlier, were much resented: attempts to enclose commons already in popular use, and the enclosure of plough-land for sheep farming.[1] This last type of enclosure, which often meant turning out whole families and even villages from their homes and jobs, caused so many complaints that one could easily imagine no other sort was going on. In fact, however, 'depopulating' enclosure of this kind was largely confined to the South Midlands; the less harmful types were the more usual, but less was heard of them.

Enclosure

*   *   *   *   *

The 'depopulating' type of enclosure was one of the causes of that growth in 'vagabondage' which so worried Tudor statesmen. Together with the break-up of the manorial system, the ban on the nobles' private armies and the casting adrift of monastic servants at the dissolution of the monasteries, it put a fair number of men out of their former occupations, and so led to wandering

Vagabond-age

[1] See page 74.

in search of work or plunder—mainly the latter. To deal with this, the government at first relied on severity.

Early measures against 'sturdy beggars'
Under Henry VIII, 'sturdy beggars' were to be branded with a 'V' and sent back to their native parish; under Somerset persistent vagabonds might be handed over to farmers as slaves. Very early, however, it was seen that though such methods might succeed with the work-shy, they were unsuitable for the sick, the elderly and the smaller number who were anxious to work but unable to find any.

Elizabethan remedies
It was in 1563 that Elizabeth's government seriously began to grapple with these problems. One law declared that no more tilled land was to be enclosed for pasture. Another enabled the parish authorities to help the sick or feeble poor by levying 'a poor-rate' on all house-holders.

A poor-rate
Statute of Apprentices
A third, known as the Statute of Apprentices, laid down very strict regulations about labour. Men were to work in the districts in which they were born; if they entered a craft they were to serve an apprenticeship of not less than seven years; and if they could not prove themselves tradesmen they must seek work as agricultural labourers at wages to be fixed by the justices of the peace—or suffer the stocks and a flogging. This last law was far too sweeping to be fully enforced; but taken as a whole the three measures did something to meet the problems of poverty and vagabondage and to keep the country stable.

Other statutes dealing with the poor were passed as time went on, and finally, in 1601, one of the last Acts of Elizabeth's reign summed up the successful features of earlier measures and laid down what was intended to be a permanent poor-law for the entire country. By this

The Poor Law of 1601
the J.P.s in every county were to appoint for each parish two, three or four prosperous householders to assist the churchwardens as 'overseers' of the poor. These overseers could levy a compulsory 'poor-rate' on the

inhabitants of their parish. With the proceeds of this the overseers were, among other things, to buy stocks of material on which the able-bodied unemployed could be set to work. Begging was prohibited, and those too infirm for work were to be cared for in almshouses—if their parents or children could not support them. Pauper children were to be apprenticed to a master. As for the 'sturdy beggars' who declined honest work, these were no longer to be bored through the ear with an inch-wide iron (a punishment which had replaced branding with a 'V'). Instead the work-shy offender was to be "stripped naked from the middle upwards and openly whipped until his or her body be bloody", and then sent back to the parish of his birth (or failing that to his last-known residence), and there 'disciplined' in a special 'house of correction' or the common jail. After suitable 'discipline' sturdy beggars were to be set to work, but if they returned to the life of the vagabond there were further punishments still in store: banishment, service in the galleys, and death.

So the Tudor poor-laws ended by distinguishing clearly between four classes of pauper—children, the aged and infirm, the genuinely unemployed, and the wilfully idle—and laying down a suitable treatment for each. All this helped to cope with some of the worst difficulties of the time, and to preserve peace and order in the Elizabethan countryside.

2. *Industry and Foreign Trade*

Though some sections of the people suffered real distress, Elizabethan England as a whole was a country of rapidly increasing wealth. The main source of this, apart from increased production from the land, was the making and export of woollen cloth. All over the country, men and women spun yarn in their spare time.

Increase in national wealth

Cloth industry

In fine weather, a spinning-wheel outside a cottage door was one of the commonest sights in England. Much of this yarn was bought up by merchants known as clothiers, who distributed it to the many full-time and part-time weavers, paid them wages for their work, and collected and sold the woven product. Probably more of this cloth—including new and lighter kinds, much

A Cottage Housewife

From a ballad sheet. Spinning was usually done outside the cottage door in fine weather. Note the early form of spinning wheel worked not by a treadle but by hand.

favoured by the Elizabethans—was being sold within Britain than ever before; but no longer did the Netherlands provide the same easy overseas market as in the earlier half of the century. Currency changes, the Dutch revolt, and the war with Spain all made the lot of the English exporter difficult.

New industries   Of the other industries, some, such as silk-weaving and lace-making, had been recently introduced by

Protestant refugees from abroad. Others were old- established, but were now fast expanding. There was, for instance, a great increase in coalmining—the coal was used both for domestic heating and for industry (e.g. in the making of salt, sugar and soap) but only in areas near the coalfields or in direct touch with them by sea or river. Great encouragement, too, was given by the government to the mining of copper, tin, zinc and lead. The smelting of iron, the making of cutlery, glass and paper, the casting of guns, the building of ships—these and many other industries developed apace. A great new fishing industry, too, was growing up—for herring in the North Sea, and for cod right across the Atlantic, off Newfoundland. All these occupations being either new or based outside the towns, escaped regulation by the now declining craft gilds.[1]

On the whole the newer industries were important for the home rather than the foreign market—for despite all difficulties cloth-making was still responsible for something like four-fifths of England's exports. Mainly to sell cloth, Elizabethan Englishmen extended their country's foreign trade in many fresh directions. Much of this trading was done through companies, of which the greatest was now that which had long handled the export of cloth to the Netherlands and Germany—the Company of Merchant Adventurers. The members of these Companies traded either as individuals within the company's rules (as did the Merchant Adventurers) or else on the new 'joint stock' principle (by which the trading was done as a common enterprise and the various individuals shared in the profit or loss in proportion

---

[1] In London (and later in other towns) the influence of the great livery companies was now becoming strong. Though concerned with certain trades such as the goldsmiths' or mercers' their members were mostly rich merchants rather than craftsmen. The main function of the livery company was not so much to regulate its own trade as to play a part in the government of the city.

to their stake in the venture). To make up for the risks of foreign trade, in either case the company operated under a charter from the Crown granting it a monopoly of English commerce with the area concerned. Such was the pattern on which was formed in Mary's reign (following the voyage of Chancellor) the Muscovy Company for trade with Russia, and then under Elizabeth the Eastland Company for trade with Poland, Scandinavia and the Balkan countries, the Levant Company for trade with Turkey and the Near East, and—the greatest of all, near the very end of the reign—the East India Company, a joint-stock enterprise, for trade with India and beyond. The new markets opened in this way helped English trade to survive such blows as the loss of Calais, the French wars of religion, and the exclusion of English merchants from the Spanish Netherlands.

3. *Discovery*

Discovery Much of the growth in overseas trade came about because of the vigour with which Englishmen had now flung themselves into the quest for new lands and fresh routes to the East. Something has already been said of Hawkins and Drake, but these were only two among scores of Elizabethan sea captains with a thirst for wealth and adventure. Of the others, five at least must be mentioned in even the briefest account of the Elizabethan age.

Gilbert One of these is Sir Humphrey Gilbert. A Devonshire man, M.P. for Plymouth and a step-brother of Sir Walter Raleigh, he early gained a reputation as a soldier. His real life's work, however, centred round his belief in a North-west Passage to the Far East—he wrote a pamphlet to prove its existence—and his conviction that England should control any such passage by planting colonies at suitable points in North America. In such colonies, urged Gilbert, could be settled "needy peoples of our country which now trouble the commonwealth". After some years he at length obtained a royal charter permitting North-western discovery and colonization, but his first voyage accomplished little.

Gilbert's second voyage, undertaken in 1583, brought him fame and death. Arriving at Newfoundland (which had been discovered by John Cabot nearly a century earlier and which was now visited annually by fishing fleets from several nations), he claimed the island in the Queen's name and set up the first English colony in North America. The colonists (who had brought not only necessities but also "music in good variety, not omitting the least toys, as morris dancers, hobby-horses, and May-like conceits to delight the savage people. . . .") quickly set to work to prospect for precious ores. Meanwhile Gilbert sailed on to make another settlement, but lost a large ship carrying colonists off what we now call Nova Scotia. So he turned for home, by that time with only two little vessels. He himself insisted on sailing in the smaller, a tiny pinnace—'frigate' the Elizabethans called it—of ten tons. Then came a tempest in the Azores. *[Colony in Newfoundland]*

> The frigate was near cast away . . . [reported the captain of the larger vessel] yet at that time recovered; and giving forth signs of joy, the general (Sir Humphrey) sitting abaft with a book in his hand, cried out to us . . . "We are as near to Heaven by sea as by land". The same Monday night, about twelve, the frigate being ahead of us . . . suddenly the lights were out . . . in that moment the frigate was devoured and swallowed up of the sea.

The settlement in Newfoundland soon succumbed and many years were to pass before a permanent colony took root; but from Gilbert's venture sprang a much greater interest in the whole idea of colonization.

Another pioneer in North American discovery was the Yorkshireman, Sir Martin Frobisher, who first won *[Frobisher]*

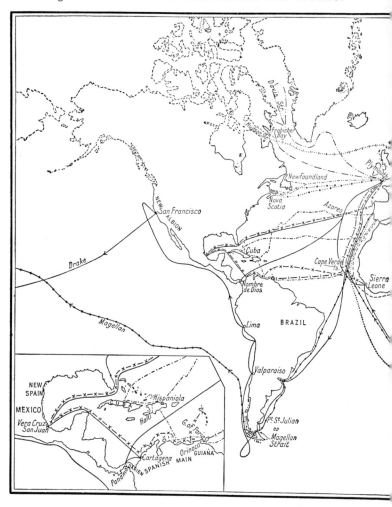

Elizabethan

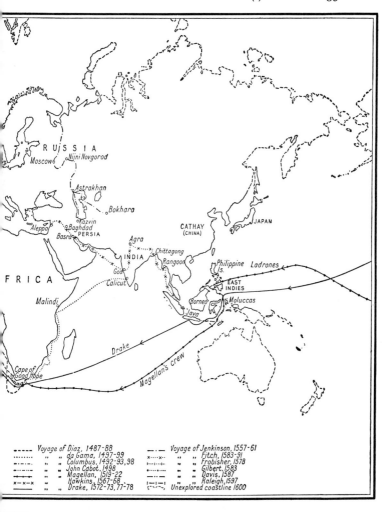

RUSSIA
Moscow
Nijni Novgorod
Astrakhan
Bokhara
Aleppo
Kazvin
Baghdad
Basra
PERSIA
Agra
Chittagong
INDIA
Rangoon
CATHAY
(CHINA)
JAPAN
Goa
Calicut
Philippine Is.
Ladrones
EAST INDIES
Borneo
Moluccas
Java
FRICA
Malindi
Drake
Magellan's crew
Cape of Good Hope

---- Voyage of Diaz, 1487-88
.... " " da Gama, 1497-99
-.-.-.- " " Columbus, 1492-93,98
—..—.. " " John Cabot, 1498
+—+—+ " " Magellan, 1519-22
x—x—x " " Hawkins, 1567-68
.... " " Drake, 1572-73,77-78

—.—.— Voyage of Jenkinson, 1557-61
x----x " " Fitch, 1583-91
..........." " Frobisher, 1578
••••••••• " " Gilbert, 1583
—..—..— " " Davis, 1587
!-!-!-! " " Raleigh, 1597
⌐¬⌐¬⌐ Unexplored coastline 1600

vages

fame as a privateer. Like Gilbert an ardent believer in a North-west Passage, he at length secured financial backing and the Queen's licence for a small expedition. He sailed in 1576, investigated an opening in Baffin Land, and returned to declare that he had discovered the Passage—though had he investigated much farther he would have found it blocked by land. With him he brought back a piece of black mineral which he believed, and an assayer soon pronounced, to be gold ore. The result was the formation of a Cathay (China) Company, with a charter from the Queen, and a rush by Court and City alike to invest in it. Thus financed, Frobisher made a return voyage on which he took possession, in the Queen's name, of the country round **Frobisher Bay**. Of the Esquimo inhabitants, his companions reported that "there is no flesh or fish which they find dead (smell it never so filthy) but they will eat it as they find it . . . a loathsome thing, either to the beholders or hearers".

From this expedition Frobisher returned with three shiploads of the mineral. Only minute quantities, if any, of gold had been extracted from this when he left for a third voyage in 1578, his object being now to colonize as well as exploit the newly discovered territory. This time he found a real strait, later known as Hudson Strait; but the discovery attracted little notice—for Frobisher came back with several shiploads of the mineral, only to find that no gold worth mentioning had been produced from the earlier lot, and that the company had gone bankrupt. This fiasco ended Frobisher's North American ventures; but he later played a prominent part in the raids on Spanish possessions, and was knighted for his services at the time of the Armada. He died from a wound received while fighting the Spanish invaders of Brittany.

Davis A third name, linked to those of Gilbert and Frobisher by the quest for a North-west Passage, is that of the great seaman John Davis. A Devonshire man and a friend of the Gilbert family, Davis voyaged three times in successive years in search of the Passage, sailing between Greenland and the lands north of Labrador. He made many fresh observations and discoveries, established the true relation between Greenland and North America, and twice thought that he had hit upon the Passage—the second time when he had reached the record latitude of 73° N. in Baffin Bay. Finding there open, ice-free sea, he beat on against contrary winds till shortage of food forced him to turn back. "I have been in 73 degrees", he recorded on his return, "finding the sea all open and forty leagues between land and land. The passage is most probable, the execution easy."

After this, Davis took part in the fighting against Spain, including the defeat of the Armada, and in an unsuccessful attempt to enter the Pacific through the Strait of Magellan and discover the North-west Passage from the Pacific end. This voyage, on which the Falkland Islands were discovered, vividly illustrates the hardships which the Elizabethans were prepared to suffer in quest of new lands and trading routes. During the return journey Davis's men began to die of hunger:

> Their sinews were stiff and their flesh dead, and many of them were so eaten with lice, as that in their flesh did lie clusters of lice as big as peas, yea and some as big as beans. Divers grew raging mad and some died in most loathsome and furious pain. It were incredible to write our misery as it was: there was no man in perfect health but the captain and one boy. . . . To be short, all our men died except sixteen [of 91], of which there were five able to move. . . .

Besides undertaking such voyages, Davis invented a quadrant and wrote *The Seaman's Secrets*, the first English treatise on navigation—previously we had relied on translations from the Spanish. In his last years he sailed three times to the East round the Cape of Good Hope, in the service, among others, of the newly formed East India Company. He met his death at the hands of Japanese pirates off Sumatra.

Gilbert, Frobisher and Davis all spent much effort trying to find a passage to the East by way of North America—a passage which was not discovered till the 19th century, and which then proved impossible as a normal route. Gilbert's half-brother and fellow-Devonian, Sir Walter Raleigh, also voyaged to America, but to much more rewarding parts. A man of action with a wealth of other talents—he was also a fine poet and wrote a *History of the World*—Raleigh had already made his mark as a sailor and soldier before he attracted the attention of the Queen. His tall, handsome figure and quick intelligence rapidly gained Elizabeth's favour, and his first venture in colonization—in Ireland—was assisted by a large grant from the Queen of forfeited Irish land. Following this, he helped to finance Gilbert's last voyage, and on Gilbert's death secured from Elizabeth the right to plant new settlements in America. Between 1584 and 1587 he sent out four expeditions, including two under his cousin Sir Richard Grenville; and to the territory which they explored—the coast from Florida to North Carolina—he gave the name Virginia, in honour of the unmarried Queen. Two settlements of a hundred or more souls were made, but both proved short-lived. The first, planted by Grenville on Roanoke Island, off North Carolina, broke up the following year when Drake anchored off the coast and allowed the hard-pressed colonists to return home with him—only a fortnight, as it happened, before Grenville returned to the colony with supplies and reinforcements.

These schemes of American colonization were interrupted by the Armada. Shortly afterwards, Raleigh lost

Raleigh

Colonies in Virginia

the Queen's favour by wooing one of her maids of honour. From his semi-retirement he emerged in 1595 to lead an expedition to Guiana, on the northern coast ^{Guiana} of South America. He was inspired by his belief, gathered from the Spaniards, that in the highlands up the Orinoco lay an empire of fabulous wealth, ruled by El Dorado, the gilded king. To this empire he did not manage to penetrate—in fact it did not exist—but he returned convinced that he had seen gold mines on the banks of the Orinoco, and that he was on the brink of a great discovery. The following year, serving under Essex, he led the great raid on Cadiz, but later quarrelled with Essex and helped to foil his rising. Soon after the accession of James I he was arrested on a charge of having conspired to place James's cousin, Arabella Stuart, on the throne; and in the Tower he remained for the next twelve years, until the tragedy of his final expedition to Guiana and later execution.[1]

Lastly—though his voyages took place earlier than ^{Jenkinson} those mentioned above—must be included the name of Anthony Jenkinson, a pioneer of travel into Russia and ^{Russia} thence to the Near and Middle East. Between 1557 and 1572, as the envoy both of the Queen and of the Muscovy Company, Jenkinson helped to develop regular commerce with the Russians—of whose habits and customs he and his companions left picturesque descriptions. From Russia, after sailing down the great rivers, he twice crossed the Caspian—once to reach as far as Bokhara and on the other occasion to penetrate to Persia, where he stayed some months at the court of ^{Persia} the Shah. Ignoring all dangers from unknown territory and fierce tribesmen, he did more than any other Englishman of his time to open up trade with this part of the world. The list of the countries he visited during his twenty-six years of travel is too long to quote in full,

---

[1] See page 201.

but besides Russia, Armenia, Persia and the lands of Asia Minor it included Flanders, Germany, Italy, France, Spain, Portugal, Rhodes, Malta, Sicily, Cyprus, Crete, Greece, Turkey, Syria, Lebanon, Palestine, several parts of North America, Norway and Lapland! As a voyager to the East he was to be surpassed in later Elizabethan times only by Ralph Fitch, who crossed Mesopotamia, travelled through India, and visited Burma.

With men of the character of Jenkinson, Davis and the rest, it was no wonder that England was able to discover new markets overseas to take the place of those she was temporarily losing on the Continent. Largely thanks to this, her export trade continued to survive, and her wealth to grow. And it was no wonder that the Elizabethan parson Richard Hakluyt, when publishing his great collection of accounts of the *Principal Navigations, Voyages, Traffiques and Discoveries of the English Nation*, should have been moved to make the proud inquiry in his preface:

Hakluyt's *Voyages*

> Which of the kings of this land before her Majesty, had theyr banners ever seene in the Caspian Sea? Which of them hath ever dealt with the Emperor of Persia, as her Majesty hath done, and obtained for her merchants large and loving privileges? Who ever saw before this regiment [rule], an English Lieger [ledger] in the stately porch of the Grand Signor at Constantinople? Who ever found English Consuls and Agents at Tripolis in Syria, at Aleppo, at Babylon, at Balsara, and which is more, who ever heard of Englishmen at Goa before now? What English shippes did heretofore ever anker in the mighty river of Plate? passe and repasse the unpassable (in former opinion) straight of Magellan, range along the coast of Chili, Peru, and all the backside of Nova Hispania, further than any Christian ever passed, travers the mighty bredth of the South sea, land upon the Luzones [Philippines] in despight of the enemy, enter into alliance, amity

and traffike with the princes of the Moluccas, and the Isle of Java, double the famous Cape of Bona Speranza [Good Hope], arrive at the Isle of Santa Helena, and last of all returne home most richly laden with the commodities of China, as the subjects of this now flourishing monarchy have done?

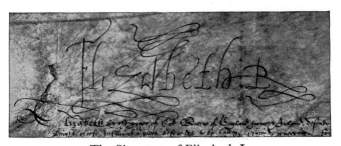

The Signature of Elizabeth I

The combination of boldness, artistry, and complexity well expresses the character of England's greatest queen.

CHAPTER SEVENTEEN

ELIZABETHAN ENGLAND (II)

1. *Houses, Furniture, Dress*

New
building

THE clearest sign of England's increasing wealth under Elizabeth was the immense amount of new building which took place. Towns spread beyond their old boundaries; villages grew into towns; fine new manor houses appeared in all parts of the country; everywhere rude hovels gave place to well-built houses and cottages in timber, 'half-timber' or stone. Indeed, one of the most striking changes in Elizabeth's reign, according to a contemporary, was the huge increase in the number of chimneys. These were replacing the old means of emitting the smoke—a hole in the roof. Made even more desirable by the growing use of coal for heating, and at the same time made possible by the greater use of brick, chimneys were in themselves a sign of the improved standard of building—and wealth—of the Elizabethan age.

Chimneys

Glass
windows

Apart from their chimneys and superior construction, possibly the greatest improvement in these new houses was the increasing use of glass for windows. In the Middle Ages glass had been imported from Italy and was very expensive, with the result that it was used only for costly buildings like the great churches. The ordinary cottager had made do with a slit in the wall, a small window of horn, or a lattice of reeds. Now the manufacture of glass in England brought glass windows into common use. Usually made of very small leaded panes, they let light into the home—and so gave rise to

The Great Bed of Ware

This magnificent four-poster, a unique affair capable of sleeping a family, is mentioned in *Twelfth Night* and is now in the Victoria and Albert Museum.

healthier domestic conditions and a new desire for household things that were beautiful as well as useful. In the early Tudor period, when windows were still small and scarce, they were often taken away by departing tenants; but during the reign of Henry VIII it was ruled that windows were a part of the building. By the end of Elizabeth's reign only the houses of the poor were without them.

With better houses went another sign of the nation's Better increased wealth—better furniture. Rough stools and furniture trestles, almost the only common articles of wooden furniture in the 15th century, were replaced by well-made oak chairs and tables; and tired Elizabethans— always excepting the poor—no longer flung themselves

Dining at Home

A woodcut from a ballad sheet. Note that the diners are sitting (or in the case of the youngest, standing) on stools, not chairs; and that the man has his hat on.

down to sleep on a rush-strewn floor or a straw palliasse with a covered log for a pillow, but climbed instead into **Beds** the comforts of a proper *bed*, with a flock or feather mattress and bolster. Moreover, if the bed were one of the elaborately carved 'four-posters'—which cost a good deal and were sufficiently prized for people to mention them in their wills (Shakespeare left his widow his "secondbest bed")—the occupant(s) could draw the curtains and enjoy a certain amount of privacy even if (as was likely) other people were frequently passing through the room.

A country manor house The furniture of a typical Elizabethan house of the finer kind, such as a country manor house, now gave a **Coverings** degree of comfort previously unknown. Coverings, for instance, were more varied, and more widely used, than ever before. For the stone or wooden floors, rushes mixed with herbs were still the usual covering; but rush-mats were becoming common by the end of the reign. The small tables and seats were often covered with fine carpets—which were far too valuable to put on the floors. For the walls of the main rooms there were coverings of many kinds. In the 15th century people who could afford them often had hangings of brightly dyed woollen cloth, but now these were varied with tapestry (a sign of wealth), painted canvas, paintings done directly on the plaster, and the extremely popular oak panelling.

In the bedrooms there were the four-posters with their silk or embroidery hangings, less important beds of a trestle type, and truckle-beds (with a low frame and castors) for servants and children. These truckle-beds were often stowed away under a larger bed in the daytime, to be pulled out at night. Bedclothes consisted of linen sheets, blankets, and sometimes fur rugs. Of other bedroom furniture the main items were usually a clothes press, a table, a stool or two, a polished metal mirror (glass by the end of the reign), and a jug and basin. *Bedroom furniture*

Downstairs, the heart of a great Eilzabethan house *The hall*

A Privy (Private) Chamber

From a ballad sheet. Smoking was first introduced in the late 1560's— probably by John Hawkins's men—and became fashionable in the 1570's.

was the hall, where the family and their servants ate. This had a dais at one end, screens and a passage at the other—as may still be seen in most of the halls of the Oxford and Cambridge colleges. It was furnished with long tables and benches, stools, a few chairs (which were much less common than stools, and regarded as seats of honour), and some chests and cupboards, including court (= short) cupboards for displaying plate. Arms or armour might decorate the walls, to gleam brightly at night by the light of candles (which had now replaced rushes). At the meals, to which the men sat down wearing hats, platters and trenchers of wood were

Cutlery, etc. now giving place to plates of pewter or silver. Spoons in these metals were now also common, but forks, recently introduced from Italy, were still very rare. When knife

Middle House, Mayfield

A fine example of Elizabethan half-timber construction—in this case with additional wooden facings to produce a striking effect in complicated black-and-white pattern. Comfortably placed merchants or lawyers often occupied houses of this size.

An Oak Draw-Table

I.e. with extending leaves. This fine specimen, with its bulbous legs
fashionable in the Jacobean period, dates from 1610 and is now in the
Victoria and Albert Museum.

and spoon could not cope, even Queen Elizabeth picked
up the chicken bone in her fingers.

Among the other rooms downstairs in a large house Parlour
would be a parlour, for the use of the family, and furnished with stools, a chair or two, chests, cabinets and
probably a small table. Downstairs in some great houses,
upstairs in others, might also be a long gallery containing Long gallery
some of the best furniture of the house and any musical
instruments—perhaps an organ or a pair of virginals.
A room of this kind was commonly used for entertaining,
and was much favoured by the children of the house for
their games.

The kitchen in a great house was the capital of an Kitchen, etc.
empire which included the pantry, the buttery, the

dairy, the still-room (for distilling), the laundry and the bake-house. The kitchen, with its spits for roasting, cauldrons for boiling, and brick-ovens for baking, usually boasted a bewildering array of pots and pans; and the dairy was equally well furnished with churns, tubs, crocks, vats, presses and the like. Beyond these outbuildings was **Garden** the garden, valued in earlier times mainly for its herbs and fruit, but now also with a section laid out purely for the sake of appearance. In this part of the garden, very formal and symmetrical, were grown the flowers—often in knot-shaped beds with dwarf edgings of box.

Sanitation However well designed in other respects, even the greatest Elizabethan houses were planned with little heed to sanitation. In the general absence of piped water, there were no bathrooms; when people wanted a bath they had one in a wooden tub—in winter before a fire. Washing was done in basins, or out of doors; but soap was expensive unless made at home. Toothbrushes were unknown, but teeth were rubbed with cloths—and picked. Scent was used a great deal, to disguise unpleasant smells. Remarkably enough, a water closet was invented towards the end of the reign by a godson of the Queen—who installed one in Richmond Palace; but it was looked upon merely as a curiosity and not generally imitated for another two centuries. Instead there were earth and other closets in cellars and courtyards, only occasionally dug over or cleared out, and a very general use of pails—which in towns were freely emptied into the street. On the whole the Elizabethans, like all previous generations, were content to live at close quarters with their muck, on the time-honoured principle that "the more the dirt is moved, the more it stinketh".

Life in a spacious, well-furnished country house of this time offered a rich variety of interest. For the owner there were all the affairs of the estate, together possibly with the duties of a lord of the manor and a justice of the peace. For his wife, there was the supervision of a Wifely range of tasks far beyond the ordinary cooking and duties cleaning to which we are accustomed. A country gentleman's wife was expected to know how to salt fish, to cure hams, to preserve fruit, to pickle vegetables, to make jams, to bake bread, churn butter, brew ale and cider. She must know how to dry herbs, make soap, distil perfumes, make pastilles for burning to sweeten the air, cure feathers for mattresses and pillows, make and mend clothes. She must be expert with her spinning-wheel, and skilled in home-made remedies—for she was also the family doctor. In all these tasks, except the last, she would have much help, both from servants and family. When her husband was away, it might even fall on her to manage the entire estate. Only in one thing, possibly, was she called upon to do less than the modern housewife: 'wash-day' usually came not once a week but about every three months!

As with houses and furniture, so with dress. Interest Dress in personal attire reached new heights in Elizabeth's reign, and was by no means confined to the female sex. Noblemen and courtiers especially demanded colour and richness in their clothes—not merely in minor items like gloves, stockings and hats, but also in the main garments of doublet, trunk-hose (breeches usually ending above the knee), and cloak. Those who could afford it usually had these garments made of velvet or silk imported from Italy or the East and ornamented with fine embroidery and precious stones. Such tastes, however, were expensive. A handsome doublet jewelled, might easily cost £100—perhaps the equivalent of one or two thousand in our own money—and, like the bedstead, would be worth special mention in one's will.[1] Costly,

[1] It is unfortunately impossible to give any general factor by which prices in olden times can be multiplied to bring them up to a modern equivalent.

Doughton Manor　　　[*Country Life*
A good example of an Elizabethan manor house constructed in stone.

too, were the rich jewels in rings or on gold chains, which were worn quite as much by men as by women.

Among the clothes were two articles at first seen only in fashionable circles but later to become much more widespread. These were the very high ruff made of fine lawn starched and wired, and worn about the neck of both sexes, and the women's 'farthingales' or hooped petticoats. Grandeur of dress, however, was a badge of gentility and wealth, and not for the mass of the people. Many ordinary folk had a best garment or two in which silk or velvet or embroidery might appear, but mostly they wore simple, if colourful, garments of wool, often in cloth of their own making. Extremely sober clothes worn by a member of the upper or middle ranks of society were usually the mark of a Puritan.

2. *Some Elizabethan Customs*

To see a little more of Elizabethan life, let us follow the story of a boy born into the family of a well-off country gentleman. That story might, of course, take many

An imaginary country gentleman

different shapes. It could, however, go something like this.

John was by no means the first arrival, for his mother had already borne twelve children. Only five of these, however—two boys and three girls—had survived infancy. At the confinement, the midwife attending John's mother in the house encountered some difficulty, whereupon John's father at once had the church bells rung to ease matters. Safely delivered, John was quickly put to a 'wet nurse'—for his mother had too many cares to feed him herself. At times he also sucked from a *Infancy* feeding-bottle made from a cow's horn. Very soon came his christening, which was made the excuse for a great celebration; and for some months he lived a pampered life, reclining in a cradle on rockers and playing with rattles and bells.

Before long the fussing stopped. From the age of three *Education* or four John was expected to concern himself seriously with his education. He was supposed to master his first lessons from his horn-book (a piece of wood imprinted with the alphabet and figures, and covered with transparent horn); to suffer whipping with good grace; and to begin to call his father 'sir' and his mother 'madam'. A few more years and he was sent away to stay with one of his father's friends in the nearest town so that he might attend the grammar school. There he toiled from 6 a.m. to 5.30 p.m. at Latin and Greek (for it was classical, not English, grammar that was studied at a grammar school), and at mathematics, rhetoric and logic—to say nothing of listening to innumerable sermons. By thirteen years of age he was considered fit to go to the university at Cambridge where, however, he still lived under strict regulations, expected to work from 5 a.m. to 5 p.m., and having to be indoors by 9 p.m. and sleep under the eye of his tutor. Nevertheless he contrived to enjoy himself, and to acquire the habit of hard drinking.

Marriage   It was shortly after he had come down from Cambridge, at the age of sixteen, that John was married to a girl of thirteen carefully selected by his parents. She was the daughter of a well-off merchant, the first of his family to become a gentleman: and she had a substantial dowry. The betrothal had taken place some years beforehand; but had either John or his bride objected strongly to the match their parents would not have forced it upon them. After the wedding ceremony at the door of the church and the prayers inside, the festivities at home provided great fun. As usual the young men vied for the bride's hair-ribbons and garters; and after some hours of feasting, dancing and merry-making, the whole company trooped upstairs, saw the young couple tucked up safely in bed, and retired downstairs to continue the party. The next day John and his wife did not go away but stayed on in the house of the bride's parents. Then, their honeymoon over, John took his wife back to live with him in his parent's home. Bride and groom were well pleased with each other—very fortunately, for to untie their marriage knot would have required nothing less than a special Act of Parliament. Among her special attractions to him were that she had naturally fair hair and a strawberries-and-cream complexion. She therefore required none of the fashionable aids to the type of beauty favoured by the Elizabethans—aids such as white lead to whiten the face and neck, or cochineal mixed with gum to redden the cheeks and lips.

Legal studies   At the age of eighteen John went to London, there to keep terms and read law at one of the Inns of Court. He did not intend to become a lawyer, but a knowledge of the law would be useful to him later as an estate owner, and possibly as a justice of the peace and one of the Members of Parliament for the county. Meanwhile his wife and baby—for they already had their first child—remained in his parent's house and saw him only during the vacations. Very often the hundred-mile journey to London proved hard on account of the weather but on his stout mount John always got through, riding thirty miles or so in the day, and resting at night in one of the excellent inns. In this way he fared better than a wealthy friend of his father's who owned one of the recently introduced coaches, with open sides and no springs, and who had found it liable to be stopped by the mud in winter and overturned by the potholes in summer. He fared better, too, than the poorer folk who travelled—when they did travel—in the country carrier's cart, together with vegetables, animals, and goods of all kinds. *Travel*

John had barely finished studying law when his father began to suffer increasing pain from a stone in the kidney. Being a courageous and strong-minded old gentleman—he seemed old, for he was now in his sixties—he decided to undergo all the risks of an operation. Anaesthetics being unknown, he dulled his senses a little with alcohol, submitted to be held down by three of his strongest servants, and was opened up by a surgeon of good reputation. The pain was well-nigh unbearable, but the surgeon was skilful, and succeeded in extracting the stone. Unfortunately, however, the surgeon's instruments, though he knew nothing about this, now carried germs which had not been destroyed by the wash and wipe he had given the knives after his last case. Instead of healing, the wound became infected, gangrene developed, and within three weeks John's father was dead. *Father's illness and death*

As John's two elder brothers had died in their teens— one from plague, the other from smallpox—John was the heir to the property. He at once ordered full mourning for his father. The room in which his father had died, the hall and the main staircase were all draped in *Funeral* black; John and his sisters donned black clothes, which they wore for the next three years; and John's mother put on 'widow's weeds', which she decided to wear for the rest of her life. Within a week the coffin—the dead man's position in life demanded that he be 'chested', though poorer folk were buried in only a shroud—was being borne to the parish church, beneath the stone floor of which it was to lie. The service over, the family returned to the house that was now John's, to partake of substantial refreshments with the other mourners, and to see that charitable gifts of food, drink and money were distributed to the poor. In such fashion did John, at twenty-one, enter into his estate—which he continued to supervise and enjoy until, worn out with the burden of advancing years at the age of fifty-seven, he in turn made his last journey to the parish church.

CHAPTER EIGHTEEN

ELIZABETHAN ENGLAND (III)

1. *Ideas*

BEFORE we leave John, let us see a little of what he A country believed as a mature man. First and foremost, of ^{gentleman's} ideas course, he believed in the Christian religion in its Religion most literal form. He believed unquestioningly that God had made the universe (in seven days); that Man had been expelled from Paradise and become liable to sin because Eve had successfully tempted Adam; that to save Man from the punishment due to sin God had sent to earth his son Jesus Christ; and that through Christ's atonement in his own person for the sins of mankind, it was possible for Man, if he believed and acted aright and God favoured him, to avoid the everlasting torments of Hell and instead enjoy perpetual bliss in Heaven with the Creator. Believing these things, John in his reflective moments regarded earthly fortune and misfortune as rather unimportant. What happened to one in this world, which was temporary, mattered very little compared with what would happen in the next, which was eternal. Being a normal man, however, John was not often in reflective mood. He therefore set more store on worldly goods, and his family, and the pleasures of eating and drinking, than might have been imagined from his sincerely held religious beliefs.

Because of his religion, and also because of what he knew of history and public affairs, John linked up the idea of God very closely in his mind with the idea of Order. God had created Order from Chaos; and there Order was always the danger of a return to Chaos through the sins of Man and the promptings of Satan. Similarly with the state: the power of the monarch (which corresponded down below to that of God up above) brought order, but only while it kept uppermost over rebellious forces—whose triumph would mean disorder. This was why it was so important to John that men should know their place and station in life and keep to it; for failure to respect due authority could only lead to confusion and disaster.

The ladder or chain of Creation

In fact, John mentally pictured the differences in rank between men as only one group of rungs in an immense ladder—or perhaps one group of links in an immense chain—which stretched from the lowest part of Creation to the highest. At the bottom were the lifeless things, such as the metals, or the four elements of earth, water, air and fire—yet each in due degree, for gold was nobler than iron, air than earth. Next came the plants in due degree—the oak, for instance, was nobler than the bramble. Beyond the plants came the animals, from the lowest (like the starfish) through the intermediate groups (including the ant) to the highest (such as horses and dogs). Then came Man, in all his many degrees, and beyond Man the Angels, also of many kinds. At the top was God, the Creator of all, who saw below an infinite series, of which each part had a special excellence (stones, for instance, though more lowly than living things, were more durable), and of which each part in some way served the part above (plants, for instance, nourished animals, and animals nourished men). To John, religion and Order were thus very much akin; for God's plan showed Order in all senses of the word—command, sequence, arrangement, control.

The spheres

According to John's idea of things, the Heaven in which God resided was outside the Universe he had created. The universe itself consisted of ten concentric spheres, decreasing in size towards the inmost (like the toy boxes which fit inside each other). All these spheres revolved, the angels turning the outer one—the *primum mobile*—and this controlling the movements of the rest. As they revolved, they made a heavenly music, too fine to be heard by the human ear. In order from the *primum mobile* inwards these spheres were those of the Fixed Stars, Saturn, Jupiter, Mars, the Sun, Venus, Mercury, the Moon, and the Earth—which was thus at the centre of the universe and the point round which all else revolved. This did not imply any superiority, however, on the part of the Earth. On the contrary, everything in the spheres from the *primum mobile* to that of the Moon was eternal and perfect; only beneath the Moon, in the sphere of Earth, were things changeable and imperfect. This was because only in the sphere of Earth were the four elements not perfectly fused. They were in layers, with earth at the bottom, water next, air next, and fire (as might be seen in meteors) on top of all; but as some were at enmity with others (water with fire, for instance), the arrangement was being constantly upset. So the Earth was a changeable, far from perfect place, in John's philosophy—and this was amply confirmed from his everyday experience.

It was of these same elements, thought John, that all The elements things on Earth were made. A good mixture of them produced something lasting, like an oak or a diamond; a poor mixture something which passed quickly away, like frost, or a butterfly. Similarly with Man: it needed a good mixture to produce a healthy man of long life. This correct mixture, moreover, had to be maintained, for in the human body the elements had counterparts which were constantly striving to come out on top and overthrow the proper balance. These counterparts were known as humours, and the way in which they were Humours

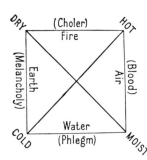

mixed, or *tempered*, decided a man's *temperament*. They were liquids manufactured by the liver, from food passed to it by the stomach—food made, of course, from the four elements. There was the humour of Melancholy (which corresponded in coldness and dryness to the

Medicine   element of Earth), the humour of Phlegm (cold and moist = Water), of Blood (hot and moist = Air) and of Choler (hot and dry = Fire). If one of the dry humours became too prominent, thought John and his doctors, the correct remedy was a purgative; if one of the moist humours, bleeding.

These ideas of John's about the humours came from a Greek physician of the 2nd century named Galen, just as his idea of the revolving spheres came from a 2nd century Greek named Ptolemy. They were rather out of date, but John was not in touch with the newer thought of the day. Like most country gentlemen, he had not read any of the Elizabethan books on the astronomy of Copernicus, which put forward an entirely different

Alchemy   heavenly system with the Sun at the centre. Similarly he was a believer, though many more studious Elizabethans nowadays were not, in the possibilities of alchemy. He thought it quite on the cards that someone would eventually distil something which would become the philosopher's stone, capable of banishing baseness from metals (and therefore of turning lead into gold). He thought it rather less likely, however, that the other object of alchemy would ever be achieved—the distillation of an elixir which would remove baseness from the body, and so prolong human life.

Truth to tell, although John was intelligent and had

received an excellent education, he was by modern standards extremely superstitious. Because of his idea of the heavens, he imagined that, by the Will of God, stars from afar were influencing not only the movements of the Earth and its surrounding elements but also indi- Astrology vidual human destinies. He even believed that each part of the body was to some extent governed by one of the planets or signs of the zodiac. Aries, for instance, governed the head and face, Capricornus the knees. He therefore thought that skilled astrologers could cast horoscopes showing the heavenly influences affecting an individual—who could then act at the best moment for success, when the conjunction or coming together of certain stars strengthened the forces in his favour. Not everyone, however, followed John in this belief: for some learned and critical people were beginning to lump astrology and alchemy together as bogus studies practised by knaves to deceive fools.

Most of John's other superstitions were widely shared not only by the ignorant but by the intelligent and thoughtful. He believed whole-heartedly in elves and Fairies, etc. fairies, fiends and hobgoblins. He believed that ghosts walked the earth, between midnight and the first cock-crow, and were then able to communicate with men. He believed that there were sorcerers, able by their incantations and knowledge of black magic to summon spirits from Hell to do their bidding. He believed that witches, in secret compact with the Devil, could fly on Witchcraft broomsticks, sail in eggshells, raise storms, blight crops, and cast evil spells alike on man and beast. Nor was it surprising that he did so, when even so learned and talented a man as King James VI of Scotland had had four women of North Berwick burned for practising witchcraft against him. They had attempted—they ad-mitted under pressure—to destroy James and his bride at sea, by casting a cat with a spell upon it into the water and so raising a tempest. When this had not produced the desired result, they had melted a waxen image of the King. John could only agree with King James that such creatures must be ruthlessly hunted down, and their practices stamped out.

All told, John had many beliefs firmly based on reason and good sense, and many that the civilized world has since agreed to regard as unfounded. It is not difficult to believe in witches and ghosts and hobgoblins, we must remember, when one lives in deep country, with few roads, few people and no street lamps!

2. *Recreation*

Elizabethan contrasts

Elizabethan England was in many ways a land of contrasts. There was the contrast between the poverty of some sections of the people and the growing wealth of the country as a whole; the contrast between a high standard of culture and a general belief in superstition; the contrast between the healthy life of the country and a high death-rate in the insanitary and disease-ridden towns. There was also the contrast between the homebound life of the women and the much wider opportunities open to men. Perhaps there was no greater contrast in Elizabethan England, however, than that between the spirit of Puritanism and the spirit of carefree enjoyment.

Sports and pastimes

Elizabethan England was a great country for vigorous sports and pastimes and for celebrating such old customs as gave a good excuse for feasts and frolics.[1] Among sports there were hunting the deer, the hare and the

---

[1] So far as feasting is concerned, the scale of eating among the well-to-do may perhaps be judged from one writer's recipe for a summer feast for fifty persons. He advises a first course of twenty dishes—they were all set on the table at once for the guests to help themselves—of the following kinds: a dish of salad, of capon, pike, turkey-chicks, bream, wild ducks, quails, meat, venison, brawn, a swan, 'a fawne or kid with a pudding in

otter, hawking, fowling, fishing, tilting, shooting, archery (which was ceasing to be a serious branch of national
defence), skating, cudgel-playing, and wrestling. Among
games there were tennis (a sport of the wealthy—not the
modern lawn tennis), bowls, ninepins, stoolball and
football—the last-named legally forbidden in the interests of archery and public order, but in fact played
everywhere by large numbers on each side, using a
pig's bladder for a ball and on a 'pitch' extending
perhaps over three or four fields, a stream or two, and
the whole length of the village street. Of sporting
spectacles the most popular were cock-fighting and the
baiting of bulls or bears with dogs—Elizabeth herself
delighted to watch bear-baiting, and sometimes provided it as a diversion for visiting ambassadors.

Among the festive occasions specially celebrated were Festive
Hallowe'en, Christmas, Twelfth Night, St. Valentine's occasions
Day and May Day. The last-named was honoured by
the young people of the village visiting the woods over-
night and returning at dawn with boughs and garlands
to decorate a maypole, round which they then danced.
Another regular time for dancing, as for most other
popular pastimes, was the ordinary Sunday afternoon,
after divine service in the morning. All these festivities,
together with the 'Church-ales' (festivities to raise 'Church-ales'
money for the church) and the not infrequent marriages,
christenings and funerals, were needless to say accompanied by a great deal of heavy drinking. And though
wine flowed freely only in the town taverns and the
houses of the well-to-do, beer (the staple drink for
children as well as adults) in those days really *was* beer,

his belly', a lomber pie, a venison pie, a chicken pie, a bustard, a
pheasant, a potato pie, young chickens, and a 'set custard'. To follow
all this there should then be a second course of twenty dishes, including
salmon, neat's tongue, and 'sowst pigge', and a third course, of ten
dishes, to include buttered crabs, pickled oysters, and 'a dish of Harti-
choakes'.

and the effect of the stronger brews was soon visible even on such hardened consumers as the Elizabethans.[1]

The Puritan attitude What was regarded by the bulk of the population as honest enjoyment, however, was viewed very differently by the Puritans. With the actual nature of some of these diversions many Puritans had no quarrel, but nearly all Puritans resented the fact that they took place so largely on Sundays—for the Puritan, with his belief that the Bible was the literally-inspired word of God, was determined to make Sunday the equivalent of the Jewish Sabbath, a day of complete rest from all worldly pursuits. Some Puritans, too, disapproved of almost all games and sports as distractions from the things of the spirit and the hard daily toil which was the best recipe for keeping men (and women) out of mischief.

A Puritan on football How much one Puritan, at any rate, disliked some of the traditional English pastimes may be seen from Philip Stubbs's *Anatomie of Abuses*, published in the 1580s. Here is Stubbs on football:

> For as concerning football playing, I protest unto you it may rather be called a friendly kind of fight, than a play or recreation; a bloody and murdering practice, than a fellowly sport or pastime. For doth not everyone lie in wait for his adversary, seeking to overthrow him and to pick him on his nose, though it be upon hard stones, in ditch or dale, in valley or hill, or what place soever it be he careth not, so he have him down. And he that can serve the most of this fashion, he is counted the only fellow, and who but he? So that by this means, sometimes their necks are broken, sometimes their backs, sometimes their legs, sometimes their arms, sometime one part thrust out of joint, sometime another, sometime their noses gush out with blood, sometime their eyes start out, and sometimes hurt in one place, sometimes in another. But

---

[1] Good beer could be had for a penny a quart. This sounds very cheap; but to earn a penny, in addition to her food, a woman employed on odd jobs might have to work for a whole day.

Kemp's Dance

Will Kemp, a famous actor and clown, betted that he could dance all the way from London to Norwich to the music of pipe and tabor (drum). He took nine days to do it. He won his bets, and afterwards wrote an amusing account of the episode.

whosoever scapeth away the best goeth not scot-free, but is either sore-wounded, and bruised, so as he dieth of it, or else scapeth very hardly. And no marvel, for they have sleights to meet one betwixt two, to dash him against the heart with their elbows, to hit him under the short ribs with their gripped fists, and with their knees to catch him upon the hip, and to pick him on his neck, with a hundred such murdering devices. And hereof groweth envy, malice, rancour, choler, hatred, displeasure, enmity and what not else; and sometimes fighting, brawling, contention, quarrel-picking, murder, homicide and great effusion of blood, as experience daily teacheth.

The Puritans, like everyone else, drank strong liquor, for there was as yet no tea or coffee to replace beer as the national drink. They drank it, however, in moderation. Very properly, Stubbs has no patience with drunkards:

And on drunkenness

A man once drunk with wine or strong drink rather resembleth a brute beast than a Christian man. For do not his eyes begin to stare and to be red, fiery and bleared, blubbering forth seas of tears? Doth he not froth and foam at the mouth like a boar? Doth not his tongue falter and stammer in his mouth? Doth not his head seem as heavy as a millstone, he not being able to bear it up? Are not his wits and spirits, as it were, drowned? [etc.]

Puritanism and the theatre

Puritan anger reached its height, however, against those recreations which drew large crowds and so exposed ordinary folk to contact with the least respectable sections of the people. For this reason, and because it attracted so many citizens from their work, they hated not only bear-baiting but also one of the chief glories of the age—the theatre.

Origins of Elizabethan drama

The origins of Elizabethan drama include the medieval 'miracle' (or 'mystery') plays presented first by the clergy and later by the craft gilds (e.g. the story of the Ark, performed by the Shipwrights' gild); the late medieval 'morality' plays (in which qualities like pride or virtue are treated as persons); and the comic 'interludes' sometimes presented between the miracle and morality plays. Such plays were still acted in the early part of Elizabeth's reign, though less widely than before the Reformation. Then came a new source of inspiration—the old Latin plays, which as part of the movement of the Renaissance were now being studied, and acted, in the big schools. From acting Latin plays, schoolboys next began to act English plays—works which sometimes followed a classical model very closely, yet developed a life and style of their own. Some of these schoolboy acting teams—in particular certain choirboys—soon developed into expert companies and drew large crowds. They were not, however, without rivals; for groups of professional performers, who had long travelled the country giving entertainments of song, dance and mime, also took to acting plays. The themes of these plays came not only from the classical drama but also from the interludes, from English history (which was just becoming a subject of study) and from the general life of the time.

In presenting these plays the professional actors met great difficulties, since they were classed with rogues and vagabonds unless they could obtain the patronage of some nobleman and call themselves—for example— 'The Earl of Leicester's Men'. The best patronage of all was that of the Court, where the new plays were from the beginning as popular as they were soon to become outside. Normally the professional players acted in the courtyards of inns if the city authorities would consent; but fear of public disorder, of the apprentices deserting their work, and of plague being spread among the crowds of spectators, often caused that consent to be withheld. In 1576, however, a wooden building called 'The Theatre'—the first in England—was built near Shoreditch, just beyond the boundaries of the City of London. And from the building of 'The Theatre'— which was soon followed by others, such as 'The Curtain', 'The Globe', and 'The Fortune', all just outside the sphere of the City authorities—English drama rapidly rose to heights which it has never since attained, let alone surpassed.

After the first outstanding group of playwrights, including Christopher Marlowe, had shown in the 1580s the power and possibilities of English drama written in blank (unrhymed) verse, there emerged a whole series of great dramatists, of whom the peak and crown was of course William Shakespeare. They were fortunate in living at a time when the English language, recently enriched by many phrases of Latin and Greek origin as

The players' difficulties

'The Theatre', 1576

Great dramatists

Shakespeare, 1564-1616

The English language

a result of the Renaissance, had just reached its full glory, and so when men could become almost intoxicated with the new beauty of words. Besides the drama there was also great writing of many other kinds—

including great narrative poems like Edmund Spenser's *Faerie Queene*, thousands upon thousands of beautiful lyric poems, and much fine prose, as in the essays of Sir Francis Bacon. In a class by itself as a masterpiece of

prose was—and is—the Authorized Version of the Bible— produced (like some of the very greatest of Shakespeare's plays) not in the reign of Elizabeth but of her successor.

The Elizabethan era was a time not only of great literature but also of great music. The richest outpouring came, as with the plays, from the 1580s onwards. Superb music was written for the main keyboard instru-

ments of the time, the organ and the virginals,[1] as well as for the two most popular stringed instruments—the lute and the viol. The latter was made in different sizes, the whole range, normally played together, making up what was known as a 'chest of viols'.

Perhaps greatest of all, however, was the vocal music. Some of this was written for church use, particularly by Orlando Gibbons and by the Catholic composers, Thomas Tallis (one of the earliest of the great Tudor musicians) and William Byrd. Some, as in the lovely 'ayres' of John Dowland, was intended for solo voice with lute accompaniment. But the most common form of all was the unaccompanied part-song, usually known to us as the madrigal, for singing in the home. In beauty, variety and profusion the Elizabethan and Jacobean madrigals have never been surpassed, and those who wrote them helped to make their period the finest in the whole of England's musical history.

---

[1] An instrument in which the strings, being plucked by a quill (instead of hit by a felt-headed hammer as in the modern piano), gave forth a much thinner sound.

The Swan Theatre

This sketch, from a letter written in 1596 by a Dutch traveller named Johannes de Witt, is famous as being the only contemporary drawing known to exist of the interior of an Elizabethan theatre. Note the platform stage jutting right out into the auditorium, the enclosing circular walls fitted up with galleries, and the balcony at the back of the stage, which could be used either for actors or spectators. In at least two respects, however, the drawing is probably inaccurate. The roofing should extend further forward, to reach almost to the edge of the stage, and between the doors at the back of the stage should be a curtain which could be drawn back to reveal **an** inner room.

A musical
nation

Elizabethan music was not merely the concern of a few talented people. It went deep down into the life and heart of the nation. Part-singing—as with the Welsh today—was a common accomplishment, and anyone of good education was expected to be able to 'bear his part'. Public concerts entirely devoted to music did not yet exist but music appeared constantly in other entertainments—witness the many lovely songs in Shakespeare's plays. Sir Francis Drake, a true Elizabethan in this as in other things, was so fond of music that he carried a company of musicians round the world with him in the *Golden Hind*. Indeed, so keen was the appetite for music that even in the barbers' shops—another Elizabethan luxury—a lute was often provided, in case a waiting customer should wish to play or sing or pay a boy to do so.

Another very striking thing about Elizabethan music is that, as with Elizabethan drama, there was no sharp distinction between the 'popular' and the 'good'. Unlike the position in our own time, the popular was then good, and the good popular.

The Eliza-
bethan Age

The Elizabethan period, though marred by much poverty, ignorance, cruelty and superstition—as indeed are most periods—was among the most glorious in English history. It was an age of deep feeling, or ardent patriotism, of pulsating vigour and high adventure. In the course of it English trade expanded rapidly, English wealth grew apace, the Spanish enemy was humbled, the British Isles became more united. Despite strong religious passions on either side, the people were held together by the new Church settlement; and throughout all the long reign the monarch, mean, tantalizing and unfair as she was, retained her grip over the country's destinies and her hold on her people's affections. This she did through her superb intelligence, her humane disposition, her high spirits and courage, and her deep political wisdom. The Elizabethan Age produced great literature, great music, fine building, great feats of daring and discovery. Very little of all this would have been possible had not the country enjoyed that internal peace and wise government which were the supreme gift of a great ruler.

CHAPTER NINETEEN

JAMES I AND THE CLAIMS OF PARLIAMENT
(1603–1625)

1. *Religion and Taxation*

The new
monarch

HE was of a middle stature, more corpulent through his clothes than in his body, yet fat enough, his clothes ever being made large and easy, the doublet quilted for stiletto-proof, his breeches in great pleats and full stuffed. . . . He was naturally of a timorous disposition, which was the reason of his quilted doublets. His beard was very thin; his tongue too large for his mouth, which ever made him speak full in the mouth, and made him drink very uncomely, as if eating his drink, which came out into the cup at each side of his mouth. His skin was as soft as taffeta, which felt so because he never washed his hands, but only rubbed his finger-ends slightly with the wet end of a napkin. His legs were very weak . . . that weakness made him ever leaning on other men's shoulders. . . . He naturally loved not the sight of a soldier, nor of any valiant man. . . . He was so crafty and cunning in petty things, as the circumventing any great man, the change of a favourite, etc. in so much as a very wise man was wont to say, he believed him the wisest fool in Christendom, meaning him wise in small things, but a fool in weighty affairs.

Such, according to one of his courtiers, was the man who in 1603 succeeded the greatest Queen in history.

James in
Scotland

It was scarcely surprising if James (who was also kindly, sensible and scholarly) had not the reckless courage of his mother Mary Stuart. Declared king as a baby, he had been brought up amid the strife and treachery of contending factions of nobles. By playing off one party against another he had eventually been able to win a fair measure of power, and even to assert his authority over the Scottish Church—the Presbyterian organization of which he had weakened by restoring the abolished office of bishop. By the time he came to the throne of England he was master, if not undisputed master, in his native realm of Scotland.

This dour struggle for power coloured James's whole outlook. He had seen his kingdom torn between conflicting creeds, his parliament merely a battleground for the opposing factions. He had therefore every reason to think that order and good government could only be guaranteed if the king's authority were complete and unquestioned. James, in other words, believed very strongly in the 'Divine Right of Kings'—the theory that the king derives his authority from God, that mere mortals cannot tamper with the hereditary succession, and that as the king owes his power to God, so he must account for his actions to God alone. Should a wicked king commit unjust acts, these must be suffered as a punishment from God—for any resistance to the king would cause more trouble than it would prevent.[1]

It was with a firm belief in Divine Right and a bitter past experience of Presbyterianism that James approached his first problem in England—that of religion. All parties had high hopes of him, but the most clamorous were the Puritans. James's mind was in fact made up in favour of Elizabeth's existing system, which would leave him with power over the Church. Nevertheless he was ready to make minor amendments and so called a

James's views

Divine Right

Religion

---

[1] The Tudors had also thought (and acted) along these lines, but did not express the theory so frequently, systematically or tactlessly as James, who delighted to write long and over-scholarly discourses for the instruction of his subjects.

Hampton
Court
Conference,
1604
conference at Hampton Court to let the Puritan wing of the Church state its case. The Catholics were not allowed to champion their cause in public; but as they did not seem dangerous and James was not of a persecuting nature, he was quite willing to leave the laws against them unenforced.

The Hampton Court Conference left no doubt where James's sympathies lay. He rejected almost all the alterations demanded by the Puritans—in good-humoured fashion until their spokesman was rash enough to plead that certain matters should be decided by the bishop 'with his presbyters' (councils of elected ministers and lay-elders). At the word 'presbyters', James burst out:

> If you aim at a Scottish Presbytery, it agreeth as well with a monarchy, as God and the Devil. . . . Then Jack and Tom and Will and Dick shall meet, and at their pleasure censure me and my Council. . . . Then Will shall stand up and say "It must be thus", then Dick shall reply and say "Nay, marry, but we will have it thus".

After this, James summed up his views in the famous phrase "No bishop, no king". The king, in other words, could not rule unless he could control the Church through his chosen instruments the bishops. As he departed, James then uttered a fatal threat—that he would make the Puritans conform to the official doctrines or else "harry them out of the land". Only in one respect did the Conference prove useful: the Puritans asked for an improved translation of the Bible and to meet this request steps were taken which resulted
Authorized
Version of
the Bible,
1611
in the publication of that wonderful work of scholarship and literature, the Authorised Version.

James
attacks the
Puritans
James lost no time in trying to carry out his threat. Despite the fact that many Puritans wanted only minor alterations, and that his first House of Commons showed Puritan sympathies, he issued a proclamation that the

clergy should conform to all rules of the Church service, or else lose their livings. Three hundred of Puritan views dared to refuse and duly paid the penalty. So far from crushing Puritanism, however, James's action merely began to change it from a force largely inside the Church to a force largely outside. Puritanism continued to grow, and some Puritans at least, such as those who emigrated to Leyden, in Holland, and later sailed to America in the *Mayflower*, preferred to risk untold hardships and dangers rather than remain where they were not free to worship in their own way—or to force their opinions on others.

Equally unsuccessful was James's policy towards the The Catholics Catholics. When he stopped enforcing strictly the laws against them there was a large increase in the number of those who stayed away from Church. Alarmed, James then switched back to strict enforcement: fines were levied and priests executed. This soon spurred some of Gunpowder Plot, 1605 the English Catholics to violent action. Sincere men, believing that the reconversion of the whole English people to Catholicism would fully justify the slaughter of a few hundred individuals, they planned to blow up parliament when James was opening it, and when Prince Henry (the Prince of Wales) was also likely to be present. In the resulting confusion they intended to seize power, make a puppet-ruler of one of James's younger children, and direct England back into the Catholic fold.

Of these intentions the government became aware. One of the conspirators warned a noble relative not to attend the opening of parliament—and the noble relative informed the King's ministers. But the devoted agent of the plotters, Guy Fawkes, still stuck to his task. An English Catholic who had gone abroad for the sake of his religion, he had become a soldier, and had now returned with but one object in mind. At eleven o'clock on the night of November 4th, 1605, a few hours before the time for the opening of parliament, and when enquiries made during the afternoon had already warned Fawkes that discovery was likely, he was arrested just outside a lumber room in the vaults of the House of Lords. Within, under a great pile of firewood, were thirty-six barrels of gunpowder, covered with iron bars to increase the force of the explosion. The next day the leading conspirators, including their guiding spirit Robert Catesby, spurred into the country in a wild hope of raising rebellion. They were quickly rounded up and either killed on the spot or, like Fawkes, in due course suffered the dreadful death of traitors.

The effects of the plot long survived the plotters. The conspiracy caused the laws against Catholics to be still more strictly enforced, and helped to make 'No Popery' one of the strongest sentiments of Englishmen for generations to come. The annual burning of effigies of Guy Fawkes—in the 17th century often stuffed with live cats to produce realistic squeals of anguish—shows how deeply the Gunpowder Plot impressed itself on the memory of the nation.

All James's good intentions about religion were thus wasted. He had offended the two extremes, Catholic and Puritan, who between them made up a large part of the population. Unfortunately this was not all. In two other matters—taxation and foreign policy—he also ran up against strong opposition.

Other matters of dispute

Taxation

James was soon in trouble about taxation. The value of money was still falling with the continued flow of gold and silver into Europe from the New World, and as prices rose to counterbalance the decline in the worth of the currency, so James found himself less and less able to make ends meet. Extravagance at Court and lavish gifts to handsome male favourites such as George Villiers, later Duke of Buckingham, did nothing to replenish the

Buckingham

royal coffers, and though the country was at peace James found himself worse off than Elizabeth had been even when at war.

Unfortunately for James he could extract very little from parliament in direct taxes, for parliament had a habit of making conditions before meeting such re-

The Pope in Council

This was an extremely popular Protestant engraving—in fact one of the first engravings to be widely bought in England. It depicts the Pope plotting both the Armada and the Gun-powder Plot, and was first issued after the latter event. It continued to be published again in various versions whenever there was a Catholic scare throughout the 17th century, and was reissued as late as the days of the 'Popish Plot' in 1679–81 and the 'Glorious Revolution' in 1688.

quests, and this James could not allow. So instead he tried to get money by means beyond parliament's control. As usual at the outset of a new reign, he had been granted for life the customs duties, including the 'tunnage' on wines and the 'poundage' on general merchandise entering or leaving the kingdom. On the advice of Robert Cecil (who as Earl of Salisbury was

chief minister for the first half of the reign) James decided to increase the rates at which these duties were levied. As a result parliament was soon in violent 'Imposi- protest against these new increases, or 'impositions'.
tions'

2. *Foreign Policy and Colonization*

Foreign   The quarrel about impositions lasted almost the entire
policy   reign. Similarly, James's foreign policy caused constant criticism in his parliaments. He began, on Salisbury's advice, by making peace with Spain—a decision which greatly disappointed men like Raleigh. In fact, James found it convenient very quickly to imprison Raleigh on a charge of treason.[1]

Thirty Years   The events which caused most trouble, however, arose
War,
1618–1648   from the marriage of James's daughter Elizabeth to a German Protestant, Frederick, Elector Palatine of the Rhine. In 1619 this prince rashly accepted an invitation from the persecuted and rebel Protestants of Bohemia to become king of that country in place of the rightful monarch, the ruler of Austria. After a single winter's reign in Bohemia, Frederick was chased by an alliance of Catholic powers not only from Bohemia but from his own territory of the Palatinate. These were the opening moves of the Thirty Years War, which involved half Europe and ended only when the German Catholics and Protestants—the former supported in the main by Austria, Spain and Bavaria, the latter by France, Denmark and Sweden—had fought themselves to a standstill, and when something like one-third of Germany's population had perished by fighting, famine or disease.

In this situation James was expected by many of his
James's plan subjects to support his Protestant son-in-law; and James
to recover
Palatinate   himself was very anxious that Frederick should at least recover the Palatinate (which was held by forces from

[1] See page 163.

Spain and Bavaria). James foolishly imagined that this could be done by diplomacy. The Spaniards, he thought, might see that the Palatinate was restored to his son-in-law if an alliance between England and Spain, long contemplated, was now sealed by the marriage of a Spanish princess to James's eldest surviving son, Prince Charles.[1] This scheme ignored the fact that the Spaniards could restore the whole Palatinate to James's son-in-law only by fighting their own allies. Moreover, the prospect of the marriage was bound to alarm many English Protestants. A Catholic Queen in England would almost certainly mean toleration for Catholics and might well result before long in a Catholic monarch, the re-establishment of Catholicism, and the wholesale persecution of Protestants.

The Spanish Alliance

James was nothing if not a lover of peace. How far he was prepared to go to win the friendship of Spain had already been seen before the Thirty Years War broke out. He had released Raleigh from the Tower in 1616 to allow him to seek the gold-mine he had heard of many years earlier in Guiana[2]: but in doing this, Raleigh was on no account to fight the Spaniards. This condition had proved impossible. Guiana had become much more peopled since Raleigh's previous visit and as soon as his men neared their objective up the Orinoco, they encountered a Spanish settlement. A fight ensued. Raleigh's son was killed, the little party was unable to make its way through the dense forest to the mine against opposition, and Raleigh, after sailing as far as Newfoundland, was eventually forced by his companions to return to England—without gold. The Spanish ambassador in London had then demanded Raleigh's head; and James had allowed Raleigh to be executed on the charge of

Raleigh

[1] Charles's elder brother, the able and popular Prince Henry, had died as a young man.

[2] See page 163.

treason for which he had been imprisoned fifteen years before.

Third parliament, 1621

It was in the knowledge that James was capable of this sort of conduct that the third parliament of his reign met in 1621. James had called it in the hope of a large grant, since the course of the war in Germany demanded military preparations. The Commons showed their mettle from the start. They opened a new attack on abuses in monopolies, and before long secured the dismissal (for corruption) of the Lord Chancellor—the essayist,

Bacon

philosopher and scientist, Francis Bacon, Viscount St. Albans. Encouraged by this success, the Commons soon

Foreign affairs

turned to foreign affairs. They urged James to fight Spain for the Palatinate—which they thought could be recovered by a purely naval war!—and to marry Prince Charles to a Protestant. James at once denied their right to interfere in such royal preserves as foreign policy and the marriage of the heir to the throne, and threatened to withdraw their traditional privileges if they tried to encroach upon his. To this the Commons retaliated with

Commons' protestation, 1621

a protestation, which was duly entered into their Journal of Proceedings. It stated that their privileges were an undoubted inheritance and birthright, and that they had the power to discuss all matters of state with complete liberty of speech.

James's reaction

A few days later, James sent for the Commons' Journals. Before his assembled Privy Council he ripped out the offending page. He then declared parliament dissolved and imprisoned three members for their share in the proceedings. One was Sir Edward Coke, a bullying lawyer who nevertheless sincerely believed that even the king was subject to the ordinary common law of the land, and who for these views had already been dismissed from the position of chief justice. Another of the three was John Pym, of whom much more was to be heard in the next reign.

Mr. WILLIAM
SHAKESPEARES
COMEDIES,
HISTORIES, &
TRAGEDIES.

Published according to the True Originall Copies.

Martin Droeshout sculpsit London.

LONDON
Printed by Isaac Iaggard, and Ed. Blount. 1623.

Title Page of Shakespeare's Plays

This is the title page of the first folio edition (an almost complete collection) of Shakespeare's plays, published in 1623 seven years after his death. The engraving by Martin Droeshout is probably the best likeness of Shakespeare that we have.

Charles
visits Spain

Still short of funds, James then pressed on with his plan of marrying Charles to the Spanish Infanta. From this folly he was rescued only by the still greater folly of Charles himself. Prompted and accompanied by the royal favourite Buckingham, Charles insisted on setting off for Spain to complete the negotiations and bring back his bride. "Two dear adventurous knights worthy to be put in a new romanze", commented James. Experience of Spain, however, brought disillusion to the travellers. The strict Spanish etiquette prevented Charles from seeing the object of his attentions alone; and the Spaniards soon fell out with Buckingham, whose ideas of the respect due to him did not coincide with theirs. After several weary months, the Prince and his companion found out that the Infanta would not be allowed to sail to England until great concessions to English Catholics had been actually put into practice. At length, too, Charles realized that the Spaniards had no intention, if peaceful pressure failed, of fighting Bavaria and Austria to get back the Palatinate for James's son-in-law. Losing patience, Charles and Buckingham then departed—though not before Charles had definitely promised to undertake the marriage.

Return of
Charles

When the two travellers arrived home they were greeted with an outburst of popular affection—due in part to their safe return, but mainly to the fact that Charles had come back without a Spanish wife. Liking this newly won popularity and smarting from his treatment in Spain, Buckingham, supported by Charles, now swung round and urged James to carry out the policy demanded by parliament—the policy, not of alliance with Spain, but of war against her. Reluctantly James

End of
Spanish
negotiations

moved in this direction. Three days before Charles was due to be married, by proxy, to the Infanta, James demanded from the Spaniards a definite promise to use force, if necessary, to restore Frederick to the Palatinate.

Title Page of Ben Jonson's Works

This volume was published in 1616. The title page shows the full influence of the Renaissance in its classical columns, etc. and in its depiction of the various types of classical drama. (The figures at the top symbolize Tragi-comedy: the satyr Satire: and the shepherd with pipe and crook the Pastoral. In the oval is the artist's idea of a Roman theatre. Below we see the figure of Tragedy on the left, Comedy on the right. At the bottom on the left is the cart of Thespis, symbolizing the plays presented by travelling companies; and on the right a chorus in an open amphitheatre). But while severely classical in detail, the design has all the riotous detail beloved by the Jacobeans and is far from severely classical in spirit.

With this the whole negotiation for a Spanish alliance collapsed. Instead—against the real wishes of both rulers—the shadow of war now loomed up between the two countries.

Fourth parliament, 1624

When James's fourth parliament met, in 1624, the atmosphere was very different from that of the third. The King was now about to carry out a foreign policy approved by parliament; and he was also prepared to agree to a new law to restrict monopolies. The result was that the Commons in turn were prepared to grant taxes. They were careful, however, to earmark the grant for certain special purposes—including the war against Spain.

War with Spain, 1625

When James died in 1625 the country was thus at war again with Spain, as it had been when he ascended the throne. The twenty-odd years of peace in between had served the country well. James loved peace, and knew its value, as his motto (*Beati pacifici*, 'Blessed are the peacemakers') shows. But it was certainly an idle dream when he hoped to get back the Palatinate for his son-in-law without war.

The issue at stake between King and parliament

Although there was harmony between James and parliament at the end of his reign, it was achieved only because the King had accepted the views of the Commons. In fact, matters were already heading towards a clash between King and parliament. On the one hand, the King considered himself the sovereign power in the state, not bound by the law of the country, with parliament enjoying an occasional share in his counsels purely as a matter of his grace and convenience. On the other hand, parliament, in which the wealthy upper-middle-class was strongly represented, while admitting it was the King's business to govern, laid claim to certain definite powers and was determined to oppose policies of which it did not approve. From this to actually deciding policy was but a short step—though few in

The Staircase of Hatfield House

This is a splendid example of the fine wide oak staircases, angled and with carved balustrades, that were becoming a popular feature in the great houses built in Jacobean times.

parliament as yet realized it. And if parliament were to decide policy, what would become of the sovereign power of the Crown?

Was the King, then, to remain the supreme power in the state—or was parliament to become that power? Or was there yet a third possibility—the view of Coke, that the supreme authority, superior to King and parliament alike, lay in the common law? These were the questions, as yet but dimly perceived, which lay at the root of the disagreements between James and his parliaments. The next reign was to bring them much more clearly to the surface—and, in so doing, to produce civil war.

*　　*　　*　　*　　*

There was another development during James's reign, not so spectacular as the clashes between King and

Colonization Commons, but no less important for the future. This was the movement of British settlers overseas. The nearest place to attract British immigrants was Ulster, where an unsuccessful rising led to wholesale confiscations of

Plantation of Ulster land and the 'planting' of some of this with English and Scottish tenants. English settlement in Ireland, however, even if not done before in so concentrated a fashion, was no novelty. What was new was the successful foundation of colonies across the Atlantic—where Elizabethan attempts at colonization had quickly collapsed.

Under James, three enduring settlements were established on the other side of the Atlantic by companies set

Virginia (Jamestown) 1607 up for the purpose. The first, Virginia, sprang from commercial enterprise and soon found a profitable export in tobacco. The original expedition was sent out

Plymouth, 1620 by the Virginia Company of London, and settled at a point later called Jamestown. The second colony, Plymouth, was settled by the Puritan 'Pilgrim Fathers' who sailed in the *Mayflower*; of the one hundred and one

GROWTH OF PURITANISM

CLASHES WITH PARLIAMENT

PEACEFUL FOREIGN POLICY

COLONIZATION

LITERATURE: THE THEATRE: MUSIC

SOME FEATURES OF JAMES I'S REIGN

emigrants, about one-third (those who had earlier emigrated to Holland) were inspired largely by desire for religious freedom, and two-thirds largely by desire for land or a better livelihood. The third settlement, Bermuda, began after the shipwreck of an expedition intended for the American mainland.

Besides these lasting settlements, there were short-lived efforts by various companies to establish colonies in Guiana, Newfoundland and Nova Scotia, while on the other side of the world the East India Company set up trading centres, or 'factories', in India. The main station and the first permanent one, was at Surat. Trading posts were also established in the East Indies —where two were soon seized by the Dutch. This great new movement, where the quest for profitable trade led to 'plantations' or colonies overseas, was to continue throughout the whole Stuart period. It is well to remember that the reign of James I, in which great music, great literature, and the growing disputes between King and parliament loom so large, saw also the beginnings of the British Empire.

Bermuda

'Factories' in the East

CHAPTER TWENTY

CHARLES I AND THE BREACH WITH PARLIAMENT
(1625–1640)

1. *The Clash with Parliament*

THE situation in 1625 demanded an extremely wise Charles I and able monarch. Unfortunately the new King, while brave, dignified, of good morals, and a great patron of art and literature, was no genius as a ruler. A firm believer in Divine Right, he had very strong ideas about his royal powers—ideas quite justified by Tudor practice—and he neither could nor would understand any other viewpoint. Already as Prince of Wales he had shown his lack of statesmanship by trying to marry a princess of a nationality and religion detested by most of his subjects.

Having failed to marry a Spanish Catholic, Charles Marriage at the outset of his reign hastened to marry a French with Henrietta Maria Catholic—the fifteen-year-old Henrietta Maria, sister of Louis XIII. This completed an alliance with Spain's great rival France. As part of the marriage agreement, Charles promised to soften the laws against English Catholics—an undertaking which was bound to be resented by parliament.

Trouble was not long in coming. During the first two Charles's years of his reign Charles twice called parliament in the first parliaments, expectation of being granted for life, like every king 1625 and 1626 since Edward IV, the customs duties of tunnage and Tunnage and poundage. Both parliaments put off making any such poundage not granted grants and instead raised grievances. The main complaint in each case was against the bad organization and failure of a foreign expedition. The first parliament began by objecting to the marriage treaty and went on to criticize the loss of an expedition sent at the end of James's reign under Count Mansfield, a German mercenary, to recover the Palatinate. This expedition never got as far as Germany—it melted away in Holland through disease and desertion. The second parliament had another disastrous venture to criticize—a naval expedition against Spain. The main features of this had been forced crews, reluctant auxiliary vessels, rotten sails, and (when a landing was made at Cadiz) a night of drunkenness on plundered wine by almost the entire landed force. Behind both expeditions was the hand of the King's friend and chief minister, Buckingham. The first parliament got as far as hinting that he should be dismissed; the second parliament, inspired by Sir John Eliot, a Cornish landowner, attacked him outright. Resenting any interference with his free choice of ministers, in both cases Charles quickly dissolved parliament.

When his second parliament failed to grant him tunnage and poundage, Charles was in real difficulty. For not content with having an unsuccessful war against Spain on his hands, he had also quarrelled with his brother-in-law, and was about to plunge into war with France. Lacking money, he tried devices which only brought him—or rather Buckingham—still further unpopularity. He continued, for instance, to collect tunnage and poundage as if it had been granted; and he tried to force loans from his subjects—about eighty of whom refused to pay and were imprisoned without trial. Against a background of growing discontent Charles then began the new war by sending an expedition under Buckingham to seize the island of Rhé, off La Rochelle. The idea was to make this a base for helping the Huguenots in La Rochelle, where they were resisting the

[margin notes] Mansfield's expedition

The attack on Cadiz

Criticism of Buckingham

Tunnage and poundage collected

Forced loans. Imprisonment without trial

War with France

Expedition to Rhé

armies of the French King—for the latter's great minister, Cardinal Richelieu, was determined to take away from the Huguenots the privilege of garrisoning certain towns (including La Rochelle), which had been granted

[*Reproduced by gracious permission of H.M. the Queen*

Charles I

These three likenesses of Charles I were done in 1637 by Sir Anthony Vandyck, the great Flemish painter whom Charles welcomed to England and patronized. (He also patronized and knighted the other great Flemish master of the time, Peter Paul Rubens). The heads were done for the benefit of the great Italian sculptor Bernini, who had been commissioned to make a bust of Charles, and who could not travel to England. When he received the likenesses Bernini is reputed to have gazed at the expression on the face and cried out: "Poor unfortunate gentleman!" Note how these portraits bring out the great earnestness and dignity of Charles, but also certain qualities of smallness, weakness and indecision.

by Henry IV. But once again the English organization proved hopelessly at fault. After a successful landing, the expected naval reinforcements failed to appear, and the expedition had to withdraw with the loss of half its men.

For some months Charles tried to fight without proper
financial backing. This soon produced further grievances. To hold the remnants of the Rhé expedition together he billeted them, often without payment, on
ordinary citizens. Since this was widely resented and
caused many disputes between troops and householders,
he also held large districts under martial law and had
cases tried in special military courts where the system of
billeting would not be challenged.

Billeting

Martial law

Harassed by these difficulties and stung by military
disgrace, Charles then once more called parliament.
The result was not surprising. The Commons came up
full of resentment against forced loans, imprisonings
without trial, billeting in private houses and martial
law. Backed by the Lords, they soon demanded, in a
document known as the Petition of Right, that the King
should recognize these practices as illegal. With this
they coupled an offer of taxes. To get the money, Charles
had to accept the petition—which he did.

Third
parliament,
1628–1629

Petition of
Right, 1628

This resounding victory did not satisfy the Commons,
who promptly renewed the attack on Buckingham.
Moreover they now claimed that a clause in the Petition
of Right forbidding loans and taxes without parliamentary consent also prevented the levying of tunnage
and poundage, which had still not been granted. Charles,
who regarded the traditional grant of tunnage and
poundage as a mere formality, was no more prepared to
agree to this than to dismiss the Duke. Instead he prorogued parliament—i.e. declared that particular session
at an end—and appointed Buckingham to lead a fresh
expedition to relieve La Rochelle. Fate decreed otherwise. John Felton, an unpaid and unpromoted ex-naval
lieutenant who had seen service at Rhé, was burning
with his own and the nation's grievances. Seeking
out the Duke at Portsmouth, he stabbed him to the
heart.

Further
demands of
parliament

Parliament
prorogued

Murder of
Buckingham

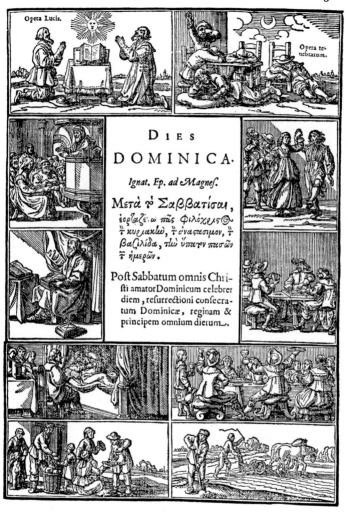

Dies Dominica (Lord's Day)

A pamphlet of 1639 setting out the Puritan view of correct behaviour for the Lord's Day. In the left hand column are the Works of Light—family prayer, church going, Bible reading, visiting the sick, relieving the poor. In the right hand column are the Works of Darkness—drunkenness, dancing, card-playing, feasting, and everyday work.

Old St. Paul's—the West Front

This drawing shows the new classical renaissance West Front added to the Gothic Old St. Paul's in the 1630's. It was the work of Inigo Jones, the first great English architect to build consistently in a classical style.

The death of Buckingham caused widespread rejoicings which Charles never forgave. It did not, however, help the expedition. Much of the English fleet (which was partly composed of 'pressed' merchantmen) again declined to attack the enemy forces, and the Huguenot stronghold had to surrender while our ships stood idly by. This final disaster was too much for Charles. Hoping as ever for further supplies, he recalled his prorogued parliament.

Surrender of La Rochelle

When the new session opened, Charles found the Commons as obstinate as ever. Indeed they raised yet another question. Led by Eliot they now launched an all-out attack against the King's religious policy— taking care, as usual, to blame this on his advisers.

Third parliament recalled

Attack on Charles's religious policy

Like his father, Charles was no lover of the Puritans.

But while James had disliked Puritanism because it would weaken royal control over the Church, Charles also intensely disliked it on religious grounds. His views were those of a small group of clergy led by his newly-appointed Bishop of London, William Laud, who was at the opposite extreme of the Church from the Puritans. Laud

Like Calvin's, only with very different results, Laud's religious policy was inspired by historical study of the Church in the first few centuries after the birth of Christ. He insisted on an amount of ceremony and ritual far beyond anything thought necessary either by Puritans or by even moderate opinion within the Church. In his own diocese, for instance, Laud ordered the communion table to be moved from the body of the church and erected at the east end as an altar, railed off from the congregation—so reverting to the old position before the Reformation and giving more importance to the priest, less to the ordinary worshipper.[1] Laud, in many ways, was Catholic but not Roman Catholic—a distinction which England found hard to grasp. And since his views were unpopular but were shared by Charles, Laud and his followers preached up the greatness of the King's power, for only through that power could they hope to impose their opinions on the whole Church. The altar controversy

It was against favours shown to Laud and his following—who were nicknamed Arminians, after a Dutchman, Arminius, whose views they were thought to

[1] According to the instructions in force at the beginning of the Stuart period, the table was to be kept at the east end (i.e. where the altar had formerly stood) and brought out into the body of the church for the actual communion. As this moving of a heavy piece of furniture was inconvenient, the instructions had become disregarded, and by the end of James I's reign the table had 'settled down' in one position. In the cathedrals this position was at the east end, like an altar, but in most of the ordinary parishes the table was still treated as such and kept in one position in the body of the church. Laud's new instructions thus applied the cathedral practice to his parishes.

share—that the Commons now turned their attack. Charles, seeing no prospect of a grant, soon sent down to adjourn parliament. But the Commons, inspired by Eliot, refused to obey the King's formal request—a request always previously treated as a command. Instead they forced the Speaker, or chairman, back into his chair (so that business could proceed), locked the door against interruption and, while the King's bodyguard was bearing down on the assembly, rushed through three resolutions. These were put by one of the members—since the Speaker would not—and carried by acclamation. They declared that anyone who introduced religious changes, or tried to extend popery or Arminianism, or advised the King to levy tunnage and poundage when it had not been granted by parliament (or paid it in the absence of parliament's consent), should be considered an enemy of the country.

The Three
Resolutions:
Parliament
dissolved
1629

For Charles this was the last straw. Weary of constant opposition and interference in affairs which he regarded as his own preserve, he resolved to call parliament no more.

2. *The Attempt to Discard Parliament (1629–1640)*

In deciding to try and rule without summoning parliament, Charles was doing nothing illegal. The law obliged the king to call parliament only when a fresh grant of direct taxation was required; and under Elizabeth I and James I there had often been long periods—seven years was not unusual—when no parliament met. The success of Charles's attempt, however, would depend on how far he could raise money by other means. And since there is nothing more costly than warfare, it would also depend on the King's remaining at peace. He therefore quickly ended the ill-starred wars with France and Spain.

Peace with
France and
Spain

The first few months Charles found difficult. Feeling ran high when, for their share in the three resolutions, Eliot and other members were imprisoned in the Tower —where Eliot later died. For nearly six months imports and exports languished as many London merchants lived up to the resolutions and avoided paying tunnage and poundage by ceasing to engage in foreign trade. Such a protest, however, was hard to maintain, and eventually nearly all the objectors resumed trade and paid up. *Imprison- ment of Eliot*

Refusals to pay tunnage and poundage

With this storm weathered, Charles proceeded to enlarge his revenue by all the means which ingenious royal lawyers could devise. For instance, by reviving a royal power neglected for over a century, Charles fined well-off freeholders who had not applied for knight- hood, and forced all freeholders with land worth more than forty pounds a year to become knights. This made them liable to extra dues on their land. Similarly, Charles's lawyers declared that the true limits of the royal forest land were those which had been in force before the days of Edward I—a decision which multi- plied Rockingham Forest by ten and made Waltham Forest cover more than half of Essex. Those whose houses or farms were on these newly declared areas were said to have 'encroached' on the royal forest, and were fined for having done so. They then had to pay again to have their land 'disforested'. *Devices to increase Crown revenue:*

(a) Forced knight- hood

(b) Enlarge- ment of royal forests

As a further piece of sharp practice, Charles's lawyers also found a way round the restrictions on monopolies. Since 1624, the Crown had been forbidden to grant monopolies to individuals except for new inventions and the like. Charles got round this by granting mono- polies, even of everyday articles such as soap, not to individuals but to companies. Like enforced knighthood and forest fines, this caused much ill-feeling. All these financial stopgaps, however, were accepted quietly compared with ship-money. *(c) Monopo- lies to com- panies*

[*Country Life*

The Double Cube Room, Wilton House

This beautiful room, in the proportion of two cubes, is in the part of Wilton House (near Salisbury) designed by Inigo Jones. The decorative plaster work, in gold and white, was planned as an elaborate setting for a splendid series of portraits by Vandyck, including some of the Stuarts. The furniture shown is mostly 18th century. Surprisingly enough the suite of rooms of which this forms a part was built during the Civil War.

(*d*) Ship-money   By recognized custom, the seaports in time of emergency had to provide ships for national defence. Sometimes, too, the coastal towns had provided money instead. In 1634 Charles asked the ports and coastal towns for ships or money on the ground that there was an emergency—for pirates abounded in the Channel and Europe was still in the thick of the Thirty Years War. The request was duly met—mostly in money, since the ships required were nearly all too big to be found or built in the harbours concerned.

Ship-money from inland towns, 1635 and 1636   The next year, 1635, Charles again asked for ship-money, and this time from the inland towns as well—on the ground that it was unfair for the coast alone to bear the burden of naval defence. This, too, was for the most part paid. But when in 1636 Charles once more asked for ship-money, from ports and inland towns alike, protest grew. Whatever the emergency, the King had had ample time to summon parliament and ask for special taxation. The ship-money was honestly being spent on ships; but clearly Charles's real intention was to increase the navy without being obliged to parliament. If he could do this, he might also build up an army in the same way—and then his path to unchecked personal rule would be easy. So there was general opposition to the tax—and among those who refused to pay was a wealthy Buckinghamshire squire, John Hampden. By a small majority the judges found against him; but that any judges at all condemned the royal viewpoint was a sign of trouble for Charles. Hampden

Yet it was not his resented financial devices which brought Charles to ruin. By 1637, when Hampden's trial began, the finances of the Crown were in a better state than at any time since the death of Elizabeth. What sealed Charles's fate was not too little success in finance but too much zeal in religion.

In 1633 Charles had appointed Laud Archbishop of Canterbury. From then on Laud had extended his activities to the whole country. By means of the Court of High Commission and the fact that the consent of the Archbishop was necessary before any book could be published, Laud attempted to silence Puritan clergy and writers. Everywhere he tried to turn the communion table into an altar and to make people bow towards this as they entered the Church. Everywhere, too, besides enforcing the laws against non-attendance at church, he strove to secure decency, order and uniformity in the service. He forbade, for instance, the use of churches for non-religious purposes, such as general meetings—and Religious policy: Laud

Attempt to silence Puritans

Church order and uniformity

at St. Paul's, in London, he stopped the time-honoured practice of strolling, gossiping and bargaining in the nave, and prevented porters using the transepts as a short cut from one street to another. This made the atmosphere of the churches more religious, but was widely resented at a time when most parishes had no other general meeting place. Laud also used the Church **Attempt to** courts to punish immorality, among the rich no less **punish** **immorality** than the poor. His aim, in fact, was not merely to stamp out Puritanism but to improve the moral standard and religious life of the whole nation.

Though a persecutor, by the standards of the time Laud was not cruel. His normal weapons against the Puritans—who would certainly have used the same, or worse, against him—were fining and imprisonment. **Puritan** Also, those Puritans who wished to emigrate were **emigration** generally allowed to do so, and in Charles's reign colonies were founded in North America—notably Massachusetts, Maine and Connecticut—with a Puritan church officially recognized by the home government. All told, some sixty thousand souls left England between **New** 1630 and 1643, of whom a third helped to settle the **England** North American Puritan colonies soon to be known collectively as New England. In fact this movement of emigration was so considerable that Charles and Laud were contemplating stopping it when they were overwhelmed by the Civil War.[1]

The punishments inflicted on the Puritans were usually severe but not savage. Sometimes, however, the normal penalties were exceeded, and the year of Hampden's protest against ship-money also saw the famous

---

[1] The Puritan colonists were quite as intolerant as Laud. The only North American colonies allowing general freedom of worship were Maryland, granted to Lord Baltimore in the 1630s as a haven for Catholics, and so called after Charles's queen; and Providence, or Rhode Island, founded in 1643 by the wise and tolerant pastor Roger Williams—who had previously been expelled from Massachusetts.

cases of Prynne, Bastwick and Burton. These three men Prynne, Bastwick and Burton —a lawyer, a doctor and a clergyman—had written and circulated fierce attacks on the bishops. They were tried before the Star Chamber (for the Court of High Commission, being a Church court, could not inflict loss of life or limb), and were sentenced to pay a fine of five thousand pounds each, to stand in the pillory, to have their ears cut off, and to be imprisoned for life. Prynne, who had already lost a good part of his ears for libelling the Queen, was also sentenced to be branded on both cheeks with the letters 'S.L.' for seditious (rebellious) libeller. In carrying out this part of the sentence, the hangman, according to a contemporary account, got one of the letters the wrong way round, and so had to burn the cheek a second time. Such punishments made a popular spectacle when inflicted on rogues, but were resented in many quarters when meted out to respectable citizens.

Between them, Charles and Laud were thus arousing National prosperity much ill-feeling. But at the same time England was prosperous and at peace, the poor perhaps better protected than ever before against the rich (for example, by government action against enclosure), and the only open signs of opposition were Puritan emigration and a general failure to pay ship-money. Charles and Laud might have survived criticism in England, had they not also stirred up revolt in Scotland.

In their passion for religious uniformity Charles and New Church regulations and prayer-book for Scotland Laud decided in 1637 to bring the Scottish service much closer to the English one. They had already laid down that Scottish ministers should wear surplices, and had tried to increase the power of the Scottish bishops. Now Charles decreed that the Book of Common Order drawn up by John Knox and generally employed in the Scottish Kirk should be withdrawn, and that instead the Scots should use a new prayer book compiled by

A Scotswoman

An Irishwoman

An English Country-
woman on Pattens

A Merchant's Wife
of London

These four engravings by Wenceslas Hollar show the varying dress of different
nationalities and classes in the British Isles during the 1640s. By this date the lace
ruff worn by the Scotswoman would have been out of fashion in England. The
Irish cloak is obviously very primitive. The pattens of the English country-woman
were high wooden platforms to keep the feet clear of the mud.

Charles's most favoured Scottish bishops in consultation with Laud. It was based on the English one—with a few alterations in a less Protestant direction.

At once the whole of southern Scotland was aflame with protest. Many Scots saw in the new prayer book —quite wrongly—a plan to introduce Roman Catholicism; and nearly all felt something English and foreign was being forced upon them. As soon as the Dean tried to read the new prayers in St. Giles', Edinburgh, a group of maidservants violently interrupted him; and when the Bishop mounted the pulpit to call for order one of the women flung a stool at him—and narrowly missed the Dean. After this, magistrates cleared the church of rioters, and the service proceeded to the sound of broken glass as the mob outside hurled stones at the windows. This lively beginning inspired a general refusal to use the new service; and soon people of all classes began to subscribe their names to a document, known as the National Covenant, in which they swore to preserve the reformed religion of the Scottish Kirk, and to resist to the utmost the King's recent changes. Scotland, though not in revolt against Charles himself, was in revolt against his religious policy.

What was Charles now to do? Being Charles, he decided to assert his rights, even though he had no proper military force. The Scots for their part soon went further by abolishing their bishops and re-establishing complete Presbyterianism. With pressed recruits and the untrained militia of the northern counties Charles then set off north. But his supporters inside Scotland were quickly beaten by the Covenanters, and on the border he encountered a Scottish army much too strong for him to attack. Leaving the Scots triumphant, he therefore disbanded the northern militia and returned south. He had, however, by no means given up the struggle. His object was only to gain time while he built up a better army—in which situation Sir Thomas Wentworth, Lord Deputy of Ireland, now became his chief adviser.

Strafford Wentworth, whom Charles created Earl of Strafford, was a very able, patriotic and forceful man. He had been one of the chief critics of Buckingham, and a strong supporter of the Petition of Right. Shortly afterwards, however, he had parted company with those who were attacking the King's ministers; for he had become convinced that parliament was willy-nilly trying to undermine the royal power in the interests of its own, and that this could only lead to weak and selfish government. Having come round to the Court point of view, he had been appointed President of the Council of the North, in which post his success was so outstanding that he was promoted to the immensely responsible position of the King's Deputy in Ireland. There too, though his methods were often harsh and unscrupulous, he had done notable work. He had put down pirates, encouraged the linen industry, attacked corruption among officials, kept firm order, and ridden roughshod over ancient laws and practices which he considered a bar to good government. This policy, which he called **'Thorough'** 'thorough' and which we should call benevolent or enlightened despotism, would now be repeated in England—and Scotland—if Strafford got his way.

Strafford advises calling parliament Strafford's first object on becoming the King's chief adviser was to raise a strong army. To get the necessary funds he advised Charles to call parliament. He did this partly because he imagined that war with the Scots might call out the true loyalty of the English people, and partly because, if parliament were approached and refused supplies, Charles would then have a better excuse to exact ship-money and the like.

The Short Parliament, 1640 So, after an interval of eleven years, Charles again summoned parliament. But when it met, the Commons

The Archbishop of St. Andrews Attacked

An illustration by Wenceslas Hollar, a Czech who stayed for many years in England, to a pamphlet entitled *True Information*, published in 1648. This gives an account of the Civil War from the parliamentary point of view. The engraving purports to show the scene in St. Giles' Cathedral, Edinburgh, when the new Scottish Prayer Book was introduced.

Soldiers turning Altars into Tables

Another illustration by Hollar to *True Information*. It shows Charles's soldiers, recruited for the campaign against Scotland, getting out of hand as they marched north. They are undoing the work of Laud by taking down altars and turning them back into communion tables in the body of the Church.

at once proceeded, under the leadership of John Pym, to raise all the grievances of the past eleven years, and to stress the part they thought parliament should play in government. They would not grant supplies until Charles had abandoned all his non-parliamentary devices for raising money, including ship-money and its military equivalent called coat-and-conduct money. Worse still so far as Charles was concerned, they began to organize a petition against war with Scotland. At

this, Charles declared the parliament dissolved. It had sat for only three weeks.

Without funds from parliament and with a forced and largely untrained army, Charles then once more tried to take the field against the Scots. On the very day he set out to join his troops at York, the Scottish Covenanter army, knowing it could depend on support from the King's critics in England, moved south over the

border. Easily occupying Northumberland and Durham and wisely coming no farther, the Scots declared they would stay there until all their terms had been met, including the payment of a large sum and the daily costs of the army while they were kept waiting.

This Scottish force Charles's troops were quite unable to confront. After some weeks the harassed King accordingly agreed once more to call parliament.

This time parliament—the Long Parliament, to use its later name—was in a much stronger position. It had behind it not only general opinion but the unofficial support of the Scottish army in the north of England. No army of any value was at the disposal of Charles. The stage was set for a new, and decisive, phase in the struggle of parliament to make good its claims against the Crown.

GRIEVANCES AGAINST CHARLES I, 1625-40

CHAPTER TWENTY-ONE

THE LONG PARLIAMENT
AND THE FIRST CIVIL WAR
(1640–1646)

1. *The Work of the Long Parliament to the Outbreak*
of War (1640–1642)

Mood of the Commons in 1640

THE men who came up to the House of Commons in late 1640 were almost of one mind. They bitterly resented the devices which had enabled the King to touch their pockets and yet avoid consulting them in parliament for no less than eleven years. Inspired by Pym and Hampden, and confident in the support, if need be, of the Scottish army, they quickly determined to sweep away everything which had made it possible for Charles to rule without parliament.

Attack on Laud and Strafford

To do this in safety, they decided as a first step that the Commons should accuse Laud and Strafford before the House of Lords as judges—a process known as impeachment. Laud the peers ordered to the Tower

Laud imprisoned

pending a full trial. On the way he narrowly escaped lynching; and in the Tower he remained until the victorious Puritans executed him over three years later. Strafford was much the more dangerous; he had suggested bringing over Irish soldiers to fight the Scots, and might well have used them to overawe parliament. When impeached he was given a fair trial by the Lords and defended himself for eighteen days with the utmost skill. Alarmed at this slow progress the Commons then passed a bill of attainder declaring him guilty of treason—to which the Lords by a narrow margin at length agreed.

The consent of the King was now needed before the bill of attainder could become an Act. But Charles had been well served by Strafford and had promised he should come to no harm. "Upon the word of a King", Charles had written, "you shall not suffer in life, honour or fortune." For twenty-four hours the tormented monarch strove to decide whether to give in to parliament or stand by his minister. Meanwhile the London mob, which was coming to play an increasing part in events, gathered round Whitehall Palace and clamoured for Strafford's blood. Influenced by the danger to his Catholic Queen, the advice of his Council, and the attitude of Strafford himself (who urged Charles to comply with parliament's will for the sake of peace) the King then reluctantly gave his assent. Three days later the executioner held up the severed head of 'Black Tom Tyrant' to the delighted gaze of perhaps the largest crowd ever to gather upon Tower Hill. *Mob violence* *Charles sacrifices Strafford*

With its main enemies disposed of, parliament could settle the old disputes in its own favour. It had already passed a bill to declare that parliament could not be dissolved without its own consent, and this Charles had accepted with the attainder against Strafford. It now went on to declare illegal all Charles's financial devices —ship-money, tunnage and poundage without parliament's consent, enforced knighthood, and the rest. Not content with this, it also passed bills to abolish the Star Chamber, the Councils of Wales and of the North, and the Court of High Commission—vital parts in the machinery which the Tudors had built up to control state and Church. All this Charles had to accept—or be refused the money necessary to carry on government and pay the Scottish army in the North. *Ship-money, etc., declared illegal* *Star Chamber and High Commission abolished*

In stripping the King of these powers, the members *Intentions of parliament* of parliament were not aware of doing anything revolutionary. They thought they were depriving the Crown only of powers which had grown up recently, in Tudor and Stuart times. There was some truth in this, but all the same they were now giving parliament (especially the Commons) an authority much greater than it had ever enjoyed before—an authority almost equal to the King's. Clearly the situation could not rest at this point.

The Execution of Strafford, 1641

Also from *True Information*. The detail is probably not authentic at all; but at least it shows the Tower and a large number of people.

Religion: the members disagree

It was not long before the next step. In the summer of 1641 parliament went on to discuss changes in the Church. At this the harmony within the Commons, and between Commons and Lords, was quickly broken—for though there were very few who approved of Laud, a large number were sincerely devoted to the Church as it existed and especially to its prayer-book service. So when the Puritans in the Commons, supported by Pym and Hampden, introduced a bill to abolish episcopacy (rule by bishops) "in all its roots and branches", it passed its second reading by so narrow a majority that it had to be dropped. Parliament, previously united on politics, had shown itself deeply divided over religion. Failure of 'Root and Branch' Bill

The next step came in November 1641, when news reached London of an Irish rebellion. Maddened by the continual seizure of their land and alarmed at the fierceness of parliament towards Catholics, the Irish in Ulster gave the lead by driving the English Protestant settlers from their homes. Similar outbreaks rapidly followed elsewhere, and before long some ten thousand Protestants perished by massacre or cruel ill-treatment. The small English forces matched atrocity with atrocity and everywhere there was chaos and terror.

In this situation King and parliament were fully agreed that an army must be raised to suppress the Irish rebels. But Pym and others then asked themselves the question—could the King be trusted with this force? Might he not use it against opponents nearer home? So Pym proposed, and by a narrow majority the Commons agreed, that the lords lieutenant who would raise this army, and its commanders, should be selected, not by the King in the usual way, but by parliament. The onrush of events, speeded by wild rumours of Catholic plots and distrust of the Queen, was driving Charles's opponents still farther along the road to revolution. An army to suppress the Irish? Parliament claims right to select commanders

In this same month of November 1641, Pym brought before the Commons a great document known as the Grand Remonstrance. After listing all the past misdeeds of the King and all the reforms achieved by parliament, it went on to demand—among other things—that the King should choose ministers acceptable to parliament, and that the Church should be reformed in a Puritan direction. At the end of a fortnight of hard debating, the Remonstrance was carried—but only by eleven votes. The Grand Remonstrance, November 1641 Parliament split

Thanks to the Puritan attack on the Church, the King now had almost half the Commons on his side against any further inroads on his powers, and by far the greater part of the Lords. This much more favourable situation, however, he soon spoilt by a very rash action—on the advice, among others, of the Queen. Against a background of growing violence in London, with clashes between 'Cavalier' officers and 'Roundhead' apprentices becoming common in the streets, Charles in the opening days of 1642 ordered his lawyers to impeach five members of the Commons and one of the Lords. He believed—not without reason—that they were about to impeach his Queen, and he determined to strike first. The five included Pym and Hampden, the charge was high treason, and impeachment—a trial before the Lords—was chosen because parliament always claimed legal authority over its own members during sessions.

Impeachment, however, was a process by which the Commons, not the King, were the accusers. So the Lords declined to order the arrest of the accused until they could be satisfied that the King was acting legally. At this, Charles, still prompted by the Queen, sent to the House to demand the arrest of the accused members. The demand was refused. The next afternoon Charles set off from Whitehall Palace with an armed retinue to make the arrest in person. Leaving his bodyguard at the doors of the Commons, he strode inside—the first time a king had ever entered that House—and occupied the Speaker's chair. But the five members, warned of the King's intention, had escaped by water. "I see all the birds are flown", exclaimed Charles ruefully, as he looked round the silent, resentful House. Then, after a few words of mixed conciliation and threat, he withdrew—having shown clearly that he would not scruple to use force against members of parliament.

Marginal notes:

Charles destroys his advantage

Attempted impeachment of five M.P.s

Charles tries to arrest them

It was this fact, coupled with renewed pressure on the Lords from the mob, which made parliament take the final step to revolution. A few days after the attempt on the five members the Commons, on the motion of Pym, proposed that the power of appointing the lords lieutenant who controlled the militia—the 'trained bands' of citizens liable for service in their own counties in emergency—should be taken from the King and given to parliament. To this the Lords after some hesitation agreed. The King at once refused his consent, but parliament acted without it by naming new lords lieutenant and ordering them to call out the militia. Parliament claims control of militia

By that time the London trained bands were already mustered for parliament and a parliamentary commander had control of Hull. Sailors from the navy also declared their readiness to stand by parliament, and thousands of armed supporters of Hampden rode in from Buckinghamshire. With London an armed camp controlled by his opponents, Charles had by then already left. He finally moved to Yorkshire. Meanwhile Henrietta Maria departed abroad, to free Charles's hands for the fight and to seek help from foreign powers. London and the navy support parliament

At York, during the next few months, the King slowly gathered supporters. Both parties made efforts to reach a settlement, but all parliament's proposals would have deprived the King of what he regarded as traditional and essential royal powers. Though few on either side desired it, civil war was clearly approaching. But as it loomed nearer, so more and more of those who had previously opposed the King rallied to his cause. Disturbed by the illegality of parliament's latest actions, or disliking the Puritanism which the majority in the Commons were now trying to force on the nation, or simply moved by feelings of loyalty, many heads of leading families, including a good proportion of the Charles at York War approaches: increased support for Charles

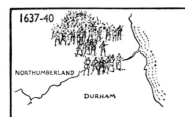

1637-40

NORTHUMBERLAND

DURHAM

Scots resist new Prayer Book

1640

Long Parliament Meets

1641

Execution of Strafford:
Imprisonment of Laud

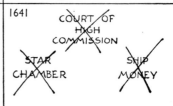

1641

COURT OF
HIGH
COMMISSION

STAR
CHAMBER

SHIP
MONEY

Charles loses many powers

1641

Parliament splits over Religion

1641

Force needed for Ireland:
Parliament demands right to select
commanders

1642

Charles tries to arrest 5 M.P.'S

1642

MILITIA
BILL

Parliament claims control of Militia.
Clashes begin

EVENTS 1637-42 LEADING TO CIVIL WAR

Lords and Commons, made their way to York. Everywhere people of influence strove to gain control of county or town for one side or the other. In July 1642 those left in parliament voted that the King, who like parliament had been trying to recruit forces, had begun war against them. Soon armed clashes occurred, and in August the King formally raised his standard at Nottingham as a sign of hostilities against the rebel majority in parliament and the capital they controlled. Events had moved forward to their logical if undesired conclusion. Between King and parliament the sword must now decide. Hostilities formally recognized, August 1642

2. *The First Civil War (1642–1646)*

In the war which followed, the main dividing line was that of religion. The King found his chief backing in supporters of the Church as it existed, while those who wished to 'reform' the Church still further—the Puritans—sided with parliament. The Catholics, who looked to Charles's Catholic queen for protection, all supported the King. The religious division

This division by religion corresponded with a rough geographical division. The King could soon count on the support of most of the north and west of England, while parliament soon held control over most of the south-east and east. This was because the south and east, as the main centres of industry and trade and the districts most exposed to new ideas from the Continent, were the chief strongholds of Puritanism. With its dislike of extravagance and wasteful pleasures, Puritanism encouraged hard work and honest money-making and so made a particular appeal to merchants and traders. The geographical division

On the parliamentary as well as the Royalist side the leaders were nobility or gentry—Pym, Hampden and Cromwell were all country squires—but the main The leaders

The Civil War

support for parliament came from the commercial classes. This accounts for the fact that within many Royalist counties the chief towns supported parliament—Gloucestershire, for instance, favoured the King, but Bristol and Gloucester supported parliament. Both sides, of course, officially fought in the name of the King —the declared object of parliament being to 'rescue' Charles from his evil counsellors. With regard to the members of parliament themselves, in the end the King had the help of about 80 peers and 175 of the Commons, parliament the help of 30 peers and 300 of the Commons. Throughout, the war was fought by two minorities—the men with strong opinions. Most of the population were not actively engaged, and the poorest classes took little part except when forcibly enlisted on one side or the other. A war of minorities

At the outset Charles suffered a great blow when the fleet supported parliament. Thanks to this, Puritan ports like Hull and Plymouth could hold out against a hostile countryside; parliament could stop foreign help reaching Charles; and London and the south-east could maintain their trade with the Continent. This last point was very important. With commerce still active and with parliament able to collect the customs duties for itself through its hold on the fleet and the ports, parliament in the long run could finance the war better than the Royalists. The latter gave their jewels and plate freely to the King, but their main wealth was locked up in land—which would fetch only low prices during such disturbed conditions. Parliament's long-term advantage in finance was to be one of the biggest factors in deciding the whole conflict. The fleet supports parliament: Effects Parliament's financial advantage

After declaring hostilities Charles moved off into the west on a recruiting campaign. He was followed by parliamentary forces mainly from London under the Earl of Essex—a Puritan and the son of Elizabeth's erring favourite. This exposed the capital—towards which Charles then headed, still followed by the parliamentary army. At Edgehill, in Warwickshire, he turned to face his pursuers. The result was a drawn battle—on the wings the Royalist cavalry, under the King's nephew, Prince Rupert (son of the Elector Palatine) charged victoriously, but carried pursuit too far instead

Edgehill, 1642

Rupert

At Ege=hill 16 peeces of Cañon shot against 80 of E: of Essex Lifegard & not one man hurte, & those 80 brake in vpon 1000 of the Kings, 4. of y^e Parliā: Reg: ran away, & 16 troops of Horse, so wee warre 6000 & they 18000, yet wee tooke y^e Standerd & Cleste S^r Ed: Varney Standerbearer in the head & Slew the Lord Lindsey Generall of the Fielde.

The Battle of Edgehill, 1642

Again from *True Information*. The representation is purely conventional, not authentic. Note the highly partisan tone of the description.

of re-forming and throwing their weight into the rest of the fight.

Despite this missed chance of a decisive victory, the King was able to continue his advance and occupy Oxford. Thence, after losing some precious days, he moved against London. At Turnham Green in the western suburbs, however, he found Essex's army back in a covering position with so strong an array of the London trained bands that he did not even attempt an assault.

Turnham Green

Instead he retired to Oxford, which became his head-quarters for the rest of the war.

The next year, 1643, Charles hoped to capture the capital by an advance from three directions. From the north was to come one army, from the south-west another, while he himself with reinforcements from Wales would bear down from Oxford. But the northern army was held up by Hull and by local forces under a Puritan squire—Oliver Cromwell—in the eastern counties; and the south-western army refused to advance very far with Plymouth unsubdued in its rear. In the same way the troops from Wales would not join the King at Oxford while Gloucester still held out.

The 'Triple Advance' strategy, 1643

The scheme upset

With his plans badly upset, the King then moved west to subdue Gloucester. Essex and the London trained bands set off after him—the shops of the capital closing to release the apprentices. Their approach scared the Royalist forces away from Gloucester, only for Charles to head once more towards London. Essex followed and came up with him at Newbury, where a day-long battle left both sides in much the same positions. Essex was critically short of food, but the Royalists were short of something still more important—ammunition—and during the night drew off.

Gloucester

First battle of Newbury

Thus far the Royalists had had the better of things. Most of the Puritan towns in the north, west and Midlands had fallen—Hull, Gloucester and Plymouth were exceptions—and outside the east and south-east the small local engagements had usually ended in Royalist victories. During the Gloucester crisis parliament therefore turned to the Scots. The Scottish army had been bought out of Northern England before the contest began, but Pym now planned to bring it back as a fighting ally of the parliamentary forces.

Royalist superiority

Parliament approaches the Scots

The negotiations were successful. The Scots promised to help parliament on conditions listed in a document known as the Solemn League and Covenant. It promised

Solemn League and Covenant between parliament and Scots, 1643

joint action to put down 'popery' (Roman Catholicism) and 'prelacy' (Church government through bishops as in the Church of England). The English parliament, in other words, was now virtually promising to make the English Church presbyterian as the price of Scottish aid.

The Scottish alliance was Pym's last achievement. He died in the closing days of 1643. By January 1644 the Scots had crossed the border, and by the spring they were besieging the northern Royalists in York. To join the Scots came one parliamentary force under Lord Fairfax and his son Sir Thomas, and another from the eastern counties under the Earl of Manchester and Oliver Cromwell. To relieve York came a Royalist army under Rupert. The dashing young prince, still only twenty-three years old, easily outflanked his opponents and entered the city without striking a blow. The besiegers then started to retire westwards; and Rupert, though he had only half his opponents' strength in infantry, was rash enough to follow and invite battle.

A few miles away from the city, on Marston Moor, the two forces clashed. Both sides were drawn up in the normal way, with cavalry on the wings, infantry in the centre. Parliament's right and right-centre were soon routed by the opposing horsemen; but on the parliamentary left Oliver Cromwell's cavalry, strongly supported by that of the Scots, overcame Rupert's cavalry in a fierce fight. "God made them", wrote Cromwell later, "as stubble to our swords". This was the first time Rupert had failed to carry all before him—but it was also the first time he had come directly up against Cromwell. Reforming his ranks, Cromwell then moved across the battlefield; with the Scottish horsemen still playing a gallant part, he shattered first the successful wing of the Royalist cavalry and then the Royalist infantry in the centre. The victory was decisive, and

Scots besiege York

Marston Moor, 1644

Charles loses the north

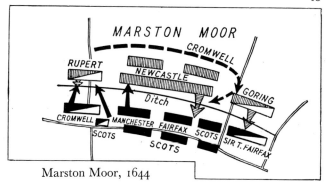

Marston Moor, 1644

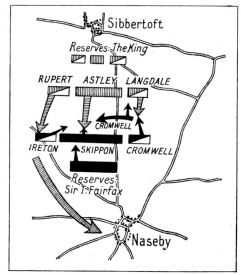

Naseby, 1645

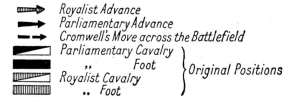

Royalist Advance
Parliamentary Advance
Cromwell's Move across the Battlefield
Parliamentary Cavalry ⎱
          " Foot   ⎰ Original Positions
Royalist Cavalry
      " Foot

when night fell the whole north of England lay at the mercy of parliament.

Parliament now hoped to complete its task by capturing the west. The Earls of Essex and Manchester, however, wasted good opportunities—Essex in the west, Manchester in a second battle at Newbury. This convinced Cromwell that parliament would never win while its chief forces were commanded by noblemen of this type, who were fighting to make Charles respect parliament and Puritanism, but were not prepared to overthrow the King completely.

As a tactful way of getting rid of the two noblemen, parliament eventually carried a 'self-denying ordinance'. By this all members of parliament, including peers, laid down their commands. About the same time, also with Cromwell's support, it was decided to create a fresh army to be paid and regulated directly by parliament—for thus far forces had been recruited and paid by individuals or a group of counties, and only engaged by parliament. Sir Thomas Fairfax, who had wasted no opportunities, was appointed General of this 'New Model Army'; and Cromwell himself was soon afterwards made Lieutenant-General, or second-in-command, with control of the cavalry.

The New Model Army, which by 1645 comprised about a quarter of the parliamentary troops, was in many respects neither new nor model. Nearly two-thirds of its men at formation were drafted in from other forces; and at least half were bludgeoned into service by the press-gang. On the other hand, the entire force was paid regularly, and so was less liable to desert than the other armies, some of whose officers had received only six weeks' pay in two years; and it could be sent, much more successfully than the local forces, to serve in all parts of the country. It was, moreover, the first really large force in English history to enjoy the advantages of

Cromwell's dissatisfaction with Essex and Manchester

Self-denying ordinance

Fairfax

New Model Army

uniform—the scarlet coat which afterwards became the standard dress of the British army—instead of merely wearing on the eve of battle some distinguishing device such as a scarf, a sprig of broom, or (on occasion) the shirt-tail pulled outside the breeches! Very important, too, was the fact that in some of the existing troops from the eastern counties, and especially in such cavalry as had already served with Cromwell, the New Model Army had a type of soldier—hardy, well-disciplined and fiercely zealous for his own religious opinions—who was uncommon in the other armies on both sides.

The New Model Army's first big battle took place in the summer of 1645 near Naseby, in Northamptonshire. It virtually decided the war. On the parliamentary left, the cavalry were routed by Rupert's horsemen— who again pursued their broken opponents and took no further part in the main battle. But on the parliamentary right Cromwell and his cavalry once more proved irresistible. After scattering the opposite cavalry he turned, as at Marston Moor, to the centre, and soon the whole of the King's infantry was compelled to surrender.[1] *Naseby, 1645*

A decisive victory

From Naseby the Royalists never recovered. A month later Fairfax and Cromwell beat the main Royalist army in the west at Langport. Extensive 'mopping-up' operations then followed; and Charles's last real hope faded when his forces were defeated outside Chester while making their way north to Scotland. *Langport*

The King's intention had been to join the Marquis of Montrose, who had raised the Scottish Highlands against the Presbyterian nobles and clergy in control at Edinburgh, and in particular against the Marquis of Argyle. *Montrose in Scotland*

[1] The worst side of Puritan zeal—the same spirit of blind hatred which led Puritan troops to smash beautiful statues of saints or stable their horses in Worcester Cathedral—was seen after the battle. The victorious soldiers slaughtered some hundreds of Irishwomen found in the Royalist camp, and slashed the faces of other female camp-followers regarded as immoral.

By a series of brilliant campaigns beginning in 1644 Montrose had got as far as controlling Glasgow and Edinburgh; but with the whole of southern Scotland at his feet his Highland followers, denied plunder, had returned to their glens. This left Montrose open to attack by a Scottish army hastily recalled from England under David Leslie, one of the victors of Marston Moor. A few days before the defeat of the King outside Chester the tiny force of the gallant nobleman was surprised and **Philiphaugh** overwhelmed at Philiphaugh, near Selkirk. Montrose escaped with a few companions. But such of his followers as fought on were killed almost to a man.[1]

By the autumn of 1645 Charles's cause was doomed, and though small Royalist forces and various isolated strongholds still fought on, the war was as good as over. **Charles surrenders to Scots, 1646** In May 1646 Charles therefore decided to complicate matters by giving himself up, not to his English opponents, but to the Scots. Riding out of Oxford in disguise, he passed through the parliamentary lines and made his way to where the main Scots army was besieging Newark, near Nottingham. At the best he hoped to make a compact with the Scots which would give him their support. At the worst, his action would be bound to cause difficulties between Scots and parliament and so weaken or divide his enemies.

---

[1] Fifty, taken prisoner, were afterwards slaughtered to satisfy demands by the Lowland Presbyterian clergy and nobility. As at Naseby, there was also a wholesale massacre of the Irish women—and, in this case, children—found in the camp of the vanquished.

CHAPTER TWENTY-TWO

THE SECOND CIVIL WAR AND THE ESTABLISHMENT OF THE COMMONWEALTH
(1646–1651)

1. *The Negotiations, the Second Civil War, and the Trial and Death of Charles*

FROM the moment Charles surrendered, the relations between King, Scots, parliament and the New Model Army (who were soon following lines of their own) became a maze of intrigue. The Scots and the majority of those still left in the English parliament were mainly concerned to see that Presbyterianism was established in England. When after long negotiations Charles refused to agree, the Scots lost patience, accepted payment for their services from parliament, handed over Charles to parliament's keeping, and marched back to their own country. *The Scots' concern: Presbyterianism* *The Scots hand over Charles to parliament*

It was now essential for settled government that parliament should come to some sort of terms with Charles. This was not made easier by the fact that Charles could still negotiate secretly with the Scots, the Army, the Irish and the French. He was well aware of the unpopularity of his opponents (who had suppressed many amusements and exacted heavy taxation to maintain their forces)—and he regarded himself as justified in seeking help wherever he could find it. At heart, too, he was resolved never to abandon his full royal authority, which he regarded as a sacred trust to be exercised for the good of the realm. So all his negotiations were *Charles's attitude* insincere, and designed only to play out time until his opponents quarrelled among themselves.

On the other side, the Presbyterian majority in parliament had made agreement very difficult by forbidding the prayer-book service and inflicting huge fines on the defeated Royalists. At the same time they were bitterly hostile to the views of their fellow-Puritans, the Baptists and Independents. Independent Puritanism was the creed of only a minority in parliament; but—much more important—it was the creed of Cromwell and the dominant elements in the New Model Army. Moreover many of the soldiers, especially in the rank and file, had developed political views of a very democratic kind, and were even demanding, against the wishes of senior officers like Fairfax and Cromwell, that England should become a republic and that all men should have the right to vote at parliamentary elections.

The result was that very soon the Presbyterian majority in the Commons decided to disband the New Model Army—with three-quarters of its arrears of pay unsettled. At the same time some of the Presbyterian leaders negotiated again with Charles and promised to support him if he would recognize Presbyterianism even temporarily. All this caused strong feeling in the New Model Army. Elected representatives of each troop and regiment were appointed to protest against the pay proposals, the army refused to disband, and on orders from Cromwell a body of soldiers seized possession of the King.

After this all parties approached Charles with solutions. To gain greater freedom of action, and because he expected—mistakenly—to be received as a friend by its governor, he escaped from Hampton Court to Carisbrooke Castle, in the Isle of Wight. There, in the closing days of 1647, he secretly struck a bargain with representatives of the Scots. By what became known as the *Engagement*, the Scots undertook to send an army into

The Presbyterian attitude

Cromwell and the Independent Puritans

Democratic views in army rank-and-file

Parliament tries to disband the New Model Army

The army seizes Charles, 1647

Further negotiations

The Engagement between King and Scots, 1647

England to support Royalist revolts and restore the King to most of his powers. For his part, Charles promised to recognize Presbyterianism in Scotland and establish it in England for three years while a permanent Church settlement was being worked out. He also agreed to suppress the Independents.

In the summer of 1648 a Scots army under the Duke of Hamilton duly crossed the border. The Scots, however, were not united in support of the expedition, which contained many raw recruits and came on the scene too late—most of the Royalist revolts having already been suppressed. Cromwell, in fact, was able to strike at the Scots when they were no farther south than Lancashire. He caught them near Preston, and in a three-day fight southwards through the county utterly defeated and scattered the entire army of invaders. *The Second Civil War, 1648*

Preston, 1648: Cromwell defeats Scots

The temper of the New Model Army was now up. Once again, they argued, the King had plunged the country needlessly into civil war. From the rank and file rose the demand that "Charles Stuart, that Man of Blood" should be brought to trial—and execution. But as the remnant of the Lords would not hear of this, and the Presbyterian majority in the Commons seemed quite prepared to go on negotiating indefinitely, that involved taking action against the greater part of parliament. Many of the New Model Army's senior officers hesitated to do this, but as the Presbyterians had negotiated with Charles to suppress the Independents most of the army leaders came to see that in self-defence they must act. In December 1648, on orders from a council of army officers, a detachment of soldiers under Colonel Pride appeared at Westminster. The Colonel did his work thoroughly. He stopped about a hundred Presbyterians from taking their seats in the Commons, and sent off another forty or so who resisted to prison. *The army demands Charles's death*

The Presbyterians still negotiate

Pride's Purge: the army expels the Presbyterian M.P.s

By 'Pride's Purge', as it became known, the membership of the Commons was reduced to less than one hundred, of whom only about sixty—all Independent Puritans—continued to occupy their places regularly. Only six or seven peers continued to sit in the Lords.

The 'Rump' This 'Rump', or relic, of the Long Parliament was now entirely obedient to the soldiers. After a last approach had failed to shake Charles's determination to preserve the Church and his own power, it duly proposed that a court should be appointed to try the King; and when the few remaining Lords refused to agree, it went on to The Rump claims power for the Commons and arranges for trial of Charles declare that the Commons, "being chosen by and representing the people" (which the Rump certainly did not!) "have the supreme power in this nation", and that whatever the Commons enacted had the force of law. At the same time it appointed one hundred and thirty-five persons to form a High Court of Justice for the trial of the King. One of the last of the army leaders to come round to this policy was Cromwell; but, as ever, once he had made up his mind he became foremost in action.

The King's trial At the trial which followed in Westminster Hall about a half of those named as judges, including Fairfax, took care not to appear. The President, Bradshaw—one of the few lawyers who consented to serve—sat in a shot-proof hat. Charles throughout refused to acknowledge any legal right on the part of the court to try him—for of course it had none; and there was great force in his argument that, if power without law may make or un-make laws, the life and liberty of every man in the country were as much in danger as his own. As Charles had committed no recognized crime, all his accusers could do was to invent a new one—high treason against the nation—and argue that Charles was guilty of this by waging war against a section of his subjects. The trial, then, was a purely political act dressed up as a legal one.

The Royal Oake of Brittayne

A very early political cartoon with a royalist viewpoint published in 1649. Soldiers directed by Cromwell (on the left, above a demon down below) are hacking down the royal oak (symbolizing Charles and the monarchy) while civilians on the right (perhaps the Commons) assist the process by pulling on ropes. Other civilians gather pickings from the branches. With the oak of the monarchy will fall the main fruit of its boughs—the Sword of Justice, the Holy Bible, the Eikon Basilike ('Royal Image'—a very popular book purporting to be the meditations of Charles I), the Magna Carta, the Statutes and the Debates of Parliament. The pigs feeding are the common people, the future victims of the action.

It was meant to have, and had, only one possible verdict. Charles (who was nothing of the sort) was declared "a tyrant, traitor, murderer and public enemy to the good people of this nation". He was to be put to death "by the severing of his head from his body".

On January 30th, 1649, outside the Royal Palace at Whitehall, Charles was led forth to his execution. From the scaffold he still proclaimed the idea of kingship which he had inherited, but which, running counter to the growing power and religious opinions of the wealthy

Execution of Charles, 1649

middle-class, had aroused the opposition of parliament and brought him low.

> For the people [said Charles] truly I desire their liberty and freedom as much as anybody whatsoever; but I must tell you, their liberty and freedom consists in having government . . . it is not their having a *share* in government. . . . A subject and a sovereign are clear different things.

This was the viewpoint which Cromwell and his soldiers had contested at the risk of their lives. Yet in destroying the King they were showing no more consideration for the wishes of the people—in fact, far less—than Charles himself had ever done.

In the final episode Charles's behaviour was throughout flawless. In the words of Andrew Marvell, a Puritan:

> He nothing common did or mean
> Upon that memorable scene,
> But with his keener eye
> The Axe's edge did try;
> Nor called the gods, with vulgar spite,
> To vindicate his helpless right;
> But bow'd his comely head
> Down, as upon a bed. . . .

When the executioner raised the severed head to show it, as usual, to the assembled multitude, the soldiers round the scaffold gave a shout of triumph. But from the mass of ordinary citizens came only a groan of pity and anger. In that expression of horror was heard, perhaps for the first time since the outbreak of the Civil War, the true voice of the English people.

2. *The Establishment of the Commonwealth*

England a Commonwealth After the execution of Charles, the Rump of the Long Parliament went on to abolish the monarchy and the House of Lords and to declare England a Common-

The Execution of Charles I

The scene in Whitehall as depicted in a Dutch print. In the ovals above are Fairfax, Charles and Cromwell. On the platform from left to right, are the two masked executioners, Charles, the Bishop of London (Dr. Juxon), and two army officers (Colonel Tomlinson and Hacker). To judge from the detail of Inigo Jones's Banqueting House, which is far from accurate, the whole thing is largely imaginary, but it gives some rough idea of the scene. There is, however, a tradition in the royal family that King Charles I was executed face upwards.

wealth. Government was to be by the Commons—which meant the Rump—and a Council of State (chosen by, and mainly from, the Rump). This arrangement appealed to very few, even in England. It appealed to fewer still in Ireland and Scotland, where Charles's eldest son was quickly proclaimed king as Charles II.

In England the new arrangements were attacked not only by Royalists but by strong parliamentarians like John Lilburne and his 'Levellers', who much in advance of their time believed that every man should have the

Lilburne and the 'Levellers'

right to vote. Lilburne's views were milk-and-water,
however, compared with those of Gerard Winstanley
and the small sect calling themselves the 'True Levellers', who also demanded an equal right to property.
When, however, a group of these men tried to put this
idea into practice by occupying some waste land in
Surrey and digging it up for cultivation under joint
ownership, they were quickly dispersed by government
troops and hostile neighbours.

Despite this opposition from many different quarters
and even mutinies by its own armed forces, the new
government had the support of most of the army leaders
and so kept a hold on England. It could not have survived long, however, had it not taken strong action
against the Royalist movements in Ireland and Scotland.
That these were crushed, and crushed promptly, was
largely due to Oliver Cromwell.

The Royalist movement in Ireland was supported not
only by nearly all settlers of English descent, but also by
many of the native Irish. The leader of this alliance was
the Earl of Ormonde, the Lord Lieutenant, a man of
fine character who on Charles I's death had immedi-
ately proclaimed Charles II. By mid-1649 Ormonde
held on behalf of Charles II almost all Ireland except
Dublin and Londonderry. So the government in London
organized a strong expedition under Cromwell—for a
Royalist Ireland would undoubtedly mean before long
a Royalist invasion of England.

Cromwell—who was extremely seasick during the
crossing—landed at Dublin in the summer of 1649. He
was anxious not to be absent long from England, his
men were burning to avenge the massacres of 1641, and
no Puritan had any sympathy with Catholics—or
Protestants who helped Catholics. All this led him to
make a dreadful example of his first opponents. On
capturing Drogheda he ordered the entire garrison,

Winstanley and the 'True Levellers'

Ireland

Cromwell in Ireland, 1649-1650

Drogheda and Wexford

England's Miraculous Preservation

Just as 'The Royal Oake of Brittayne' was a royalist cartoon, so this is a parliamentary one. Published in 1646, it depicts the Ark of England (in three compartments of House of Lords, House of Commons and Assembly of Divines) surrounded by various figures in the stormy sea. These are the royalist leaders who have conspired against the Ark, have been thrust out, and are now doomed to drown. Waving a sword on the right is Rupert; in the centre Strafford vainly discharges a musket and Laud is seen with his prayer-book; and on the left is Henrietta Maria, holding out a sealed paper. The figures in the ovals are the parliamentary commanders and the Scottish general Leslie.

some two thousand strong, to be put to the sword. A little later his troops meted out similar treatment to the defenders of Wexford. Both actions were permissible under the laws of war at the time, for parts of the garrisons had fought on after the main defences were taken; but the massacres were in striking contrast to Cromwell's normally humane behaviour in England.

Nine months' bitter struggle reduced the eastern part of Ireland, and Cromwell then returned to England, leaving others to complete the task of conquest. This they did by 1652, at the dreadful cost to Ireland of perhaps

Conquest of Ireland

one-third of her people. Moreover, to ensure obedience and to reward the English soldiers and government
creditors, the Rump (and later Cromwell) confiscated
vast areas of Irish land and gave or sold it to Englishmen. This was done throughout three of the four
provinces of Ireland, thousands of Irish landowners
being transported to the West Indies or compelled to
accept small estates in Connaught. So the Irish had to
suffer not only foreign rule but also local control by
landlords with whom they had nothing in common.
From that day to this, 'the curse of Cromwell' has remained a vivid memory in Ireland and a constant
stumbling-block to good relations between Irish and
English.

Meanwhile the Scots had also proclaimed Charles II
king. They would not, however, admit him to the
country until he had taken the covenant to maintain
Presbyterianism in Scotland, and had also sworn to
impose it on England and Ireland. Such terms did not
please Charles, who from his exile encouraged Montrose
to collect a force abroad and make a landing in the
Scottish Highlands. If Montrose could again raise the
clans against the Presbyterian lords in control at Edinburgh, Charles might then enter Scotland on his own
terms. But unfortunately Charles chose to play a double
game. While encouraging the venture of Montrose, he
also came to a draft agreement with the Scottish Presbyterians—an agreement he doubtless intended to throw
overboard if Montrose succeeded.

The news that Charles was negotiating with the
Presbyterians weakened Montrose's hand and made
some of the Highland chiefs reluctant to join him. When
he landed from the Orkneys early in 1650 his band of
followers was pathetically small, and before he could
gather much support he was defeated by the government forces. He escaped from the field, only to be given

*Confiscation
of Irish land*

*Scotland:
Charles II
proclaimed*

*Charles
encourages
Montrose*

up by a lord with whom he had sought shelter. Hanging Execution of Montrose:
was not enough to satisfy the Edinburgh authorities. He Charles ac-
was cut down after three hours, beheaded and quartered cepts terms of Presby-
—after which the Presbyterians were better placed to terians, 1650
insist on Charles accepting all their terms. This the easy-
going young man did. By mid-1650 he was ruling, or
rather reigning, in Scotland as a 'Covenanted King',
expected to repent at all times of his own and his
father's misdeeds.

The thought of Charles I's son enthroned in Scotland
and likely at any time to invade England alarmed the
Commonwealth government. Very soon Cromwell, recalled from Ireland, was leading an army north. In the
preliminary skirmishes for Edinburgh, however, he was
outmanœuvred and forced back towards the sea at
Dunbar. Here he was threatened by a Scottish force Dunbar
at least twice as numerous which took up position on the
hills dominating the town. But the Scots, anxious to
bring on a battle, descended too soon from their point
of vantage—"God hath delivered them into our
hands!" Cromwell is said to have exclaimed. The next
day the Commonwealth troops shattered the entire
Scottish army and took some ten thousand prisoners.
The English losses, according to Cromwell, amounted
to no more than twenty.

Cromwell was now faced with the prospect of further
campaigns in Scotland to round up Charles. Failing to
end these as he wished, he set a trap by leaving the
western route into England very lightly guarded. Charles Charles
jumped at the desperate chance offered him. With an invades England
army more Royalist than Presbyterian, he headed south
for Carlisle and Lancashire.

Cromwell meanwhile moved south on a parallel
course the opposite side of the Pennines. Then he struck
across westwards to Worcester, where the exhausted Worcester
invaders had been compelled to rest. The result was 1651

almost a foregone conclusion—the Scottish army was utterly routed, and Charles himself was one of the very few to escape. Wandering in disguise for many weeks with a price on his head, and once forced to hide in an

The Scots and Charles II

This satirical illustration to a broadsheet poem, published in 1651, symbolises the uncomfortable situation of the young Charles II as a 'Covenanted King' in Scotland. A Scot (labelled Jockie) turns the handle of the grindstone while a presbyterian minister holds Charles's nose down to it. The verse couplet on the left is spoken by one of the Scots; that on the right by Charles. The artist obviously has no sympathy with either King or Scottish presbyterians—perhaps he was an Independent.

oak while Puritan soldiers passed nearby, this "tall man above two yards high" (in the words of the proclamation offering a reward for his capture) at length made his way to the south coast and thence escaped to France in a small boat. Meanwhile General Monk and others

Escape of
Charles

were completing the conquest of Scotland—which was soon forcibly united to the Commonwealth. Scotland united to Common- wealth

Ireland and Scotland were not the only sources of danger to the new English government. The Commonwealth leaders also had to round up the Royalist ships— for about a quarter of the navy had broken away from Puritan control and under the dauntless Prince Rupert was now preying on English merchant shipping. The Action against Royalist ships task of bringing Rupert to heel fell largely to Robert Blake, a Puritan merchant who had sat in the Short Parliament and distinguished himself in defending Bristol and Taunton. Blake also helped to bring the islands round the British shores into submission. Blake against Rupert

At the same time there was also the question of the colonies. Newfoundland (where small communities had settled by the 1630s) and the Puritan colonies (four of which were now loosely linked together as the New England Confederacy) had recognized the Commonwealth without delay. Virginia, Maryland, the Bermudas and the West Indian possessions, however, remained Royalist—until a Commonwealth naval squadron helped them to change their minds. The colonies forced to submit

With this done, the Commonwealth had now succeeded in its first great task—the establishment of its authority throughout the British Isles and the English colonies overseas.

CHAPTER TWENTY-THREE

THE RULE OF THE PURITANS
(1651–1660)

1. *The Anglo-Dutch War and the 'Barebones' Parliament*

ONCE firmly established in power, the Commonwealth leaders were soon tempted by the strength of their army and navy into quarrelling with Holland. During the Thirty Years War, which had at last ended in 1648, the Dutch had won from Spain not only recognition of their independence but also valuable colonies in the East. By 1651 Holland, not Spain, was the greatest obstacle to English trade and expansion overseas.

The rise of Holland

To deprive the Dutch of some of their extensive 'carrying' trade, and to build up English merchant shipping to the Dutch level, the Rump in 1651 passed a Navigation Act. This most famous of its kind—there were many navigation acts before and not a few afterwards—laid down that when goods from outside Europe were imported into the Commonwealth or its colonies they must be carried in Commonwealth or colonial ships. When goods were brought into Commonwealth territories from Europe they must be carried either in Commonwealth ships, or in the ships of the country producing the goods. Dutch ships, in other words, could bring only Dutch goods to the Commonwealth and its colonies; they could no longer carry to Commonwealth ports the goods produced by other nations.

Navigation Act, 1651

The Commonwealth leaders also pressed Holland in other ways. They demanded that the Dutch should

Commonwealth demands:

recognize the 'right' of English ships acting against French privateers to search Dutch vessels for French goods. They demanded acknowledgment of the 'right' of English warships to receive in the 'British seas' a salute from Dutch and other foreign vessels—a salute which involved lowering both flag and topsail. And they insisted on compensation for a massacre of English settlers by the Dutch in the East Indies which had taken place nearly thirty years earlier. To all this the Dutch refused to agree. A state of war then gradually set in between the two nations, the first clashes arising from the refusal of the Dutch admiral, van Tromp, to give the salute in the Channel.

For over a year Blake on the one side, van Tromp (and de Ruyter) on the other, waged a ding-dong struggle in the Channel and North Sea. In the end Blake's larger ships and generally more efficient forces told, and he was able to blockade the Dutch ports. With their overseas trade cut off and the commercial life of their fine cities coming almost to a standstill, the Dutch then became eager for peace. In England too the mounting cost of the war caused great resentment, and soon after Cromwell came into power he offered the Dutch honourable terms. By these the Dutch recognized the Navigation Act, paid some of the required compensation, ceased to shelter Charles and the English Royalists, and agreed to give the salute in the 'British sea' as before. The question of the right of search was left unsettled, to cause more trouble later.

Meanwhile the Rump had done its best to retain power. Clearly it should have made way for a more representative parliament. So at least thought many of the army officers including the commander-in-chief, Cromwell—who persuaded some of the Rump leaders to agree, only to hear next morning that the Rump was debating a bill which would have prolonged its own

Cromwell dissolving the Rump, 1653

A Dutch print illustrating the famous scene when Cromwell (in foreground third from left, pointing with stick and saying 'Begone, you rogues') dissolved the Rump of the Long Parliament. In the background soldiers are pulling down the Speaker, and driving away a goose with a peacock's tail. The owl on the right, like the goose, probably represents the stupidity of the members.

power. At once Cromwell hastened to the House with a troop of soldiers. After rebuking the members for various faults, he called in his men and forcibly dissolved parliament. As he turned to depart he noticed the mace which lies on the table before the Speaker. "What shall we do with that bauble?" he exclaimed: then, motioning to an officer, "Here, take it away". The doors were **Cromwell expels the Rump, 1653** then locked behind the expelled members, and no shred remained of the old order of King, Lords and Commons. That evening a wit wrote on the door of the Commons' chamber, "This House to let, unfurnished".

Cromwell's impulsive action did not solve the ques- **Cromwell's dilemma** tion of a new form of government. The more Cromwell pondered on what was to replace the Rump, the more he realized that a really free election could only result in the triumph of the Royalists and the end of all his own power. This, he felt, he could not permit—not because he was aiming at a dictatorship, but because his victories

Oliver Cromwell

From an unfinished miniature by one of the first outstanding British artists, Samuel Cooper. In accordance with Cromwell's directions, it is not a flattering portrait—it makes no attempt to disguise the warts—but it brings out the strength, the humanity, and the deep reflectiveness of one of England's greatest men.

had convinced him that he was appointed by God to safeguard Puritanism and do the English people good.

At the same time, Cromwell sincerely believed in the need for a parliament to curb the ruler, and give the worthiest elements of the nation—in his opinion, the

Puritans with property—the chance to express their views. He knew, too, that to dispense with parliament would make a mockery of the cause for which he had fought. Torn between desire for a parliament and the knowledge that any freely elected parliament would at once restore the Stuarts and oppress the Puritans, he and his fellow commanders agreed that lists of men suitable to sit in parliament should be prepared by the Independent Puritan congregations. But there would be no election. From these lists the members of parliament would be chosen, not by the normal voters, but by the council of army officers.

The
Barebones
Parliament',
1653 This assembly of carefully picked Puritans met in 1653. It has gone down to history as the 'Barebones Parliament', from the fact that one of its members had the picturesque name of Praise-God Barebones. It was a very talented body—Monk and Blake were members, besides Cromwell—and it passed several valuable reforms, including acts for the relief of poor prisoners, the safe care of lunatics, and the keeping of parish registers of births, marriages and burials. Some of its other proposals, however, such as the abolition of tithe, could not have been carried without causing great difficulties. This led to the assembly becoming sharply divided. Fearing trouble if the extreme reformers had their way, the more moderate members then turned up in strength early one morning and voted the assembly at an end. At the same time they declared that their power reverted to the man who had summoned them—Cromwell, whose authority as commander-in-chief was now becoming more and more the only stable part of government.

2. Cromwell as Lord Protector (1653–1658)

In the interests of order, the 'moderate' leaders of the army were now beginning to favour a return to some kind of monarchy. Their idea was that Cromwell should be head of the state, but with limited authority. They therefore obtained his consent to a scheme for rule by a Lord Protector (Cromwell), a Council of State, and a single House of Parliament, with powers carefully divided between all three. The details were set out in a document known as the Instrument of Government. Among its terms, those who had supported the King in the Civil Wars were temporarily, and all Catholics permanently, barred from voting or being elected. Freedom of worship was to be enjoyed by all kinds of Puritans, but not by 'Papists' or 'Prelatists'. *The Instrument of Government* *Cromwell, Lord Protector*

The Instrument of Government had many weaknesses. It was purely a creation of the army; it had no tradition behind it; and its religious clauses offended more than half the nation. How little support it commanded was soon seen. When Cromwell, as Protector, called his first parliament, it at once tried to increase its own power—with the result that Cromwell dissolved it as soon as he legally could. *Weakness of the Instrument*

Though the Instrument—and the Protector's own position—had not been accepted by parliament, Cromwell nevertheless acted as if it had. Together with his Council he issued proclamations—only to find that many judges and justices of the peace would not enforce them. The result of this could only be chaos. So before long, Cromwell simply fell back on force. Following a Royalist revolt in Wiltshire, he divided England and Wales into eleven districts, and stationed in each a body of troops under a major-general, whose task was to see that Cromwell's and the Council's edicts were obeyed. *Cromwell rules through the army*

This the major-generals did very thoroughly. Among other things they saw that the justices of the peace and other authorities collected heavy taxes from the late Cavaliers, held hundreds of Royalists under arrest, shut down superfluous alehouses (one major-general suppressed a third of all the alehouses in Warwickshire), *The major-generals* closed the theatres and clapped the out-of-work actors into prison, and banned horse-racing, cock-fighting, and bear-baiting.[1] On orders from Cromwell, the major-generals also insisted that Sunday should become a

Puritan repression

Puritan Sabbath with work and games forbidden (even to take a walk—except to church—or to mend a dress was risky!) and that disregarded laws against drunkenness, swearing and other vices should be put into effect. They had a fine field of opportunity, for the Puritans in parliament from 1642 onwards had passed measures by which adultery was punishable with death, swearing was punishable by a scale of fines according to rank (a duke paid nearly ten times as much as a labourer) and Christmas Day and the last Wednesday in every month were to be kept as fasts. On Christmas Day, for instance, soldiers were sent round London to search the kitchens for any food being cooked. Cromwell was thus ruling by force far more thoroughly, and in a far more bitterly detested way, than ever Charles I had done.

Still, Cromwell could not be happy as a dictator. He remained anxious that an elected parliament—of Puritans—should share in the work of government. In 1656,

A second parliament

when at war with Spain, he once more summoned a parliament from which Cavaliers were barred; again nearly half the members came up opposed to the Protector. These he excluded from the House. The rest

Cromwell refuses title of king

asked him to accept the position of king (which he refused out of loyalty to, and possibly fear of, the repub-

An Upper House restored

lican section of the army), and to set up an Upper House

[1] The Puritans' main objection to horse-racing was that it encouraged gatherings of Cavaliers. Bear-baiting and cock-fighting they disliked on the same grounds, but also because of the cruelty to animals and the fact that young people might be corrupted by the bad characters among the spectators. During the period of rule through the major-generals, Colonel Pride led a detachment of soldiers to the famous bear-pit at Bankside and personally killed the bears. His men then went round the cockpits wringing the cocks' necks.

of life-members (to which he agreed). But when he allowed the excluded members to return, they promptly celebrated by attacking this new Upper House. So within a fortnight Cromwell, in a mixture of sorrow and anger, once more dissolved parliament. "Let God judge", he said, "between you and me"—to which his opponents fervently replied "Amen". He then fell back on rule through the army.

Parliament attacks Cromwell and is dissolved

Meanwhile abroad Cromwell was raising England's reputation to a height untouched since the defeat of the Armada. Having successfully ended the war against Puritan Holland, he resolved to strike at one of the great Catholic powers, and at the same time gain wealth and territory for England. At the end of 1654 he sent an expedition to capture Spanish colonies and treasure in the Caribbean. His excuse was that the Spaniards had seized our vessels in that part of the world (which they regarded as all theirs) and had handed over English merchants in Spain to the Inquisition. The expedition, which was very badly prepared, was repulsed from the city of San Domingo in the island of Hispaniola, but went on to capture an island which had practically no defenders at all—Jamaica. Exasperated, Spain treated this as war, and very soon Cromwell made the obvious move of allying with Spain's great enemy, France.

Capture of Jamaica: war against Spain

Alliance with France

The new war between England and Spain was at first fought on the sea. Among the feats of Blake was to remain at sea blockading the Spanish coast throughout a whole winter—a feat never before attempted—and then to catch the enemy at Santa Cruz, Teneriffe, and sink their entire fleet without loss to himself. A little later Cromwell sent some of the New Model Army over to support the French, who were trying to conquer the part of the Netherlands still held by Spain. Fighting with the greatest gallantry, the red-coated Puritan soldiers helped to beat the Spaniards—whose forces

Blake at Teneriffe, 1657

New Model Army in the Netherlands

included Charles's brother James and five regiments of Irish, Scottish and English Royalists. The redcoats' greatest triumph was at the battle of the Dunes, outside Dunkirk—which by the terms of the alliance then passed to English keeping.[1]

Battle of the Dunes

Spain was not the only country to feel the power of Cromwell. He had earlier curbed the rulers of Algiers and Tunis, who had been holding English sailors and ships captive. Blake crippled the Tunis guns from the sea—the first time that fire from ships afloat had ever silenced a shore battery. To put pressure on these rulers and on Spain, Cromwell not only sent a fleet into the Mediterranean but kept it there for several months, so starting what became later a permanent British practice.

Blake in the Mediterranean

Perhaps the clearest proof of Cromwell's power abroad was his protection of the Vaudois, a Protestant folk of Savoy, in the Alps. An ardently Catholic Duchess of Savoy had issued an order that those Vaudois who had moved down into the valleys and townships from their native mountain heights (where they were guaranteed freedom of worship) should turn Catholic within three days—or else lose their houses, farms and businesses. Meeting with a little resistance in enforcing this edict, her soldiers had then carried out a frightful massacre of men, women and children alike. Soon the woes of the Vaudois rang throughout Protestant Europe and in England the Puritan poet and Latin secretary of the Commonwealth, John Milton, was penning one of the most powerful sonnets ever written:

Cromwell's protection of the Vaudois

Avenge, O Lord, Thy slaughtered saints, whose bones
Lie scattered on the Alpine mountains cold. . . .

Cromwell could not send an army to the Italian Alps. But as part of the price of his friendship with France he

[1] Cromwell hoped that Dunkirk would make up for the loss of Calais. Charles II, however, soon sold it to France.

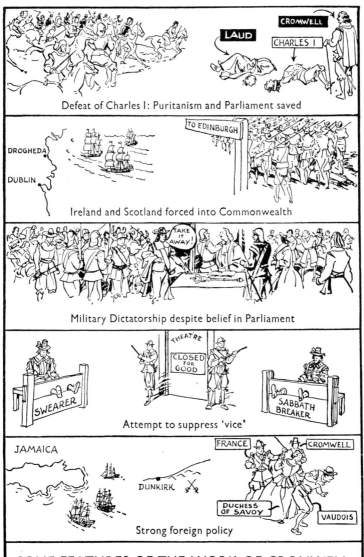

Defeat of Charles I: Puritanism and Parliament saved

Ireland and Scotland forced into Commonwealth

Military Dictatorship despite belief in Parliament

Attempt to suppress 'vice'

Strong foreign policy

SOME FEATURES OF THE WORK OF CROMWELL

insisted that France should put pressure on Savoy—and France duly did so. Without moving a man or firing a shot, Cromwell in this way stopped further violent persecution of the Vaudois and won them an enlarged area in which to live.

Cromwell's achievements

Even his bitterest opponents in England were thus forced to recognize some greatness in Cromwell. For all his deep religious convictions, they regarded him as a hypocrite—as a man who had fought and murdered the King on the ground that the King was a tyrant, only to become a far greater tyrant himself. But they could not fail to recognize his courage, his military genius, and the fact that, after two reigns in which every English expedition abroad had ended in disaster, he had taught the powers of Europe to look on England as a country no longer to be flouted but feared.

3. *The Breakdown of Puritan Rule*

Death of Cromwell, 1658

Richard Cromwell

Worn out by his labours and difficulties, Cromwell died in 1658. He had nominated his son Richard to succeed him; and Richard—'Tumbledown Dick'—duly took up the position of Protector. But though a man of ability he lacked Oliver's energy, and as a civilian squire he carried little weight with the determined, ambitious generals of the army. After a short struggle with these men Richard gave in, agreed to the soldiers' demand to recall the Rump, and recognized that the Protectorate (and with it his own rule) was at an end.

End of the Protectorate: Rump (and Commonwealth) restored

The restored Rump, now only forty-two members strong, soon began to act in its old high-handed manner. It declared all Oliver's acts illegal, and even made the major-generals liable to repay the taxes they had collected on his behalf. So the soldiers soon dissolved the Rump and returned to direct military rule—only to quarrel among themselves so badly that they had to restore the Rump again.

Army dissolves Rump and restores it again

The country was now in utter confusion. In this situation the actions of one man proved decisive. General Monk, the Commonwealth commander in Scotland, unlike most of his fellow-generals was in firm control of his own forces. Feeling himself the strongest power in the state, and unwilling to tolerate disorder any longer, Monk marched his army towards London. Of his exact intentions he gave no word. Once in London, he soon found that the Rump was violently unpopular and quite unfit to govern. He therefore demanded that the Rump should first re-admit all the Presbyterians excluded by Pride's Purge, and then make way for a new, freely elected parliament. To this the Rump was forced to agree, though it stipulated that no Royalists should be elected to the new assembly. Amid general rejoicing— bonfires were lit and Barebones' windows broken—the excluded Presbyterian members then returned and a little later the Long Parliament at last voted itself at an end.

Monk

Rump re-admits Presbyterians

End of Long Parliament

The restoration of the Stuarts was now a foregone conclusion, though on what terms was still far from certain. Charles's main task was thus to behave with discretion. Accepting good advice, Charles sent to Monk from Breda, in Holland, a statement calculated to have a wide appeal. This promised pardon to all except those specially exempted by parliament and undertook to leave to parliament the vexed question of the ownership of estates which had been sold or confiscated during the revolutionary period. In the same document Charles declared a "liberty to tender consciences" (i.e. religious toleration), and promised to embody this in such terms as parliament should approve. He also agreed to accept any measures proposed by parliament for paying off the arrears of the army.

Negotiations for return of Charles

Declaration of Breda

In the elections the vote everywhere went to those candidates who favoured the return of the Stuarts—

New elections

indeed, many Royalists who had borne arms against parliament were chosen, despite the ban against them. By Monk's decision they were able to take their seats. It was Monk's voice, too, which decided that all peers (not merely the small band who had favoured parliament) should sit in the Lords. With these questions settled, Monk communicated to the newly elected parliament the terms of Charles's declaration. This was warmly welcomed on all sides, and parliament at once voted that the government "is, and ought to be, by King, Lords and Commons". The following month Charles II landed at Dover, to be escorted to London by Monk and the Puritan regiments.

The monarchy restored: Charles II lands, 1660

The fact that all parties except a few fanatics desired or accepted the return of the Stuarts does not mean that the Puritan revolution was a failure. It broke down because it had followed, or been driven into, a course too extreme. The execution of the King cut off the Puritans from the bulk of the nation, who also hated Puritan religious zeal, Puritan suppression of amusements, Puritan taxation (needed for a big army) and Puritan military government. But though the Commonwealth died unmourned, the Puritans had in fact achieved two great objects. They had stopped Charles I suppressing their faith; and they had made certain that in future the power of the king would be restricted as never before by that of parliament.

Failure and success of the Puritan revolution

CHAPTER TWENTY-FOUR

THE RESTORATION AND THE EARLY
YEARS OF CHARLES II
(1660–1667)

1. *The Restoration Settlement*

THE prince called to the throne in 1660 was not Charles II unfitted to rule a torn and disunited nation. He had courage, strength, wit, good humour, a wide experience of men and misfortune, plenty of ability and no very firm religious opinions. He was fond of pleasure—especially walking with his dogs, rowing and sailing, horse-racing, scientific experiments, dancing and love-making—but nevertheless had a shrewd head for business. Unlike his father, he trod warily in difficult situations. Genuinely anxious to heal his people's wounds, he was still keener not to depart once more on his 'travels'.

The recall of the King settled many of the problems left by the breakdown of the Commonwealth, but by no means all. What powers, for instance, should the new Charles II monarch wield? The answer came largely by recog-bound by nizing only those acts of the Long Parliament which had Charles I's received the assent of Charles I. This, however, kept all concessions the gains wrung from Charles I before the Civil War. Charles II had no Star Chamber or Court of High Commission, nor could he levy taxes or other charges without consent of parliament. His power was nothing like so great as that inherited by Charles I. This was the first and most important feature of the Restoration Settlement.

Beyond this, there were the terms of the Declaration
of Breda to be carried out. Charles kept his promises
and allowed parliament a deciding voice in the questions he had mentioned. From Charles's proposal of a
general pardon, parliament excepted certain persons
concerned in the trial and execution of Charles I—who
were soon hanged, drawn and quartered. With regard
to the Royalist estates, it decided that only those directly
confiscated (not those sold to pay fines or help the King)
should be restored—a decision which avoided much dis-
turbance, but left many Royalists injured and angry.
And as for the army, with some small exceptions such as
bodyguard troops and Monk's own regiment, parliament was only too glad to pay it off and disband it. This
made the King's task in foreign affairs very difficult, but
after its recent experiences the country regarded a
standing army as too much of a threat to liberty.

Parliament also made an important financial arrangement with the King. It was meant to safeguard parliament's rights and at the same time to give Charles a
proper revenue. But the taxes voted—including an
'excise' on beer and various other drinks from cider to
sherbet—for most of the reign brought in nothing like
the sum intended. So the Crown remained seriously
short of money, and later parliaments took advantage of
this to force their policy on Charles.

The other great matter demanding settlement was
religion. In the Declaration of Breda, Charles had
promised "a liberty for tender consciences" if parliament agreed. But when it came to the point, the majority
in the Commons proved unwilling to meet the views of
the Presbyterian minority, even though the Presbyterians had done much to bring about the Restoration.
At the end of 1660 the parliament which had recalled
Charles was dissolved with the religious question still
quite unsettled.

The Breda promises:

(a) General pardon

(b) The land settlement

(c) The army disbanded

Financial settlement

Religious settlement

Convention Parliament dissolved

The elections for the new parliament were held while The 'Cavalier' Parliament the flood tide of Royalist enthusiasm was at its height, and the members came up full of zeal for Crown and Church. The great majority were determined above all to prevent the Puritans regaining power. The result was seen in the acts passed between 1661 and 1665, which are together usually known as the Clarendon Code. The Clarendon Code, 1661–1665: name comes from Charles's chief minister at the time, Lord Clarendon—a little unfairly, as he was by no means the leading spirit in persecution.[1]

The first of these measures, the Corporation Act, (a) The Corpora- tion Act made future membership of a town corporation dependent on taking the Church of England communion. Its intention was to drive the Puritans not only from control of the towns but also from parliament—for in many towns the corporation alone had the right to vote at parliamentary elections. It was soon followed by the second measure, an Act of Uniformity requiring all (b) Act of Uni- formity clergy to use the Church of England prayer book— which was revised to become still more unacceptable to the Puritans. The result of this was that many hundreds of Puritan ministers had to give up the livings they had held under the Commonwealth. Henceforward the best the Puritans could strive for was not control within the Church, but toleration outside the Church.

But if parliament was anxious to persecute, Charles was not. A man of no strong religious feelings, he played his part easily enough as the head of the Church of England, but in his more serious moments inclined secretly towards Roman Catholicism. This was partly because of the influence of his mother and sister, partly because of his strong belief in authority, and partly

[1] Clarendon received his title at the Restoration. As Sir Edward Hyde, and a leading lawyer, he had first opposed Charles I, then come round to his support. He had shared Charles II's exile, and advised him wisely over the Declaration of Breda.

Stag-Hunting

From a series of engravings of sports by Hollar, published in 1671. Stag-hunting continued to be a favourite British sport throughout the 17th century—as in some parts it still is. Compare with the earlier picture on page 68, where the sport is obviously much less highly organized.

Hern-Hawking

From an engraving by Hollar. Hawking also continued to be a favourite sport. In this picture two falcons are bringing down a heron (hern).

because in his escape after Worcester he had received outstanding help from Catholic subjects. Reluctant to persecute anyone, and extremely anxious to win freedom of worship for the Catholics, Charles at the end of 1662 declared that, if parliament agreed, he would in certain cases not enforce the Act of Uniformity. By this move he undoubtedly meant to benefit Catholics and Puritans alike. But so far from allowing Charles to bring in this working system of toleration, parliament insisted instead on further persecution. The Conventicle Act soon forbade conventicles (religious meetings) of more than four persons apart from members of the same household, unless the meetings were conducted according to the rites of the Church of England. And a year later came the Five Mile Act, by which no expelled Puritan minister could come within five miles of a borough, or of any place where he had once held a living, unless he would swear not to attempt any alteration in Church or state. Once again this Act, intended to reduce the Puritan ex-ministers to starvation, arose from no desire of Charles. He accepted it, and with good grace, to get more money for the war with Holland which had by then broken out.

Charles attempts toleration, 1662

(c) Conventicle Act

(d) Five Mile Act

The effects of the Clarendon Code spread far beyond the field of religion into the whole of English life. By denying the Puritans—or Nonconformists, as they soon became called—any share in government, the code made them concentrate still further on trade and industry. And because Nonconformists could not hold official positions, it made nonconformity socially inferior to membership of the Established Church.

There was one other important part of the Restoration Settlement. Under the Commonwealth and Protectorate, the parliaments of Scotland and Ireland had been forcibly united with that of England, and both countries had had the doubtful privilege of sending a

Restoration Settlement in Ireland and Scotland

few Puritan members to Westminster. At the Restoration this arrangement stopped, and the two countries became linked to England, as before the Civil War, only by their common allegiance to the Crown.

Scotland

In Scotland (where all acts of the Scottish parliament since 1640 were cancelled) bishops were once more restored, and measures were passed similar to the Clarendon Code. This anti-Presbyterian policy was now supported by most of the Scottish nobles, who were heartily tired of clerical domination, but it met with sustained—and in a later reign successful—opposition from other ranks of society. Of the Scottish Presbyterian leaders, the great Marquis of Argyle and three others were executed for co-operating with the Commonwealth.

A Scottish Clarendon Code

Ireland

In Ireland, too, the Church was restored and laws were renewed against both Catholics and Nonconformists. There were so many Catholics, however, that the rules about Church attendance could not be enforced. Probably a greater hardship to the Catholics was that many who had had their estates confiscated failed to recover them. About two-thirds of Irish land fit for cultivation remained in the hands of Protestants of English descent, with results full of tragedy for the future of Ireland.

Restoration of Church

The Irish fail to recover their land

2. *The Second Anglo-Dutch War, the Great Plague, the Fire, and the Fall of Clarendon*

Charles's marriage

Charles's reign was not many months old when King and Council turned their attention to the interesting subject of a wife for the monarch. Various foreign princesses were considered, and Charles finally agreed to marry Catherine of Braganza, daughter of the King of Portugal. This was partly because Portugal, with French help, had by now recovered her independence

Catherine of Braganza

from Spain; and Charles, who much admired the brilliance of the French Court under his cousin, Louis XIV, was eager to keep within the circle of French friendship. But it was still more because Catherine brought to Charles the largest dowry till then received by an English king—Tangier (which soon proved too expensive to garrison), Bombay, and a big gift of sugar, mahogany and money. A lasting advantage which followed was the right to trade freely with Portuguese colonies. The more human results of the match, however, were not so satisfactory. Charles, while extremely fond of Catherine, proved unable to abandon his attachments to other ladies. Catherine, while extremely fond of Charles, proved unable to supply him with an heir. *Her dowry*

The friendship with France which helped to bring about the Portuguese marriage was a settled policy on the part of Charles. One of its earliest signs was when Charles and his council, to the great popular indignation, agreed to sell France Dunkirk. The fact that France had an alliance with Holland in the early years of the reign, however, did not prevent a renewed struggle between English and Dutch. *Charles's friendship with France* *Sale of Dunkirk*

This second war with Holland came for much the same reasons as the earlier conflict under the Commonwealth. The Dutch were still England's chief rivals in commerce—so much so that the only great act of parliament of the Commonwealth which was renewed, and even strengthened, at the Restoration was the Navigation Act. Together with rivalry for overseas markets went the seizure and counterseizure of overseas possessions in America, West Africa and the East Indies. The Dutch especially resented a 'grant' by Charles to his brother James, Duke of York, of the New Netherlands—a colony between New England and Virginia. The subsequent English occupation of this territory *Rivalry with Holland* *English occupy New Netherlands, 1664* linked up the English North American colonies in one continuous seaboard—and soon led to formal war between the two countries.[1]

Second Anglo-Dutch War, 1665–1667 The naval fighting in the 'official' war began well when the Duke of York won a great victory off Lowestoft. But soon came the ravages of the Great Plague, and during the autumn of 1665 the main English fleet could Louis XIV supports Holland not leave port. The next year Louis XIV honoured his alliance by joining the Dutch—but being at heart anxious to keep in with Charles he put much less than his full strength into the war.

During the summer of 1666 the naval fighting again flared up. The English under the Duke of Albemarle (as Monk had become at the Restoration), suffered heavy losses in a terrible four-day battle off the North Foreland, but had their revenge a few weeks later very near the same spot. Very soon the English were able to raid the Dutch coast and destroy over a hundred merchantmen. But September brought another calamity—the Great Fire of London—and Charles and his ministers resolved to end the war. Before long Charles Agreement between Charles and Louis struck a bargain with Louis; France would stop helping the Dutch if Charles would make no alliance against France for a year—for the ambitious Louis had now put forward a claim to the Spanish Netherlands.

As the Dutch were also anxious to make peace the end of the war seemed in sight. To save the Crown's hard-pressed finances Charles and his council therefore decided—against Charles's own advice—to lay up the main battle fleet and trust to the harbour guns for defence until peace was signed. But the negotiations The Dutch in the Medway, 1667 dragged, and the Dutch seized their chance. In June 1667 they entered the Thames, turned into the Medway, shattered the boom which protected Chatham

[1] The capital of the New Netherlands, New Amsterdam, was renamed New York after the Duke of York.

harbour, burnt several ships, and towed away un-
molested two more, including the largest vessel of the
English fleet. Incompetence and corruption at the naval
base stood dramatically revealed: many stores suddenly
needed were found to be 'missing'.

Other Dutch raids in the next few weeks were fought
off, but Charles and his ministers were now threatened Terms of peace
by a great wave of unpopularity and hastened to end
the conflict. They agreed, among other things, to let the
Dutch carry to Britain goods they had imported from
Germany and the Spanish Netherlands, and to require
a naval salute only in the Channel. By giving way on
these points they were able to conclude a peace, known
as the Treaty of Breda, which left England with what England retains New Netherlands
proved to be by far the most valuable conquest of the
whole fighting—the New Netherlands.

The Great Plague and the Great Fire, which together The Great Plague
sapped England's fighting strength during the war, are
two of the best remembered events in English history.
The Plague, like the much more severe Black Death of
the 14th century, was of the bubonic type, distinguished
by swellings, particularly in the groin. It came from the
East, probably entering this country in a ship's cargo.
The black rat was the great carrier, and the fleas from
this animal spread the disease, which was then trans-
mitted still more widely by infection from the skin or
breath of the sufferer. There was nearly always some of
it about in Tudor and Stuart times, and a major
epidemic developed every five years or so.

The epidemic of 1665–1666 was in fact the last. It
was especially severe in London, where at its height in
the summer of 1665 it carried off a thousand people
every day. Many vivid descriptions have been written
of the melancholy sights of that dreadful summer—of
the red crosses and the "Lord, have mercy on us" on
the doors of plague-stricken houses, whence no one was

allowed to emerge; of the church bells tolling incessantly for the funerals; of the hand carts trundled through the streets in the evening with the cry "Bring out your dead"; of the bodies cast together into great pits, and of the corpses rotting in the fields beyond the suburbs; of the King and Court and most other folk of wealth and fashion deserting London, and parliament meeting at Oxford, and government in the capital left to the soldierly courage of old Albemarle.

The rise and fall of the London death figures during the Plague may be vividly followed in the diary of Samuel Pepys, a devoted official of the Admiralty.[1] So, too, can the course of the Great Fire—a fire which began in a baker's shop in Pudding Lane, in the east of the City near London Bridge, burned for three days and nights, and spread almost to the City's western boundary. Pepys's whole description, covering entries for over a week, is extremely vivid. Though much too long to quote in full, some idea of its value to the historian—and of the extent of the fire—may be gained from a few extracts concerning the first day:

Samuel Pepys

The Great Fire of London, 1666

> September 2nd 1666 (Lord's Day) . . . By and by Jane comes and tells me above three hundred houses have been burned down tonight by the fire we saw, and that it is now burning down all Fish Street, by London Bridge. So I made myself ready presently and . . . got up upon one of the high places . . . and there I did see the houses at that end of the Bridge all on fire, and an unfortunate great fire on this and the other side the end of the bridge. So with my heart full of trouble I down to the water-side, and there got a boat and through the Bridge, and there

[1] Penned in shorthand, Pepys's Diary lay undeciphered in the library of Magdalene College, Cambridge, until the 19th century. Covering the years 1660 to 1669, it provides not only a unique record of the life of the time, but also a fascinating picture of the human weaknesses of the author. The record ceases in 1669 because the writer feared oncoming blindness—a fear happily unjustified.

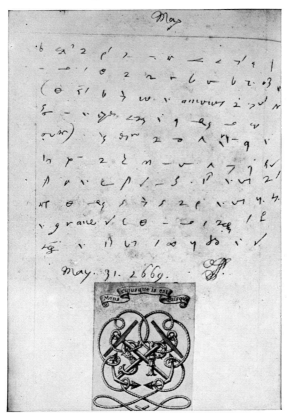

Pepys's Diary—The Last Page

This shows the shorthand in which Pepys kept his diary, varied with occasional words of longhand. In his cipher at the bottom the anchors and ropes round his initials are a reference to his position at the Admiralty.

saw a lamentable fire. . . . Everybody endeavouring to remove their goods, and flinging them into the river or bringing them into lighters that lay off; poor people staying in their houses as long till the very fire touched them and then running into boats, or clambering from one pair of stairs by the water-side to another. And among other things the poor pigeons, I perceive, were loth to leave their houses, but hovered about the windows and balconies till they were, some of them, burned, their wings, and fell down. Having staied, and in an hour's time seen the fire rage every way, and nobody to my sight endeavouring to quench it, but to remove their goods and leave all to the fire; and having seen . . . the wind mighty high and driving it into the City and everything after so long a drought proving combustible, even the stones of the Churches, I to Whitehall . . . and did tell the King and the Duke of York that unless His Majesty did command houses to be pulled down, nothing could stop the fire. . . . At last met my Lord Mayor in Canning Street like a man spent, with a handkerchief about his neck. To the King's message he cried, like a fainting woman, Lord! What can I do? I am spent; people will not obey me. I have been pulling down houses, but the fire overtakes us faster than we can do it. That he needed no more soldiers; and that for himself, he must go and refresh himself, having been up all night. . . . By this time, it was about 12 o'clock; and so home, and as soon as dined, away and walked through the City, the streets full of nothing but people and horses and carts loaded with goods. . . . River full of lighters and boats taking in goods, and good goods swimming in the water; and only I observed that hardly one lighter or boat in three that had the goods of a house in, but there was a pair of virginals in it.

Having seen as much as I could now, I away to Whitehall by appointment . . . and there met my wife—and walked to my boat; and there upon the water again, and to the fire up and down, it still progressing, the wind great. So near the fire, as we could for smoke; and all over the Thames, with one's face in the wind, we were almost burned with a shower of fire-drops. This is very true; so as houses were burned by these drops and flakes of fire, three and four, nay, five and six houses, one from another. When we could endure no more upon the

The Fire of London

This contemporary picture by a Dutch artist gives a vivid impression of the desolation. On the right, beyond the refugees, is the Tower of London, which the fire did not reach; on the left is London Bridge; in the centre is the huge church of Old St. Paul's.

water, we to a little ale-house on the Bankside . . . and there staied till it was dark almost, and saw the fire grow; and as it grew darker, appeared more and more, and in corners and upon steeples, and between churches and houses as far as we could see up the hill of the City, in a most horrid malicious bloody flame, not like the fine flame of an ordinary fire. We staid, till, it being darkest, we saw the fire as only one entire arch of fire from this to the other side the bridge, and in a bow up the hill for an arch of above a mile long; it made me weep to see it. The churches, houses, and all on fire and flaming at once; and a horrid noise the flames made, and the cracking of houses at their ruine. So home, with a sad heart.

Results of the fire

In all, the fire covered four-fifths of the City proper. Among other buildings it destroyed the Guildhall, the Custom House, the Royal Exchange, St. Paul's and eighty-eight other churches, forty-four halls of the Livery Companies, and some thirteen thousand houses. Great as was the hardship caused through loss of homes, business, rents, work and possessions—there was as yet no system of fire insurance—the fire had nevertheless one good result. Many of the destroyed wooden or half-timbered houses had harboured disease, which was less likely to gain a hold in the new brick or stone structures that, by order, replaced them. The old houses, too, had been very closely packed together and in many cases had projected into the roadway or had upper storeys overhanging their lower ones; wider spacing and plain fronts in the new buildings now allowed more light and sunshine to penetrate the streets. At the same time the opportunity was taken to do away with many narrow alleys, to build special markets for street traders, to relieve traffic congestion by widening key thoroughfares, and to lay down pipes for the better disposal of sewage. All told, the rebuilding of London was a great work, reflecting the utmost credit on Charles (who made many

The rebuilding

Pack Horses

A Stage Waggon

A Dray and a Coach

These details of transport are taken from views of Oxford and Cambridge published in 1675 and 1690.

excellent suggestions), on the City authorities (who had the entire task of organization), and on the ordinary folk who had lost their homes. So far as houses were concerned, it was more or less completed within five years of the disaster—a truly remarkable achievement.

There was, too, another consoling feature. By a fortunate accident there was living at the time Sir Chris- Wren topher Wren. Mathematician, astronomer and inventor, Wren had only just begun to interest himself in architecture; but, like several other eminent men, within two or three weeks of the fire he had prepared a general street plan for the entire rebuilding of London. Appointed one of the King's surveyors for the reconstruction—the City supplied others—he soon found that his ideas for remodelling the streets into fine thoroughfares forming a splendid series of patterns were quite impracticable: except in a few selected cases, reasons of speed and expense and ownership of the ground made it necessary to follow the outlines of the old main streets. In the reconstruction of the churches, however, Wren was able to give full play to his genius. In all, besides the Royal Exchange and other public buildings, he built fifty churches in the City, nearly all in a free treatment of the style of the classical Renaissance. Foremost, of course, is St. Paul's, with its wonderful dome that for two and a half centuries has dominated the capital's skyline and stood for Londoners as the very heart and soul of their great city.[1]

The plague, the fire and the Dutch raid on the Medway occurred in successive years. Coming so soon on top of the Civil War and all the commotion of the Commonwealth, they gave rise to a tense and nervous atmosphere which lasted for the rest of the reign. In the plague was seen the hand of God; but the fire, though an accident, was blamed on the Catholics—a belief unfortunately confirmed by an insane Frenchman, who confessed to being responsible and was executed. Someone, too, had to suffer for the Dutch raid and the many weaknesses in organization revealed by the war. In this case the victim was Charles's chief minister, Clarendon.

Fall of Clarendon, 1667 To the old statesman Charles owed much, but they had little in common, and to forestall the critics Charles cheerfully dismissed him. Then, when the Commons demanded impeachment, Charles advised him to flee

[1] Many of Wren's great churches were unfortunately destroyed in London's modern great fire—caused by German bombing in December 1940

abroad—where until his death he worked on his long, valuable and magnificently written *History of the Great Rebellion.*

But it was not only Clarendon who suffered for the disaster in the Medway. Charles found himself obliged to agree that the Commons should inspect the official accounts to see how the sums voted for the war had actually been spent. Yet one more link was being forged in the long chain of events by which parliament would eventually become the main, instead of a junior, partner in government.

The Commons inspect accounts

CHAPTER TWENTY-FIVE

CHARLES II, SHAFTESBURY, AND THE EXCLUSION STRUGGLE
(1667–1685)

1. *The Cabal, Danby, and the 'Popish Plot'*

A FTER the fall of Clarendon, there was for some years no similarly outstanding minister. During this period Charles relied for advice mainly upon five men whose initials happened to spell the word CABAL (secret council)—under which term they have gone down to history. In fact, however, they did not meet as a group; they were simply five ministers among a number of others. But as they were mostly without serious religious convictions, and as two had links with the Catholics and the other three with the Puritans, these five men could agree about one thing—the need for religious toleration. Charles's outlook being precisely similar, he made them his allies in the bold venture he was now to undertake.

The Cabal, 1667–1673

The policy of toleration

For reasons already mentioned Charles looked sympathetically on the Catholics. He also saw clearly that the interests of the nation demanded religious toleration. The Anglican (Church of England) majority in parliament, however, scorned the very idea, and was quite prepared to refuse Charles money unless he persecuted. To introduce toleration, Charles must therefore escape dependence on parliament. And this, he now decided, might be done by skilful use of his powers in foreign policy.

Charles at heart a Catholic

His weapon —foreign policy

With these intentions, Charles first made an alliance with Holland. This put difficulties in the way of further

Alliance with Holland—to put pressure on Louis

French conquests in the Spanish Netherlands. As Charles anticipated, the thwarted Louis XIV then tried to detach him from this alliance. And for deserting the Dutch, Charles could ask a stiff price.

The bargain was finally struck while Charles's beloved sister Minette (the wife of Louis XIV's brother) was visiting England. The terms were set out in a treaty signed at Dover and kept strictly secret. England would join France in war against Holland; and Charles, at a suitable time, would declare his conversion to Catholicism. This, Charles had previously given Louis to understand, would be only the prelude to the official restoration of the Catholic faith in England. For promising to act in this highly dangerous fashion, Charles would receive from Louis about £170,000 and, if necessary, the loan of 6,000 French troops. In fact, Charles can hardly have seriously intended to declare himself Catholic straight away. The French money, however, would help him while he was introducing toleration against the wishes of parliament. *Secret treaty of Dover, 1670: English alliance with France* *Charles gets money and promises to declare his Catholicism*

By 1672, Louis was ready for action against Holland and claimed Charles's help. Parliament was not in session, and the moment had come for Charles to carry out his plan. So he provoked incidents with the Dutch which in due course led to war. At the same time he issued a Declaration of Indulgence allowing the Nonconformists to worship in public and the Catholics to worship in their own homes. *Declaration of Indulgence, 1672*

Such a declaration on Charles's part, though not illegal, involved suspending some forty different laws. Much as toleration was needed, to introduce it in this way was highly unwise. Toleration for Nonconformists would seem bad enough to the Anglican squires in parliament, but toleration for Catholics would arouse their deepest distrust—especially as England had just allied with the strongest Catholic power. Charles's declaration, in fact, would be seen as merely the beginning of a scheme to turn England Catholic with French help.

Third Anglo-
Dutch War
1672–1674

Much now depended on the fortunes of war. A series of easy victories, and Charles's plan might have suc-

Charles II

This picture by Samuel Cooper shows Charles in 1665 at the age of 35.

ceeded. But de Ruyter held his own against the combined navies of England and France; and the progress of Louis XIV on land was halted when the stout Netherlanders, not for the first time, cut the dykes to create impenetrable barriers of water against the invader.

In their hour of need, too, the Dutch gave powers previously withheld to the young Prince William of Orange, great-grandson of William the Silent, and in so doing gained a leader of cool judgment and iron will. William of Orange

Charles's dream of quick success thus came to nothing, and the war began to drag. But he could not finance a long war on the fairly small sums that he could extract from Louis, and by 1673 he had to recall parliament. It offered money—but only on condition that Charles cancelled his Declaration of Indulgence. Deeply suspicious of Catholics in high places, it also passed a Test Act, making government office, civil and military, depend on willingness to take the Church of England communion. All this, to get money, Charles was forced to accept. The Test Act, 1673

Charles could now continue the war, but victory still eluded him. Unable to finance a long war, in 1674 he therefore deserted Louis and made peace. This was a popular move, for the French navy had not given proper support to the English squadrons, and France had become more detested than Holland. Apart from a small cash payment and the right to receive the naval salute in northern waters, the peace treaty brought England little advantage. The only results of Charles's ill-designed scheme were thus two years of vain warfare and (with the passing of the Test Act) toleration further off than ever. Peace with Holland

The Test Act marked the end, not only of Charles's attempt to introduce religious freedom, but also of the Cabal. The King's chief minister—the Lord Treasurer—revealed himself as a Catholic by giving up his post; and so too did Charles's brother James, the heir to the throne, who laid down the office of Lord High Admiral. Shortly afterwards James increased the public alarm still further by taking as his second wife the Catholic Break-up of Cabal and policy of toleration

Mary of Modena—a marriage which opened the prospect of a line of Catholic kings.[1]

The Protestant members of the Cabal of course were not affected by the Test Act. The most important, how-Shaftesbury ever—Lord Ashley, now the Earl of Shaftesbury—lost Charles's favour by supporting it, and was soon dismissed. By this time Shaftesbury had found out about the secret treaty of Dover, and was convinced that Charles planned to rid himself of parliament and turn England Catholic. From this time onwards his opposition to the monarch was completely open, bold and unscrupulous.

*   *   *   *   *

For the next four years Charles's Lord Treasurer and
Danby chief adviser was a Yorkshire squire whom he created Earl of Danby. Danby's policy was to preserve the privileges of the Crown by pleasing the strongly Cavalier
His policy: and Anglican majority in parliament. This meant re-
friendship
with Holland fusing toleration to both Catholics and Nonconformists,
and no
toleration and maintaining friendship with William of Orange rather than Louis XIV—whose frequent aggressions were now making Englishmen forget their old enmity to Holland. The result was the end of the Third Anglo-
Financial Dutch War, already recorded, followed by a few years
success of peace in which England enjoyed a trade boom and Charles nearly made both ends meet.

Danby's policy, however, did not secure wholehearted support from Charles, who continued to play a highly tricky game. To lull Protestant suspicions and get grants from parliament, he allowed Danby to ally England
Marriage of with Holland and marry James's daughter Mary to
Princess
Mary to William of Orange. But at the same time he made Danby
William of
Orange

---

[1] James probably became a Catholic in 1669. His first wife, Clarendon's daughter, became a Catholic soon afterwards. The children of this marriage, Mary and Anne, both remained Protestants.

Scenes from the 'Popish Plot'

Taken from an illustrated broadsheet published in 1678 and containing the story of the 'plot' in 29 pictures. This reproduces the first six, including the Pope and Cardinals hatching the plot at Rome, a recollection of the Fire of 1666, Oates telling his story before Sir Edmund Berry Godfrey, Oates informing the King and Council, and the murder of Sir E. B. Godfrey.

keep up secret negotiations with France, in the hope of obtaining money from Louis for breaking the alliance with the Dutch. Nor were Danby's ideas approved by all in parliament, for there was now a vigorous minority, led by Shaftesbury, which aimed at toleration for all Protestants and the supremacy of parliament over the king.

Shaftesbury's policy: parliamentary supremacy and toleration for all Protestants

To divide opinion still further and whip the two sides

into the wildest of passions, there occurred in 1678 the episode known as the 'Popish Plot'. Titus Oates, a hideous-looking young parson who had twice changed his religion—from Anglican to Catholic and back again —and Israel Tonge, a crack-brained cleric who was largely deceived and led on by Oates, claimed to have unearthed a Catholic plot to murder Charles, set James on the throne, and bring back Catholicism by force. According to the two informers, the Pope, the Jesuits, Louis XIV and the leading Catholic peers were all involved, and a gang of several thousand desperadoes was ready to fire London, massacre the chief citizens in their beds, and prepare the way for invasion.

These charges, which their authors and others later improved upon still further, were at once seen by Charles (whose shrewd questions trapped Oates into some obvious lies) to be a complete invention. But in general, even Oates's wildest accusations—which he put forward in the hope of reward—were readily believed. This was partly because of Oates's extreme boldness, and partly because the Catholics were thought capable of any crime for the sake of their religion. It was still more, however, because within Oates's haystack of fiction lay the grain of fact that James and others were indeed studying how to re-establish Catholicism. James's wife's secretary, for instance—by a fortunate chance for Oates—was found to have corresponded with Louis XIV's confessor on this point. Moreover, Charles II himself, as we have seen, had some years before secretly promised Louis XIV to declare his own Catholicism as a preliminary to restoring the old faith. This, of course, was not publicly known, but suspicions had been aroused, and there was fear for the safety of the Protestant religion. So the story of the 'Plot', though false in all its details, was readily believed; and soon innocent Catholics were being done to death with every cruelty demanded by the law, while Oates was enjoying handsome rewards and official quarters in Whitehall.

Belief in the Plot would never have become so widespread, however, but for the growing power of Shaftesbury. Shaftesbury was anxious to bring down Danby. So, too, after the English alliance with Holland, was Louis XIV. As soon as Danby brought this about, Louis made peace with the Dutch, stopped his grants of money to Charles, and paid Shaftesbury to whip up opposition to Danby. Soon there was produced in parliament a letter written by Danby (on Charles's orders) asking Louis for money so that Charles could avoid giving in to parliament. This at once caused a clamour for Danby's head. To save his minister from impeachment and stop further disclosures, Charles then dissolved parliament. The ultra-royalist 'Cavalier' Parliament, which had sat on and off since 1661, was at last at an end. *Louis withdraws subsidies from Charles and supports Shaftesbury against Danby*

The 'Cavalier' Parliament dissolved, 1678

This gave Shaftesbury his chance. Charles was bound to call another parliament soon in the hope of grants, for a decline in trade had reduced his revenue and Louis had withdrawn his subsidy. With feeling running strongly against the Catholics and the Catholic heir to the throne, Shaftesbury could now hope to capture the electors for his own policy of the supremacy of parliament and freedom of worship for all Protestants. For this purpose the gold of Louis XIV came in very useful. By skilful bribery Shaftesbury encouraged Oates and others to further 'revelations', built up a mob-following in London to frighten judges and juries who tried to withstand the anti-Catholic fury, and at the elections in early 1679 won a handsome majority. *Shaftesbury triumphs at elections, 1679*

Charles was now forced by popular feeling to include Shaftesbury in his Privy Council. He was not prepared, however, to accept Shaftesbury's views on the question that was now inflaming the whole nation—the question

Charles II, Louis XIV and Holland

From a Dutch print of 1677. Louis XIV, on right, offers Charles II (on horseback) gold to become his ally in the war against Dutch. The contrary policy, of alliance between Charles and Holland, would foster peace and prosperity (on left).

whether James, as a Catholic, should remain heir to the throne.

2. *The Exclusion Struggle and the Triumph of Charles*

The first 'Whig' parliament demands exclusion, 1679

The view of Shaftesbury and the majority in the new parliament was that England should not have a Catholic king. They therefore demanded that James should be excluded from the succession. Charles, on the other hand, believed that only strictly hereditary succession could preserve the monarchy and avoid disorder. Also, as a Catholic at heart, he must have hoped that an avowed Catholic would succeed him. So he announced that he would agree to limitation of James's power to appoint Catholics if he came to the throne, but could not accept

any measure to exclude him from the succession alto- Parliament dissolved: Shaftesbury dismissed
gether. And when the Commons persisted in demanding
exclusion, Charles soon brought the parliament to an
end and dismissed Shaftesbury.[1]

The King was now in very low water financially. Soon
he decided to try his luck again with a new parliament.
But the anti-Catholic panic was still at its height, and Second 'Whig' parliament, 1680–1681
the results of the voting were more than ever in favour
of Shaftesbury's candidates. Playing a waiting game,
Charles therefore refrained from calling the parliament
together and negotiated afresh with Louis.

By this time Shaftesbury had made a fatal mistake.
He had resolved, not merely to exclude James, but to
pass over James's Protestant daughters Mary and Anne
and fix the succession on the Duke of Monmouth—the Shaftesbury plumps for Monmouth
eldest of Charles's various illegitimate children. This
attractive but shallow young man was chosen because he
was a Protestant and likely to be an easy tool in Shaftesbury's hands. To make him acceptable, Shaftesbury
spread the story that Charles and Monmouth's mother
had really been married. A mysterious 'black box', it
was said, contained proof of the wedding.

Still feeling his way amid the anti-Catholic fury,
which he could not oppose openly for fear of losing his
throne, Charles kept his new parliament from meeting
for a full year. At last he allowed it to come together,
but almost at once the Commons hurried through an Exclusion Bill rejected by Lords
Exclusion Bill against James. The Lords, however, took
a different view—that the exclusion of James would lead
to civil war. After a long and heated debate, marked at
the end by several of the peers drawing swords, they rejected the measure. Soon afterwards Charles, judging

[1] The one real achievement of this parliament had been the Habeas
Corpus Act, by which a prisoner became in all circumstances entitled
to his writ of *habeas corpus*, i.e. a trial without undue delay. It passed the
Lords because one of the tellers in jest counted a fat peer as ten and
afterwards failed to correct the figures.

from this and the fairer behaviour of judges and juries
Parliament
dissolved in the trials of Catholics that the worst of the frenzy was
passing, once more dissolved parliament.

By now the followers of Shaftesbury and their opponents had earned the names by which the two main political parties were to be known for almost two centuries. Shaftesbury and the exclusionists dubbed 'Tories' and their opponents 'Tories'—an Irish term for bandits. 'Whigs' This implied that the anti-exclusionists were Catholics and cut-throats. In retaliation the anti-exclusionists began to call Shaftesbury and his followers 'Whigs'—a Scottish term for some peasants in the Western Lowlands who had recently rebelled (without success) against the suppression of conventicles. This implied that the exclusionists were Presbyterians and rebels. The two terms of abuse stuck. From then on, supporters of parliamentary supremacy and toleration for Protestant Nonconformists were 'Whigs'; supporters of the existing powers of king and Church were 'Tories'.

The Presbyterian revolt in Scotland and the violence of Shaftesbury had by now given rise to fear of another civil war. This fear worked in favour of Charles and James: better not to tamper with the succession, and leave even a Catholic monarch with his full powers, than risk the 1640s all over again. Hoping that this feeling was now stronger than the blind fury against Catholics, Charles (who needed money desperately) called yet another parliament in 1681. He summoned it to Oxford; for Shaftesbury's 'brick Protestant boys' in London were as ready to beat up members of parliament as judges and juries.

Third
'Whig'
(Oxford)
parliament,
1681 Once more, however, the elections went in favour of Shaftesbury's candidates. In a mixture of triumph (for they thought that this time Charles must surely accept exclusion) and fear (for they knew that their support of Monmouth bordered on treason), the Whigs rode into

Oxford. Many of them brought armed escorts and some uttered threats of violence which deeply alarmed peaceful countrymen. When parliament met, Charles offered a regency on his death, with James inheriting the throne but remaining abroad, and with the royal powers exercised by James's Protestant daughter Mary. Blinded by passion and sure that Charles was at the end of his tether, the Whigs refused anything less than total exclusion.

They then gathered again to hear, as they thought, the monarch's surrender. But unknown to them, Charles had just made another secret agreement with Louis— who had begun to fear that Charles might exclude James in favour of William of Orange. Promised money by Louis, Charles could snap his fingers at parliament. With dramatic suddenness—his robes of state were taken to the assembly secretly—Charles appeared before the Lords and Commons, not to accept exclusion, but to dissolve parliament. Suspecting that prosecution for treason would quickly follow, the Whig leaders then spurred out of Oxford, their plans shattered and their forces in hopeless confusion. *Charles's new agreement with Louis*

Parliament dissolved

* * * * *

Supported by French money and the loyal feelings called forth by the recklessness of the Whigs, for the remaining four years of his life Charles managed to avoid calling another parliament. The loyalty was redoubled after the discovery of a plot to murder Charles and James at Rye House, near Hoddesdon, as they returned to London from Newmarket. This plot was mainly the work of some ex-Cromwellian officers, but the investigations also revealed a plan for general rebellion involving Monmouth and some of the leading Whig peers. Among those executed as a result were two of Shaftesbury's chief supporters, Lords Russell and Sidney *Rye House plot*

Execution of Russell and Sidney

Sidney. Shaftesbury himself had died shortly beforehand in Holland, whither he had fled to escape prosecution.

Strong in the support of public opinion, Charles—and later James on his behalf—was able in these final years to pass from defence to attack. He cancelled many of the borough charters on the ground that the towns concerned had exceeded their privileges, and then usually gave a fresh charter under which no member of the corporation could be appointed without royal approval. This meant that the Crown could break the Whig hold over the boroughs and in due course produce a more favourable parliament—for the corporations elected many of the M.P.s. So Charles's last years were spent in growing personal power, much to the monarch's amusement and satisfaction. All this, however, Charles could do only by forgetting toleration and allowing the Church to persecute to its heart's content.

The end of Charles was typical of the man. Laid low by a stroke in his fifty-fifth year, he bore with the greatest patience all the remedies of the doctors, including purges, bleedings and blisterings, and through several days of intense pain retained his affability and wit. Almost at the last he apologized to his attendants, with characteristic humour, for being "an unconscionable time a-dying". Just before he died, his Catholic friends and brother smuggled in to him, in disguise, a Catholic priest who had saved him after Worcester, and had since been exempted from the penalties against Catholic clergy. Risking his life once again—for to convert to Catholicism was punishable by death—this priest received Charles into that Church to which for so long the King had at heart belonged. So it was only at death, when it was too late for his position as ruler to be affected, that Charles formally became a Catholic—a supreme example of that tact which had enabled him to retain almost every jot of his powers for a quarter of a century, in circumstances fully as difficult as those which overwhelmed his father.

The reign of Charles is difficult to judge fairly. It is very doubtful if he ever seriously planned, as 19th-century historians maintained, to set up a Catholic despotism. He was, however, determined to keep all the powers left him at the Restoration, and had no intention of allowing parliament to encroach on such matters as the choice of ministers or conduct of foreign policy. Disliking this and Charles's anxiety to tolerate Catholicism, parliament never really allowed him an adequate revenue, and this threw him, so to speak, into the arms of Louis XIV. The result was that Louis had some easier conquests than he might have done—which cost England (and Europe) dear later. In sum, much of the reign was a vicious circle, with parliament making Charles's task impossible, and Charles giving parliament good reason for doing so. By supreme skill in his closing years, and at the cost of submission to France and the Church of England, Charles came out the winner. But with the Commons' financial powers it was very doubtful if any later monarch—least of all James—would have equal success in resisting the advance of parliament. *Charles's intentions*

Charles successful in retaining royal powers

The reign of Charles is best remembered by the turmoil of plague, fire, Dutch wars and 'Popish Plot'. Fortunately there were other things less dramatic but no less important. There was constant commercial and colonial progress, including the formation of the Hudson's Bay Company, the conquest of the New Netherlands already mentioned, the settlement of the Bahamas, and the foundation of North and South Carolina, Delaware and Pennsylvania. There was great architecture by Wren, great poetry by Milton and John Dryden, brilliant and witty drama by Dryden and William Wycherley. There was a great popular religious work— *Other aspects of reign*

Commercial progress

Colonies

Title Page, Ogilvie's *Britannia*

Published in 1675, *Britannia* was the first English road-atlas. The title page depicts various forms of travel, aids to navigation, and scenes likely to be met with *en route*.

Pilgrim's Progress—written by John Bunyan, a wandering Baptist preacher who spent nearly half the reign in Bedford gaol. And above all, there was the new scientific movement represented by the foundation in 1660 of the body soon to be known as the Royal Society, with the King as patron.

Architecture and literature

Science: The Royal Society

Some of the early members of this society had already met together at Oxford during the Commonwealth. At Gresham College in London they now formed an organization under royal patronage with the prime object of investigating the forces of nature and gaining useful, accurate practical knowledge of their workings. In almost every sphere of science—chemistry, astronomy, medicine, botany and, above all, in mathematics and physics (where Isaac Newton soon was to reign supreme) —the members did work of the highest value. Witness, for example, an early experiment in blood transfusion, as recorded by that enthusiastic member Samuel Pepys:

> November 14, 1666. At the meeting at Gresham College to-night . . . there was a pretty experiment of the blood of one dogg let out, till he died, into the body of another on one side, while all his own ran out on the other side. The first died upon the place, and the other very well and likely to do well. This did give occasion to many pretty wishes, as of the blood of a Quaker to be let into an Archbishop and the like: but may if it takes, be of mighty use to men's health, for the mending of bad blood by borrowing from a better body.

Far more important than any particular discovery or invention, however, was the spirit in which the researches were undertaken. In this society—Fellowship of which is still one of the greatest honours open to a scientist—men met, not to wrangle on the matters that were inflaming the nation, but to increase the sum of human knowledge. In this spirit, they considered an immense range of topics, including agriculture, trade,

Title Page to *Pilgrim's Progress*

From the third edition, published in 1679. It shows Bunyan
dreaming his immortal story of Christian's journey. Guided
by the Bible, Christian leaves the City of Destruction, and
Hell yawning beneath, and toils his way up the hill to the
City of Light.

St. Stephen's, Walbrook

One of Wren's most beautiful churches, built just near the Mansion House in London in 1672–77. Note the classical Renaissance architecture and the dome (good practice for the later St. Paul's!). This church was bombed during the Second World War, but has now been repaired and re-opened.

THE KING —
EXECUTIVE
POWER

PARLIAMENT —
FINANCIAL
POWER

Restoration Settlement

NEW AMSTERDAM
NEW YORK

Wars with Dutch

LORD
HAVE
MERCY

Plague and Fire

TEST
ACT

DECLARATION
OR
INDULGENCE

Royal Efforts to bring in Toleration

THREE CHEERS
FOR MONMOUTH

OATES

'Popish Plot' and Exclusion Struggle

HUDSON
BAY

PENNSYLVANIA

NORTH CAROLINA
DELAWARE
SOUTH CAROLINA
BAHAMAS

Colonization

MILTON
BUNYAN
DRYDEN
PEPYS

Great Literature and Architecture

Growing Interest in Science

SOME FEATURES OF CHARLES II'S REIGN

architecture, history, geography and grammar. Only two subjects, in fact, were forbidden—religion and politics. The King himself, though only a dabbler in science, had something of this desire to rise above the prejudice of the age; and partly thanks to his sympathy the new movement of scientific inquiry and experiment was able to ignore and survive the furious controversies of the reign. From the advances made in the later Stuart period there was to be no turning back, and within two centuries the results of scientific inquiry, as applied in England and elsewhere, had changed the life of the greater part of mankind.

CHAPTER TWENTY-SIX

JAMES II AND THE
'GLORIOUS REVOLUTION'
(1685–1688)

1. *Monmouth's Rebellion and the King's First Efforts
for Catholicism*

James II

THE new king bore little resemblance to his brother. Where Charles had been affable and easy going, James was abrupt and severe. In his earlier years he had done well as a military commander and as Lord High Admiral; but by the time he became king at fifty-two his mental powers were already in decline. His main passions for many years had been the Catholic religion, the royal rights, the navy, and a series of lady-friends so plain as to make Charles remark that they must have been recommended by James's priests as a penance. As a further point of difference from Charles, James frequently repented his sins, and on occasion chastised himself with a whip.

James's advantages

Despite his Catholic faith, James began his reign with many advantages. The nation was still in a very loyal mood, and the citizen's duty not to resist the king was more widely preached from pulpits than ever before. James, it was thought, would keep his Catholicism to himself. In the absence of a son it would be only a few years before a Protestant—his daughter Mary—was safely on the throne.

The King's first actions were popular enough. He announced that he would preserve the Church and state as already established, and agreed to be crowned

according to the rites of the Church of England.[1]
Together with the strength of loyal feeling and the
'remodelling' of the corporations at the end of Charles's
reign, this helped to produce an overwhelming Tory
majority in his first parliament. As James admitted,
there were "not above forty members but such as he
himself wished for". *A Tory parliamen*

Even before parliament met, however, there came
signs of James's fierceness and folly. One was his
appointment of the able but brutal and subservient
Judge Jeffreys to the Privy Council. Another was the
punishment which he allowed to be inflicted on Titus
Oates for perjury—life imprisonment, regular exposure
in the pillory, and a whipping across the whole of London involving some three thousand lashes. This was
meant to kill Oates, but he survived—to be released and
given a pension by the Whigs in the next reign! Equally
vindictive, and far less excusable, was James's treatment of respectable Nonconformists for attending conventicles: in England many were again imprisoned and
in Scotland a new death penalty was strictly enforced,
even against women. This persecution James encouraged, not because he liked the established religion,
but because he regarded most Noncomformists as
rebels. *James's severity* *Persecution of Non-conformists*

James began on good terms with parliament, which
quickly voted him supplies. Its sitting was then interrupted by an event which rallied the nation still further
round the King—the Duke of Monmouth's rebellion. *James begins well with parliament*

In exile in Holland, Monmouth and other leading
exclusionists had resolved on a desperate venture. Together with Scottish exiles led by the Earl of Argyle
(son of the Marquis executed at the Restoration), Monmouth and his group planned a double invasion of *Monmouth's rebellion*

[1] The ceremony omitted, however, the communion service and the
presentation of the Bible.

The Flogging of Oates

A Dutch print published in 1685 and showing the villainous Oates undergoing
his punishment at the cart's tail.

Britain. Argyle, as the head of the great clan of Campbell, would land in the west of Scotland; Monmouth
would sail a week later for England. Argyle duly reached
Scotland, failed to raise the Highlands, and moved
desperately towards Glasgow. A week before his forces
finally dispersed and he himself fled in a vain attempt
to escape capture and execution, Monmouth and about
one hundred and fifty followers, delayed by contrary
winds, put into Lyme, in Dorset.

Such was Monmouth's popularity in the west (where
he had journeyed triumphantly at the time of the
Exclusion Bills) that large numbers of labourers in
Dorset and Somerset soon rallied to his banner. If they
had scythe or pitchfork they were accepted, but many
without weapon of any kind had to be turned away.
Unemployment and distress also helped to swell Monmouth's ranks with these poorer workers; the upper
classes, who had more to lose, took care not to join.

Having formally claimed the throne, Monmouth
moved west with some five thousand untrained men.
He failed to capture Bristol, in desperation turned for
London, then fell back on Bridgwater. Near by, on

Argyle

Monmouth
lands

Sedgemoor,
1685

Sedgemoor, he made a night assault in an attempt to surprise his pursuers, but his men were held up by an unreported water-course. Under heavy attack from the royal troops, they stood their ground until their ammunition gave out and the royal artillery came into play. The Mendip miners were still fighting when Monmouth, seeing that the battle could have only one end, put spurs to his horse and fled. Three days later he was taken near the New Forest, a trembling fugitive in a ditch.

James now enjoyed a terrible revenge. During the pursuit scores of captives were at once strung up and quartered as a warning to others. Then, by due process of law, a more systematic massacre began. One of the first to suffer was Monmouth himself. The dejected Duke tried to avoid his fate by a grovelling submission, even hinting that he would turn Catholic, but died Execution of bravely when he found that no entreaties could melt the Monmouth heart of James. He had need of all his courage. Jack Ketch the executioner lost his nerve, struck repeated blows with the axe, and finally used a knife to sever head from body.

If James was ice, his Lord Chief Justice, Jeffreys, was 'The Bloody fire. Jeffreys went on circuit of the counties affected by Assize' the rebellion. Everywhere he bullied juries, cursed the prisoners, made brutal jokes, and pronounced sentence with undisguised malice. In Winchester he condemned a much respected lady to be burned alive for sheltering a fugitive, and only the strongest pleas to the King secured a reduction of the sentence—to beheading. In Dorset he condemned a woman who had spoken treasonous words to be whipped through all the twenty-five or so market towns of the county, and a young man to be similarly punished every year for seven years. All told, he caused over three hundred of the rebels to be hanged—most also suffered the full penalty of quartering—and over eight hundred to be transported as slaves to the West Indies. Vengeance on this scale was something which had not been seen in England for a century, and was never to be seen again.

James's
revenge in
Scotland

In Scotland similar punishment was meted out to the supporters of Argyle. Hundreds were executed or transported, many of the women sent overseas were branded on the cheek, and in one day thirty-five prisoners at Edinburgh suffered the loss of their ears.

His revenge complete, James determined to build up such a military force as would make further revolts impossible. From some six thousand troops the royal army grew to nearly thirty thousand. About half of these were encamped during the summer on Hounslow Heath, only a few miles outside London—for the special purpose, it soon seemed to Londoners, of dominating

James builds
up the army

the capital. As if the general fear of a standing army were not enough, James also tried—unsuccessfully—to win converts to Catholicism within its ranks, and, in defiance of the Test Act, appointed Catholics as officers.

Catholic
officers and
Irish troops

In addition he enlisted Catholic troops in Ireland and brought them over to England—an action bound to cause the utmost alarm.

A warning
from France:
The Edict of
Nantes re-
voked, 1685

The danger to Protestantism of a Catholic king with a large army was all too plain, and was now made even more obvious by events in France. For many years the French Catholic clergy had petitioned Louis XIV against the freedom of worship allowed to the Huguenots by the Edict of Nantes issued in the reign of Henry IV. Desiring the honour (and convenience) of having no heresy in his kingdom, Louis had begun a campaign to make his whole people Catholic. It involved the use first of the royal lawyers, then of the royal money, then of the royal troops. Finally, to a chorus of praise from his bishops, Louis grandly announced that, as heresy had practically ceased to exist, the Edict of Nantes was no longer necessary, and would be revoked. Huguenot churches were to be demolished, Huguenot children to be brought up as Catholics. Huguenot ministers were to leave France within a fortnight; any other Huguenots who tried to emigrate would be sent to the galleys or (by a later decree) put to death.

The number of Huguenots was apparently larger than Louis imagined, for some three hundred thousand eventually escaped and carried their faith abroad. Among them were some of the most industrious and skilful sections of the French nation, so that France's loss proved a great gain to countries like England and Holland, which accepted the refugees. And these refugees bore living witness to the intolerance of a great Catholic king. Their arrival in England would not lessen suspicions of the intentions of James II.

Angered by the revocation and alarmed by the granting of commissions to Catholics, parliament now petitioned James to reduce his army and dismiss the Catholic officers. This was the death-blow to the hope he had so far entertained—that parliament would assist him in his plans by repealing the Test Act. He at once refused the petition, and never called parliament together again. He did not, however, change his aim. If he could not win a more favourable position for the Catholics with the help of parliament, he must do so by other means.

James falls out with parliament

2. *The Declaration of Indulgence, the Birth of James Edward, and the Revolution of 1688*

After his dismissal of parliament, James moved still faster along his chosen path. As his next step he set up a new court to control the Church, similar to the abolished Court of High Commission. Its chairman was Jeffreys, now promoted Lord Chancellor. This James followed by appointing Catholics to the Privy Council, to the magistracy, and to Oxford University, all in

A new Court of High Commission

James's Catholic appointments

defiance of the Test Act. He even chose Catholic sympathizers for important positions in the Church of England.

Opposition from Church All these actions aroused great opposition in the Church—among those very men who were normally the strongest supporters of the royal power. Feeling the need James turns to the Nonconformists for popular support, James therefore turned to a large section of the nation, who, like the Catholics, had no cause to love the Church—the Nonconformists. If the Anglicans would not co-operate with him to help the Catholics, perhaps the Nonconformists would. Advised Penn by William Penn, a Quaker who like the rest of his sect had suffered persecution, and who ardently believed in Declaration of Indulgence, 1687 freedom of religion for all, James in 1687 issued a Declaration of Indulgence. It gave freedom of worship to both Catholics and Nonconformists, and at the same time suspended the laws debarring them from civil and military office.

James's intentions This declaration raised very important questions. Thousands of unfortunate people were released from prison by what at first glance might seem a wise measure of toleration. Yet clearly James was no real believer in toleration—for until the very moment of the declaration he had persecuted the Nonconformists to the utmost. The declaration, in other words, resulted not from a change of heart but from a change of tactics. With the help of the Nonconformists James might break down the Anglican monopoly in Church and state; that done, the task of establishing a Catholic supremacy would be much easier. This is to judge James, not by his words, but by his character and his ideas of duty to his faith.

Doubtful legality of the declaration Moreover, though the declaration gave relief to many ill-used people, the King's right to issue it was by no means clear. There were good legal grounds for his power to dispense with the operation of a law in the case of any given individual—as when he appointed individual

PHILOSOPHIÆ

NATURALIS

PRINCIPIA

MATHEMATICA.

Autore *IS. NEWTON*, *Trin. Coll. Cantab. Soc.* Matheseos Professore *Lucasiano*, & Societatis Regalis Sodali.

IMPRIMATUR

S. PEPYS, *Reg. Soc.* PRÆSES.

Julii 5. 1686.

LONDINI,

Jussu *Societatis Regiæ* ac Typis *Josephi Streater*. Prostant Venales apud *Sam. Smith* ad insignia Principis *Walliæ* in Cœmiterio D. *Pauli*, aliosq; nonnullos Bibliopolas. *Anno* MDCLXXXVII.

Title Page, Newton's *Principia*

Newton's *Principia* (or the Mathematical Principles of Natural Philosophy) was published in 1687. In it he stated the laws of motion of earthly bodies and showed that the heavenly bodies obeyed the same laws. The title page shows that it was issued with the approval of the Royal Society, whose president at the time was Samuel Pepys.

Catholics to important positions despite the Test Act. But from this to suspending the law entirely (in this case the whole of the penal laws, the Clarendon Code and the Test Act) was a far step. Charles II had issued such a declaration and had been forced to withdraw it. If this decided the law, the declaration was illegal. In any case, there might clearly be grave dangers to liberty if the king could suspend laws previously approved by king and parliament.

So there were plenty even among the Nonconformists who doubted whether the declaration was the right way to introduce toleration. In these circumstances it was only a partial success. James therefore decided to issue a similar declaration including a promise to call parliament within six months. When this attracted little attention he ordered it to be read by the clergy in every church in the kingdom.

A second declaration —to be read in churches, 1688

This rash decision stung the clergy to revolt. They had preached up the duty of obedience to the King until it was almost an article of faith, but when they came to the point they were not prepared to help the King undermine the powers of their own Church. In large numbers the bishops disregarded the order to circulate the declaration, and when the fateful Sunday came for the first reading in London, in only seven of the capital's churches was the King's order obeyed. In Westminster Abbey most of the congregation rose and marched out as soon as the reading began. Meanwhile, two days earlier, the Archbishop of Canterbury (William Sancroft) and six other bishops had petitioned the King to withdraw the declaration, on the ground—infuriating to James—that it was illegal.

The clergy disobey

The bishops' petition

Going from folly to folly, James next decided to treat this statement as a seditious libel—a libel on the Crown which might weaken the subject's allegiance. The seven bishops were arrested, confined to the Tower, and then

Trial of the seven bishops

put on trial. This turned them into popular heroes; and when the jury returned a verdict of 'Not Guilty' there were rejoicings such as London had not seen since the Restoration. Even James's soldiers at Hounslow raised a great cheer—an ill omen for the King.

A little before the trial there occurred the event which *Birth of a* settled James's fate. His wife, Mary of Modena, gave *son to James, 1688* birth to a son. This meant that his Protestant elder daughter by his first marriage—Mary, wife of William of Orange—was no longer the heir. The new prince would certainly be brought up as a Catholic; and a largely Protestant nation would now have to look forward to a line of Catholic kings. A few days after the birth, and on the day when the rejoicings at the acquittal of the bishops left no doubt about the feelings of the English people, an invitation was therefore sent in secret to William of Orange.

This invitation asked William to come to England *Invitation to* with a force to protect the rights of the Protestant *William of Orange* Church and of his wife Mary—for it was everywhere put about and believed (quite unwarrantably) that James's son was someone else's child smuggled into the Queen's bedroom in a warming pan! The invitation was signed by seven prominent men including leaders of both parties, and was carried by an admiral disguised as a common sailor. It informed William—who had been sounded for several months—that an overwhelming majority of the people would welcome him. Even at this stage, however, James might have saved his throne if he had played his cards with any skill; for rebellion was greatly dreaded by the people and the invitation did not go so far as to ask William to take his father-in-law's place. But James continued to make mistake after mistake, while William made none at all.

William's readiness to intervene in England arose *William's* mainly from his hopes of bringing England into a firm *intentions* alliance with Holland against France. His life's work was to defy Louis XIV and prevent France from over-running Holland and the Spanish Netherlands. Seeing which way events were moving, Louis had warned the Dutch against any invasion of England and had offered to lend James a French naval force. But the French king's open support (which would be much resented in

Fireworks on the Birth of Prince James Edward

This shows a fine set-piece over the Thames during the official (and short-lived) celebrations at the birth of James II's son and heir. Firework displays, popular in England from Tudor times onwards, reached almost the status of a fine art in the late 17th century.

England) annoyed the normally subservient James, who replied that he had no need of Louis' help. Shortly afterwards Louis withdrew for other work the French army which had been stationed on the borders of the Netherlands.

James rejects help from Louis

William was now free to move. Borne by a 'Protestant wind'—it took him down the Channel past James's fleet and then backed conveniently just when he had overshot

William free to sail

his landing place—William set off for England. On November 5th, 1688—an encouraging anniversary—he and some fifteen thousand soldiers, including many English and Scots who had been serving in Dutch pay, arrived safely in Torbay.

Meanwhile James had at last seen the danger signals. In the month before William's landing he abolished his new Court of High Commission, dismissed many Catholics, restored to their fellowships at Magdalen College, Oxford, a group of dons whom he had earlier dismissed for refusing to elect a Catholic as master, and even gave back old privileges to the boroughs. All was in vain. James's concessions were seen for what they were—a sign of weakness. They merely encouraged leading men of both parties to join the invaders.

William's declaration made only one main demand— the calling of a freely elected parliament to discuss matters between James and his people. This James refused to do unless William departed. He then joined his forces at Salisbury and prepared to resist the invaders. Meanwhile the western gentry, after a little delay, were gathering around William, whose supporters were also gaining control of the key cities in the north and Midlands. It was now up to James to put everything to the test of battle; but disheartened and fearing to be trapped if he advanced west, he decided instead to retire on London. At this, some of his principal commanders went over to William. The deserters included one of the victors of Sedgemoor, Lord Churchill, whose wife had great influence over James's second daughter, Anne.

From then on, James's troops were in no position to resist William's advance on the capital. Soon even Anne had left to join William's supporters, and James was contemplating flight. Having smuggled his wife and infant son aboard a vessel bound for France, he tried to follow by another ship—after causing as much confusion

Monmouth's Rebellion

Standing Army Increased

Catholics appointed to State offices

Declarations of Indulgence

Trial of Seven Bishops

Birth of Prince James Edward

Landing of William of Orange

Flight of James II

THE REIGN OF JAMES II

as possible by throwing the Great Seal into the Thames and ordering his troops to disband. His plan, however, miscarried. He was brought back to London, and then wisely allowed by William to escape once more. Flight of James

James's final folly of taking flight solved most of his opponent's difficulties. William then called together a representative assembly of Peers and Commons, and at their request ordered elections for what in all but name was a new parliament.

On this Convention, as it was called, fell the duty of making some permanent arrangements for government. Many of the Tories in it wanted to save their faces by making Mary a regent, while James abroad kept the empty title of king. William, however, would have none of this. Nor, if Mary were made queen outright, would he consent to be only a Prince Consort or, as one peer put it, "Gentleman Usher" to his wife. Instead he gave it to be understood, with Mary's full approval, that if he were not made king he would return to Holland—a move which would have plunged the country into chaos. The threat was enough. Both parties joined in declaring that James had abdicated, and that William and Mary should be joint monarchs. They became so, however, only on certain conditions—conditions which, as we shall see, limited the royal power more strictly than ever before. The 'Convention' Parliament, 1689 William's attitude—king or nothing William and Mary joint monarchs—on conditions

Meanwhile, in France, James had regained his nerve and Louis' friendship, and was planning the recovery of his lost kingdom.

CHAPTER TWENTY-SEVEN

WILLIAM III,
THE REVOLUTION SETTLEMENT, AND
THE FIGHT AGAINST LOUIS XIV
(1689–1702)

1. *The Revolution Settlement and the War Against France*

WILLIAM and Mary became monarchs on three main conditions. The sovereign must never again keep a standing army in peace-time without parliament's consent. He must not 'dispense' with legal penalties in wholesale fashion, still less suspend laws altogether. He (or she) must neither be, nor marry, a Catholic. These conditions, later enacted in the Bill of Rights, were meant to stop future kings behaving like James II.

The Bill of Rights, however, was only part of the Revolution Settlement. Quite as important were the arrangements about money. Parliament took care to grant the Crown a fairly small sum for ordinary revenue, and to grant it for only one year at a time. The effect of this was that parliament had to meet every year, and long periods without parliament became impossible.[1] This financial stranglehold parliament tightened still further as the reign proceeded. It earmarked grants for definite purposes, and then insisted on auditing accounts to see that the money had been spent in the way intended.

An important decision, too, was taken about religion.

The Bill of Rights, 1689

Financial settlement

Annual grants— frequent meetings of parliament

Appropriation of supplies

Auditing of accounts

[1] In the same spirit parliament gave the king and his officers powers of discipline over the military forces for only one year at a time.

To stop the Nonconformists grasping at James's offer of religious freedom, some of the leaders of the Church had promised to support a properly legal scheme approved by parliament. The promise was now fulfilled in a measure usually known as the Toleration Act. The effect of this was to allow freedom of worship to all except Catholics and Unitarians.[1] Nothing was given beyond the bare right to hold services. Nonconformists and Catholics alike remained subject to the various laws, including the Test and Corporation Acts, intended to exclude them from public office. *Religious settlement* *Toleration Act, 1689: Catholics and Unitarians excluded*

Scotland had a Revolution Settlement of her own. The Scottish parliament offered the throne to William and Mary and accompanied the offer by a 'Claim of Right' which went further than the Bill of Rights. An important feature was that the Crown should give up controlling the Church of Scotland through bishops and should recognize it as fully Presbyterian. All this William accepted, and by mid-1689 his government was in full control of the Lowlands. *Scotland* *Claim of Right* *A Presbyterian Church*

The Highlands were another story. Here old loyalties —to the Catholic religion, among other things—were strong; and here there soon developed the movement known as Jacobitism, or support of James.[2] It was headed by Graham of Claverhouse, Viscount Dundee, a soldier who had earlier distinguished himself by his brutal zeal in hunting down Covenanters. The movement rapidly gained strength, and when government forces marched north, Claverhouse's Highlanders surprised and scattered them in the valley of Killiecrankie. But in the hour of victory Claverhouse was killed, and a few days later the government troops had their revenge. The clansmen *The Highlands: Jacobitism* *Jacobite victory at Killiecrankie, 1689*

[1] Unitarians believe in the unity of God as opposed to the normal Christian doctrine of the Trinity—i.e. the three-fold idea of God as Father, Son and Holy Spirit. They thus regard Christ as supreme prophet and perfect man rather than divine.

[2] James = Jacobus (Latin).

Defeat of
Jacobites

dispersed, and the danger to William's government was over. Jacobitism, however, remained as a dormant force to be readily awakened later.

By the end of 1689 William was generally acknowledged throughout Scotland, but parts of the Highlands were still not properly under control. Eventually the government ordered a number of chiefs to take an oath of allegiance by December 31st 1691. When that day dawned, only Macdonald of Glencoe, who had held back out of bravado, had not made his submission. During the day he appeared at the newly built Fort William to take the oath, only to find that there was no magistrate present before whom he could swear it. Alarmed, he set off for the nearest town where he could expect to find a sheriff. Snowstorms held him up and he did not arrive until January 6th. A sheriff then took Macdonald's oath, but warned him that the higher authorities might not accept it.

The Massacre of Glencoe

This indeed proved to be the case. William's chief Scottish adviser, the Master of Stair, saw in Macdonald's lateness a heaven-sent chance to teach a troublesome Highland clan a lesson. In this he was supported by the heads of the great clan of Campbell, who had suffered from Macdonald's raiding. So Stair informed William that Macdonald of Glencoe had failed to appear by the appointed time, and got permission to inflict a spectacular punishment—the extirpation of Macdonald's 'set of thieves'. Interpreting this as freedom to wipe out the entire clan, Stair then planned a most brutal and treacherous massacre. A troop of soldiers under Campbell leadership was billeted on the Macdonalds. When they had been there some days, and won their hosts' confidence, they arose one night and set about their task—to butcher every man, woman and child in the valley under the age of seventy. Fortunately they did their work clumsily, and many of the intended

victims escaped. Enough, however—thirty-seven in all
—were shot or hacked down to make the deed one of
the blackest in all the turbulent history of Scotland.

Even so, the struggle in Scotland was as nothing The struggle in Ireland
compared with that in Ireland. When James fled, his
Catholic Lord Deputy, the Earl of Tyrconnel, retained
control of Ireland on his behalf. The Protestants of
Ulster rose to support William, but were soon forced to
take refuge in Enniskillen and Londonderry. Such was
the position when, within three months of leaving Eng-
land, James landed in Ireland to reassert his title to the James lands 1689
throne.

Once in Ireland, James soon called an Irish parliament in which the overwhelming majority was Catholic.
It cheerfully passed an Act of Attainder (involving the
death penalty and confiscation of estates) against some
two thousand leading Protestants; but it was much less
interested in the all-important matter of military support for James. As a result troops from England were
able to break the boom on the River Foyle and relieve Relief of London-derry
Londonderry—which had endured one hundred and
five days of siege and bitter hardship—and shortly afterwards the garrison of Enniskillen also won a notable
victory. By mid-1690 English forces had regained the
whole of Ulster, but progress was slow and James's
army was still almost intact. William himself then came
on the scene. In one swift attack he shattered James's Battle of Boyne and flight of James, 1690
defensive line on the Boyne and captured Dublin—
after which James once more fled to France.

The last Irish forces were defeated at Limerick in Treaty of Limerick
1691. The terms of surrender included a rather ambigu-
ous clause which the Irish took to mean that any penal
laws against Catholics would not be strictly enforced.
However, William's parliaments in both England and
Ireland insisted on severity. By the end of his reign Irish Restrictions on Irish Catholics
Catholics could not vote at elections, sit in parliament

or town corporations, or serve as jurymen, soldiers, sailors or schoolmasters. They were debarred from certain trades, forbidden to buy land, and at death had their estates divided among all their sons. Catholic worship, however, was permitted, and not all the restrictions were enforced.

Control of
Irish trade

William's reign also saw measures intended to limit Irish trades or industries—notably those concerned with salt, beer and fine cloth—for the benefit of their English counterparts. This harmed the Protestant settlers quite as much as the native Irish. On the other hand, where Irish industries, such as coarse friezes and linen, did not compete with England's, they were sometimes positively encouraged. Nevertheless the effect on the Irish of these laws was very galling. Ireland was being treated as a colony. Her interests might be considered, but only if they did not conflict with those of England.

*   *   *   *   *

The Anglo-
Dutch alli-
ance against
Louis

William's life work was the defence of Holland against France. Already he had built up three coalitions to resist Louis. Now, with Louis supporting James II, William could link England with Holland in a great alliance which also included the Emperor, Spain, and states in Germany and Italy. Ringed with hostile powers, Louis would find his days of easy conquest over.

The fight at
sea

The ensuing war raged over many parts of Europe. At first William was on the defensive, concentrating against James II and the French in Ireland. Also, from 1690, when the French beat an Anglo-Dutch fleet off Beachy Head, he had to face a period of French superiority at sea. Two years later, however, in trying to clear

La Hogue,
1692

a way for invasion, the French encountered off La Hogue an Anglo-Dutch force under Admiral Russell nearly twice their own strength. The Allied victory was decisive: for the rest of the war no French battle fleet put to sea.

CANAÏLLÉ
T. CANAEL UYT

De Engelfche en Hollandfche

Rabble—Out of the Channel !

From a Dutch print and poem celebrating the naval victory of La Hogue in 1692. Dutch and English sailors together dispose of the enemy—the French and the Jacobites.

From then on, the French struck at sea mainly against Allied merchantmen. French 'privateers'—privately owned or leased ships sailing with a government commission to attack enemy vessels—inflicted grave losses on British commerce (like the German submarines of later wars), but could not make up for the lack of a strong French navy. From 1692 the Allies enjoyed all the advantages of naval superiority, such as ability to bombard or blockade enemy ports and maintain expeditions oversea. Thanks to this, William could make great use of English troops in Flanders, and even for some months support Spain and Savoy by keeping an English fleet in the Mediterranean.

French privateering

Allied naval superiority

English fleet in Mediterranean

The fighting on land marked a new stage in the development of the British army. As parliament was

The fight in Flanders

fully agreed on the need to resist James and Louis, William could keep larger numbers of British soldiers on the Continent, and for a longer period, than ever before. They fought for the most part in the Spanish Netherlands—the modern Belgium—where campaign after campaign was waged for the many fortified towns. In this slow and elaborate siege warfare William proved a brave leader of almost superhuman determination, William as a but not an inspired general. In sixteen campaigns he won only one clear-cut victory. All the same he kept the French from overrunning the Spanish Netherlands and stopped them reaching Holland. It was in these campaigns that British regiments won some of their earliest battle honours and began those great traditions which have done so much to foster the pride and strength of the British army.

William as a general

British regiments

For nearly nine years the great struggle continued. Then, in 1697, Louis agreed to make peace on terms fairly favourable to the Allies. He did so not merely because he was hard pressed financially, but also because there was looming up a question of supreme importance which Louis, the Emperor and William all wanted to settle without further years of conflict. That question was nothing less than the future of the whole Spanish empire. The Spanish king, the decrepit and half-witted Charles II, was dying childless; unless the great powers could agree about the succession, there was bound to be a fight for the spoils. With this in mind, they made peace at Ryswick, in Holland. The French agreed to restore all their conquests except Strasbourg, to recognize William as king of England, and to give no help to his enemies—including James II. The Dutch were to be allowed to garrison a number of towns in the Spanish Netherlands to form a 'barrier' against any further French aggression. For eight years' fighting these gains may seem meagre. In fact, however, they

A new question— The Spanish succession

Peace of Ryswick, 1697

French recognize William III

The Dutch 'barrier'

meant that William had successfully defended his two countries and the revolution of 1688 against the strongest power in Europe.

2. *Finance, Political Parties, and the Question of the Spanish Succession*

The long years of fighting cost William's government some £40,000,000. Such a sum could never have been spent on a war by Charles I or Charles II, because parliament would never have voted it to monarchs whose policy they distrusted. But as the great dispute about the right to impose taxation had been settled in favour of parliament, and as parliament and William were agreed about the need to resist Louis, parliament was now prepared to vote much bigger grants than ever before. Such grants were earmarked ('appropriated') specially for the war, and parliament was careful to see that the money was spent in the way intended.

Finance

Large grants from parliament

Even so, it would have been impossible, without a tremendous outcry and struggle, to raise these sums by ordinary taxation. New customs duties and a new land tax helped to increase revenue, but the government also had to borrow on a much larger scale than ever before. No longer was it a question of seeking loans from a few companies or individuals, as monarchs had done in the past. The government now set out to tap the whole lending power of the general public.

Land tax

Loans

Of the various schemes that were tried, one—the most successful—had a long-enduring result. It gave birth to the Bank of England. In 1694 a group of Whigs offered to raise over a million pounds and lend it at eight per cent interest to the government; subscribers to the loan were given the privilege of forming the first English bank on joint-stock lines, with the right of issuing notes and dealing in bills of exchange. This government-favoured bank soon proved to have advantages over the

Bank of England

various private banks which had sprung up since the Restoration. It gave many services in the war, and Recoinage helped in the recoinage of 1696 (when the old coins, often 'clipped' and so short of their proper value, were called in, and a new coinage was issued with milled edges to prevent clipping). When peace came it was rewarded by increased privileges. From then on the Bank of England became the 'bankers' bank', and the one responsible for handling the financial transactions of the government—including, of course, further loans

The foundation of the Bank of England and of regular public borrowing had extremely important results. It made government borrowing much easier, because so long as the government paid the interest the subscriber was content—he had invested his money, and was getting a guaranteed return. If he wanted his money back, he could always sell his share in the loan to someone else; and if a time came when the whole of the loan had to be repaid, the government could always do so by arranging a fresh loan. So, by this system of National Debt, as it was called, governments could borrow almost indefinitely, as long as they could find enough money from taxes to pay the annual interest. That is why the National Debt has increased from £14,000,000 at the end of William III's reign to over £27,000,000,000 in 1955. In other words the National Debt has enabled governments to do expensive things (such as fight wars) by putting much of the financial burden on future generations—who are highly taxed to meet the interest charges and pay off the loans.

Advantages of National Debt The National Debt, with the Bank of England to handle it, was a powerful weapon from the time of William III onwards. Without it, Britain could never have won nearly all her wars and built up a great empire. But it also greatly helped the growth of English trade and industry. With properly organized government borrowing, interest rates fell, banking began to be a special occupation, and the ordinary individual or company could borrow much more easily to start, or support, a business. In the same way, Scottish trade benefited from the foundation of the Bank of Scotland in 1695. _{Bank of Scotland}

The National Debt had another and more immediate result. People of all views took advantage of the good investment offered. And once they had lent their money, it was very important to them that James II should not recover the throne, in case he repudiated these debts incurred by William. So the National Debt not only helped to defeat James and Louis in the field, but also fostered loyalty to the new government. It was a bulwark which protected the revolution of 1688 against enemies both abroad and at home. _{Another result— support for William}

*   *   *   *   *

The Whig and Tory parties, it will be remembered, had come into being over the question of excluding James from the throne. Both parties were now agreed in accepting William—and on both sides some of the leaders remained secretly in touch with James. In both parties, too, the leaders were noblemen or gentry with large estates, and members of the Church. _{Whigs and Tories: (a) Resemblances}

Beyond this, the two parties differed. The Tories were content to leave the king as the mainspring of government; the Whigs wanted parliament to become this. The Tories wished to keep the Church strong and privileged, and some even wanted to repeal the Toleration Act; but the Whigs looked with a fairly friendly eye on the Nonconformists (who supported Whig views about Crown and parliament). The Tories were strongest in the countryside, where there were few Nonconformists; the Whigs in the towns, where there were many. The _{(b) Differences}

Tories tended to think of what was good for the land-owners; the Whigs paid more heed to the interests of the merchants.

The King's power still great

The parties, however, were by no means highly organized bodies of the sort we know today. The executive power—the power of enforcing the laws and the decisions of the government—was still the king's. And it was still up to him to choose what ministers he liked. Because the Tories took the more generous view of the king's rights, William at first tended to draw most of his ministers from them; but later, as the war with France dragged on, William turned to the Whigs, who were more enthusiastic for it than the Tories.[1] His ministries, however, were never completely made up of members of one party, nor was the majority in the ministry automatically chosen from the majority in the

A movement towards party government

Commons. But towards the end of the reign the monarch found that things went much more smoothly if his ministers were chosen mainly, if not entirely, from the majority party in the Commons.

The reign of William thus marked some big steps towards party government. Party government in its fullest sense, however, could only come when the king had lost nearly all his power, and this was by no means yet the case. Indeed, William was very far from being a figurehead. Apart from choosing his own ministers, he kept foreign policy so much in his own hands that he made treaties without telling his ministers all the details in advance. In addition, he five times refused to consent to bills which had been passed by both Houses—an action which Charles II had dared to take only once.[2] On the other hand many measures, such as a Triennial

[1] The Whigs were keener on the war because of their trading connections—there were valuable colonies and trading rights at stake. The Tories also objected more strongly to the increased taxation caused by the war—for the main direct tax fell on land.

[2] The last exercise of the royal veto was by Queen Anne, in 1708.

Act to ensure a new parliament every three years, were eventually forced on him against his wishes.

In the three or four years following the Treaty of Ryswick, William found his conduct very much under fire. With a Tory majority in the Commons, parliament

Greenwich—The Painted Hall

This fine hall, completed in 1703, was part of the naval hospital which William and Mary commissioned Wren to build. The wall panels and ceiling were painted later in the 18th century by Sir James Thornhill. The building is now part of the Royal Naval College.

insisted that William's army should be cut down, his Dutch guard dissmissed, and his grants of land to Dutch friends cancelled. In addition a measure known as the Act of Settlement, by limiting the future rights of foreigners and foreign-born monarchs in England, aimed a great deal of indirect criticism at his work as king.

The Act of Settlement: a Hanoverian succession for England

The main purpose of the Act of Settlement was to provide for the succession. Mary had died childless in 1694, and though her sister Anne was the recognized heir, she was well into middle age, and her last surviving child had just died. The act laid down that after the death of Anne the Crown should pass to the Electress Sophia of Hanover (the daughter of James I's daughter Elizabeth and the Elector Palatine) and her heirs. James II's descendants were thus barred from the throne. To make doubly sure, the act also provided that every future sovereign should join in the communion of the Church of England.

The succession to the Spanish empire

The peace which so sharply revealed the country's feelings about William did not last long. As Charles II of Spain neared death, the question of his successor reached the point of crisis. By 1700 the claimants had

Charles of Austria and the Dauphin

been reduced to two. One was the Archduke Charles of Austria, second son of the Emperor, the other the Dauphin, son of Louis XIV To avoid war, William III and Louis then agreed that the territory at stake should be divided between these two candidates, but this overlooked Spain's pride in preserving her empire. Just

The will of Charles II of Spain: all to Philip of Anjou

before he died, the Spanish king signed a will which left the whole inheritance to the Dauphin's younger son, Philip of Anjou, on condition it was not united to France. If Philip refused it, the whole was to go to the Archduke Charles.

Louis accepts the will

Louis XIV could not allow all these lands to pass into the hands of a rival power. He accepted the will on behalf of his grandson. This made war between France and the Emperor inevitable. England and Holland, however, might perhaps have remained neutral had not Louis moved French troops into some of his grandson's

Louis occupies Dutch 'barrier'

new territory and so made it clear that he intended to treat the Spanish dominions as his own. Among other places he occupied the 'barrier' towns held by Dutch garrisons in the Spanish Netherlands. As a result William was able to form a new league against France, usually known as the Grand Alliance of the Hague. By this England and Holland promised the Emperor to join him in war against France unless Louis gave the Archduke Charles some agreed share of the Spanish possessions. For themselves, England and Holland were to have commercial privileges in Spain and whatever they could get of the Spanish New World. Grand Alliance of Hague: the Spanish empire to be divided

England was now once more practically committed to fighting against Louis. Opinion in England, however, was still divided about the need for war. At this stage further actions by Louis closed the English ranks. He banned the entry of British goods into France and asked his grandson to enforce a similar ban in Spain and Spanish America. Almost as bad, when James II died in France, Louis at once proclaimed the dethroned monarch's son King James III of England. This quickly brought the peace party round to William's policy, with the result that England could throw her full weight into the forthcoming struggle. Louis excludes British goods
Louis proclaims James III
England united for war

Preparations for the fighting were proceeding fast when early in 1702 William's horse stumbled over a molehill in the park at Hampton Court. From this accident William's worn and wasted body never recovered. He died as the armies of his Grand Alliance were about to enter upon one more stage of his life's work of resisting French aggression.[1] Death of William 1702

*　　*　　*　　*　　*

William was far from being a well-loved ruler. He was reserved and somewhat haughty, and the early William's achievement

---

[1] One of the Jacobite toasts was to the mole which brought about William's death—"the little gentleman in black velvet". Anne's opinion of William appears in confidential letters, in which she refers to him as 'Mr. Caliban'.

Henry Purcell
by John Closterman

Robert Boyle
by Friedrich Kerseboom

William Congreve
by Sir Godfrey Kneller

Sir Isaac Newton
by Sir Godfrey Kneller

These are four of the many great men of the later Stuart period—a musician, two
scientists and a dramatist. Note the long curled wigs fashionable at the time.
Kneller, a German, settled in England and succeeded Sir Peter Lely, a Dutchman,
as the favourite Court and society portrait painter.

death of Mary—a brave, good and charming woman—robbed him of one who could have done much to soften feeling against him. He gave his confidence to very few friends, and those mostly Dutchmen—for many of his English ministers were still intriguing with James II. Yet this repeated faithlessness in his ministers he consistently ignored—he reckoned that in the end they would see that the interests of England lay, like those of Holland, in resisting the aggression of France. Despite his constant suffering from asthma and a tubercular lung, his patience and courage never faltered. With as little fondness for England as England had for him, he still served her well, ruling with mercy and justice, accepting with good grace whatever restrictions on the royal power he could not prevent, and saving not only England, but also Holland and most of Europe, from succumbing to France. And in saving England, he saved, too, something for which he had no great liking or admiration—that parliamentary supremacy over the king which was the final outcome of the revolution of 1688.

Looking back over the reign, we can see more clearly what were the main results of that revolution. One stands first and foremost. The king still remained the mainspring of government, but parliament, by its power of the purse and its frequent meeting, was now in a position to win control of policy and become the dominant partner. In any case, the old ideas of Divine Right were now dead—a monarch had been set aside, and a new one appointed on the terms set down in the Bill of Rights. If he broke those terms it was obvious that he, too, might be set aside. *Results of 1688 Revolution:*

(a) Increased power of parliament

(b) End of Divine Right

There were other results only a little less important. An advance was made towards party government. The great principle of toleration in religious affairs was established, even if Catholics and Unitarians were denied its benefit. Closer union between England and *(c) Advance towards party government*

(d) Religious toleration

Increased Power of Parliament

TORY
FOR
KING AND PARLIAMENT
CHURCH
AND
COUNTRY

WHIG
FOR
PARLIAMENT AND KING
TRADE
AND
TOLERATION

Increased Importance of Political Parties

PRESBYTERIAN

BAPTIST

INDEPENDENT

Beginning of Religious Toleration

Long Struggle against France

SOME RESULTS OF THE REVOLUTION OF 1688

Scotland was made easier, between England and Ireland more difficult. And finally, the revolution ushered in a long period of war with France, in which Britain reached forward towards her full destiny in commerce and empire.

CHAPTER TWENTY-EIGHT

ANNE: THE OPENING YEARS OF THE WAR OF THE SPANISH SUCCESSION AND THE UNION WITH SCOTLAND

(1702–1707)

1. *The Opening Years of the War*

Anne

THOUGH happily married to the kindly but somewhat sottish Prince George of Denmark, Queen Anne was already a pathetic figure when she came to the throne. Her body was swollen with gout and dropsy, and often swathed in bandages; she had suffered greatly from the loss of her dozen or more children; and her conversation was so limited that interviews at Court were an ordeal for all concerned. Her main comforts she found in religion, one or two private friendships (notably with the wife of Churchill, now Earl of Marlborough), and the pleasures of the table. But though slow and dull, Anne did not lack good sense. Devoted to the Church and so inclined to favour the Tories, she nevertheless tried to prevent both parties going to extremes, and nearly always took a broad and wise view of the nation's interests.

The Spanish Succession

For almost the entire length of Anne's reign England was engaged in the War of the Spanish Succession. William III had already arranged for England and Holland to join Austria against Louis, and Anne completely accepted his policy. And she was, of course, delighted with his choice for commander-in-chief—

England declares war, 1702

Marlborough. Within two months of her accession, England and Holland on the same day formally declared war against France. Scotland, too, was committed by the Queen to the struggle.

In England the Whigs were the party keener on the war, but the moderate Tories—with whom Marlborough was most in sympathy—also gave it full support. The extreme or high Tories—some of whom were Jacobites—were less enthusiastic, and were against sending a large army to the Continent. Because the high Tories put less energy into the fight against France than into their efforts to keep down Nonconformists, Anne had to shed them from her Council as the war proceeded.[1] Parties and the war

The leading minister in this Council—or Cabinet as it was now coming to be called—was the Lord Treasurer, the moderate Tory Lord Godolphin. His partnership with Marlborough and his management of the Queen, the Cabinet and finance proved so successful that he held office from the start of the reign until 1710. He began, as was natural in view of Anne's sympathies, with a Cabinet almost entirely Tory, and ended—the result of his and Marlborough's determination to carry on the war vigorously—with a Cabinet almost entirely Whig. Sometimes the unofficial term 'Prime Minister' was applied to him; but the Queen still presided at the formal weekly meeting of the Cabinet and the leading minister still depended on the favour of the Crown rather than on control of a party.[2] Godolphin

Secure in the support of the Queen and Godolphin, Marlborough set about his task. In addition to Holland and Austria, his allies included Hanover and some The alliances

[1] The high Tories were particularly anxious to stop the practice known as 'occasional conformity' (by which many Nonconformists took the Church of England communion once or twice a year in order to qualify for office under the Test and Corporation Acts).

[2] Party groupings were still very fluid and the House of Commons contained many members who did not yet think of themselves in terms of Whig or Tory. One observer, listing the M.P.s, divided them into "Churchmen, High Churchmen, Low Church, Nonconformists, Courtiers and Sneakers".

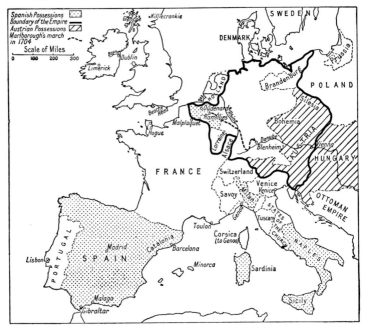

Europe at the outbreak of the War of Spanish Succession, 1702

other German states. In the opposite camp were France, Spain (where Louis' grandson was now ruling as Philip V) and Bavaria.

Task of the British army The task of the British army was to help defend Holland, and, if things went well, drive the French from the Spanish Netherlands. The officers were mostly experienced, but many of the troops had been 'pressed' into service because they were criminals or without means of support. Their general, Marlborough, combined a keen brain with a handsome appearance and exceptional charm and tact. His command extended to the Dutch forces, but his power to use these was subject to many restrictions.

During 1702 Marlborough successfully defended Holland although the Dutch four times spoiled his plans by refusing to risk their army in attacks. Meanwhile an Anglo-Dutch fleet under Sir George Rooke had a great success at Vigo, where it destroyed or captured an entire Spanish treasure fleet with its escort of French warships. From then on the main efforts of the French at sea were confined once again to privateering—which they did to such effect that they seriously interrupted English east-coast trade, at one time making the price of Newcastle coal almost prohibitive in London. *The war in 1702: Marlborough repels French Vigo*

French privateering

Encouraged by Vigo, Portugal now joined the Allies. She entered the war, however, only on condition that England and Holland should recognize the Austrian Archduke Charles as king of Spain and should send troops to the Peninsula to drive out Philip V. So England and Holland were now committed to win for the Austrian Archduke not merely the outlying parts of the Spanish empire, but Spain itself—an even harder task.[1] *Portugal joins Allies: Charles to have Spain*

Again repeatedly baulked by the Dutch, Marlborough vainly strove during 1703 to make headway against the French armies in the Spanish Netherlands. Meanwhile mortal danger began to threaten Austria from the linking up of a French army with that of the Bavarians. In the spring of 1704 Marlborough therefore decided to march his Anglo-Dutch army from Holland to the rescue of Vienna. He well knew that the high Tories at home and the Dutch would never agree to such a move, so he kept his intentions a close secret. Only Anne, Godolphin and a few of the leading Austrians—includ- *1703*

1704: the threat to Austria

Marlborough's scheme

[1] The British friendship with Portugal has remained unbroken ever since this alliance. Among the terms of the treaty, English cloth was admitted at low duty into Portugal in return for the admission of Portuguese wine at low duty into England. This clause operated throughout the eighteenth century, and explains why our ancestors of that time drank so much port—and suffered so much gout.

ing their famous general and professional soldier, Prince Eugene of Savoy—were fully acquainted with the plan The Dutch—and most of the English ministers—he deceived by seeking permission to move up the Rhine and invade France.

The march to the Danube

The decisive moment came soon after Marlborough had passed Heidelberg. Instead of striking across the Rhine into Alsace, he wheeled his Allied army southeast, and Europe saw with astonishment that he was heading, not for south-eastern France, but for Bavaria and Austria. During the last week in June, while high Tories in England vowed to have his head, he reached the Danube. Quickly he relieved Vienna, but he had still to meet the main French and Bavarian armies.

Vienna relieved

Blenheim, 1704

The great clash took place, between roughly equal forces, in and around Blenheim on the Danube.[1] While Eugene fought a holding action to the north, Marlborough directed the main struggle round Blenheim village. The result was clear-cut. When sunset came, the Franco-Bavarian armies were in flight, leaving nearly ten thousand French infantry trapped in the village. All told, the enemy probably lost four-fifths of their troops, and within a month the rest had been chased across the Rhine. At one stroke Marlborough had saved Austria, knocked out Bavaria, and ended the war in Germany. It was indeed "a famous victory".

End of war in Germany

The war in Spain

Meanwhile fighting had begun in the Spanish Peninsula. As one of the very first episodes, Sir George Rooke, commander of the Anglo-Dutch naval force, sent a squadron under Admiral Byng to storm Gibraltar. Heavy bombardment and a landing on the isthmus by the newly formed Royal Marines enabled the sailors to get ashore almost without opposition, and soon the

Capture of Gibraltar. 1704

---

[1] The Allied forces present numbered some 52,000, of which about 9,000 were British. Nearly all the other regiments, including those in Eugene's army, were paid for either by England or Holland.

town and harbour were safely in their hands. At the cost of little more than sixty dead Britain had seized one of the keys to the Mediterranean.

During 1705 and 1706 Allied forces made some progress in Spain and once got as far as Madrid; but by 1707 Philip has recovered his ground, and the conquest of Spain was little nearer. Elsewhere in Europe, however, the events of 1706 practically decided the struggle. Alarmed by the mounting cost of the war, Louis XIV ordered his commander in the Spanish Netherlands to bring everything to the test of a great battle. Nothing could have pleased Marlborough more. At Ramillies he Ramillies, routed his Franco-Bavarian opponents so completely 1706 that they lost over half their men. Soon the French were driven from almost the entire Spanish Netherlands, and The Spanish the first great purpose of the war was achieved. Netherlands conquered

Hard on top of this came equal success by Eugene at Turin, in Italy. The dispirited French army fled across Turin, 1706: the Alps, and without its support the French garrisons the French driven from in the Spanish possessions of Milan, Naples and Sicily Italy could be rounded up at leisure. The second war objective—the expulsion of Louis' troops from Italy—had also been accomplished.

Unfortunately these triumphs only encouraged the Allies to persist in trying to win Spain as well for the Austrian Archduke. As Marlborough and Godolphin Marlborough were both set on this, they came to rely at home much and Godol- phin more more on the Whigs, whose trading interests made them dependent on Whigs anxious to see Spain and Spanish America under weak Austrian rather than strong French control. So the two friends were soon forcing Anne to appoint Whigs to positions in the Cabinet. In fact they needed Whig support against the high Tories not only over the struggle abroad but also over the proposed union of the English and Scottish parliaments—a matter which now seemed almost about to cause a war nearer home.

2. *The Union with Scotland*

The history of Scotland under William III had been one of growing irritation with England. With the Claim of Right recognized and the Presbyterian system fully guaranteed, the Scottish parliament had developed a new spirit of independence. With great freedom it Scottish criticism of William III appointed largely on the advice of English ministers) and expressed the general Scottish opinion that William was neglecting his northern realm. Behind this was not only national pride but also resentment at the comparative poverty of Scotland, and the fact that William seemed powerless to secure what she most wanted—the right to enjoy free trade with England and the English colonies.

In the closing years of William's reign there had occurred what the Scots regarded as a specially striking example of England's commercial enmity. A 'Company of Scotland Trading to Africa and the Indies' had been formed, with the intention that half its capital should be subscribed in England. But the English East India Company opposed the scheme strenuously, and English participation in it was stopped. The Scots then went The Darien scheme company tried to found a colony on the Isthmus of Darien, about one hundred and fifty miles south of the present Panama. Ignoring the fact that the spot chosen was ridden with malaria and in Spanish territory, the company sent out three expeditions, all of which came to grief through fever and the Spaniards. The fault was the company's own; but when the shareholders' money was lost, Scottish popular opinion laid the blame on the English government, which besides stopping English participation had also (since England was then at peace with Spain) forbidden the governors of all the English colonies to help the Scottish settlers.

The Darien affair, coming on top of other reasons for discontent, caused so much criticism in the Scottish parliament that William began to regard as unworkable the whole system of two separate parliaments under a single king. At the same time many Scots began to demand either a complete union between the two countries, with a single monarch, parliament and trading system, or else total separation. Naturally William did not favour the latter. In his final message to parliament at Westminster he recommended union. Anne agreed, and in 1702 commissioners from both countries were appointed to discuss terms. *Complete union—or separation?*

Though many on both sides of the border could see the advantages of union, there were also plenty who opposed it. Scottish Jacobites would not willingly accept a Hanoverian successor to Anne; English high Tories greatly disliked the thought of recognizing Scottish Presbyterianism. Many Scots, too, bitterly resented the fact that their representatives had not been consulted over the decision to commit Scotland to war against France. In sum, national feeling was still unprepared for union, and in 1703 the commission's meetings were adjourned. *Opposition to union* *Union commission adjourns, 1703*

There followed three years of pressure and counter-pressure by the two countries. The Scots gave warning that on Anne's death they would choose a different monarch from the new English ruler unless England had meanwhile satisfied them about future government and trade. They also raised a militia to resist any English attempt at imposing Anne's successor by force. Anne had at first to accept this in order to get money from the Scots for the war, but after Blenheim the English government took a stronger line. By the Aliens Act of 1705 England stated that if the Scottish parliament did not agree to settle the crown of Scotland on the recognized English ruler when Anne died, every Scot would *Scottish pressure* *A Scottish militia* *England's retaliation— the Aliens Act* be treated as an alien as far as England was concerned, and all the main Scottish exports would be banned from England and Ireland.

Against the Aliens Act the Scots at first reacted strongly. More and more Scotsmen began to drill under arms, and the two countries seemed to be drifting towards war. Feeling ran at its highest when the Darien Company, annoyed by the East India Company's hostility, brought a charge of piracy against an English captain and crew who had put in to Leith, and against all justice secured convictions. The unfortunate Captain Green and two of his crew were duly executed on Leith sands before a fiercely exulting crowd; but fortunately this blood-letting satisfied the desire for revenge, and before long the Scottish parliament agreed to negotiate once more. It also allowed Anne to appoint the commissioners—an important step, since this meant that men favourable to union would be chosen.

Captain Green

A fresh commission, 1706

Within nine weeks the negotiations resulted in a complete scheme of union. The main terms were that Scotland and England should be united under one monarch, one parliament and one flag, that there should be no trade barriers between the two countries, and that the Presbyterian Church should alone be recognized in Scotland. In addition, Scotland was to keep her own laws and legal system, except where these conflicted with later laws made by the united parliament. Scotland was to have forty-five members in the Commons, and sixteen peers in the Lords; as a poor country she was to pay only one-fortieth of the land tax though she had one-eighth of the population. To smooth the path of these proposals through the Scottish parliament, England also gave the Scots some £400,000 towards reduction of national debt and compensation of Darien shareholders.

Proposed terms of union

The reception of these proposals in Scotland was

mixed. In general, they were regarded as fair; and in any case Scotland could defy England only at the price of subservience to France. All the same, there were still plenty ready to fight rather than suffer the least loss of Scottish independence. While the Scottish parliament was debating the proposals, extreme Presbyterians from the west were marching on Edinburgh to protest against union with a non-Presbyterian country, Jacobites in the north-east were preparing for action, and the anti-English mob in Glasgow rose and held the town until suppressed by Scottish dragoons. The Edinburgh mob, too, threatened trouble, and soon English troops were marching north, ready to cross the border if hostile forces captured the capital. It was in this atmosphere that Scotland's representatives, by a clear majority but against bitter opposition, finally decided to accept the scheme of union.

Opposition to proposals

The terms accepted

A little later those same proposals were put through the English parliament. Despite many laments from opponents in Scotland—who discovered a specially evil omen in the stranding of 'thirty-one whales' on the sands of Kirkcaldy—on May 1st, 1707, there came into being the new United Kingdom of Great Britain. That day Queen Anne, accompanied by four hundred coaches, drove in state to Wren's mighty church of St. Paul's, then nearing completion, "to give thanks for the greatest of all the victories with which God had blessed her reign".[1]

The United Kingdom, May 1st, 1707

[1] G. M. Trevelyan: *England under Queen Anne.*

CHAPTER TWENTY-NINE

ANNE: THE LATER YEARS OF THE WAR, AND THE HANOVERIAN SUCCESSION
(1707–1714)

1. *The Whigs and the War*

THE year 1708 brought the Allies a further run of successes. These included the capture of Minorca by British forces, the interception of a French expedition under James Edward Stuart destined for Scotland, and a great victory by Marlborough at Oudenarde, in the Spanish Netherlands—a victory which opened the way to the invasion of France. All this helped to give the Whigs, the keenest supporters of the war, a majority in the general election held in England during that year.

Minorca

Oudenarde, 1708— France open to invasion

Whig success at polls, 1708

This swing to the Whigs made Godolphin and Marlborough more and more dependent on them. Already two of the leading moderate Tories, Robert Harley and Henry St. John, had objected to Godolphin's offering any posts to Whigs, and had been dropped from the ministry. Six months after the election Godolphin now had to go much further. Against all the wishes of Anne, he found himself obliged to appoint extreme Whigs to some of the principal posts. Of the Queen's ministers only Godolphin himself, Marlborough, and one other could now be counted as Tories.

Dismissal of moderate Tories Harley and St. John

Almost a Whig Cabinet

The link between Godolphin and Marlborough on the one hand, and the Whigs on the other, was that they were all determined to carry on the war until the Archduke Charles had driven Philip V from Spain. This

Whig policy in Spain

would have been sensible enough had the Allies continued to make progress in Spain, or had they been able to drive on towards Paris. But after 1708 the Allies in fact made few gains, and the war began to drag on fruitlessly. This gave the displaced Tory leaders a chance to urge the opposite—and increasingly popular—policy of making peace, even if some of the Allied aims were not achieved.

In 1709 the Allies opened negotiations with Louis XIV. France was in desperate straits and the French king was willing to accept almost any terms. But the negotiations broke down because the Allies, while powerless to expel Philip V, still insisted that Spain should go to Charles. By this time the war was becoming widely disliked in England, for taxation and the national debt were both increasing fast, and large sums were being raised by taxes on everyday articles like beer, coal and candles. To add to the discontent, a great frost in early 1709 lasted several weeks and was followed by a run of poor harvests, causing hardship, scarcity and a continued rise in prices. *Unsuccessful peace negotiations, 1709*

Discontent in England

The invasion of their country, and the knowledge that their king had done all he honourably could to conclude peace, rallied the French people behind Louis XIV. Soon Marlborough found himself faced by a new French army. With Eugene's co-operation he attacked at Malplaquet, just inside France, and once more beat his opponents. But this time the French inflicted far more casualties than they themselves suffered; and Paris was still almost as far off as before. *The French rally*

Malplaquet, 1709—a fruitless victory

This lesson was lost on Marlborough and the Cabinet, who still continued the struggle. At this rate the war might have gone on for many more years but for the fall of Godolphin's ministry. The story behind this shows us some of the ways of 18th-century politics. Anne had always distrusted extreme party men and she especially resented the presence in the Cabinet of the extreme Whigs, who tended to put parliament before the Crown. *Anne's dislike of extreme Whigs*

She was also angry with Godolphin and Marlborough for working with them. Nothing might have come of Anne's feelings but for the fact that, tired at last of the Duchess of Marlborough's stormy temper and constant support of the Whigs, she had dismissed her old friend and become dependent on a lady-in-waiting named Abigail Masham. The quiet and humble bearing of this lady—a refreshing change from that of the Duchess—concealed a talent for intrigue, and she used her growing influence over Anne to help Robert Harley, one of the dismissed moderate Tories. It was Harley who, admitted to Anne's apartments by Mrs. Masham, now advised the Queen how to change her ministers.

Anne dismisses Duchess of Marlborough

Abigail Masham

Robert Harley

The change of ministry was achieved gradually and while parliament was not in session. First Godolphin was dismissed, then one by one the Whigs; Marlborough was kept because he was still unrivalled in the field. Mainly moderate Tories—including, of course, Harley, who became Lord Treasurer in Godolphin's place—were appointed to the vacancies. When the whole character of the ministry had changed, and its influence could be used whole-heartedly on the Tory side, a fresh general election was held. The result, produced by Crown influence and the rising discontent under the previous ministry, was a decisive victory for the Tories.[1]

Dismissal of Godolphin and Whigs, 1710

Appointment of Harley and moderate Tories

Tory success at polls

2. *The Tories, The Peace of Utrecht, and the Hanoverian Succession*

The Tories negotiate with France

Almost as soon as they came into power Harley and other Tory chiefs opened a secret negotiation with France. The decisive steps were taken in 1711. Harley,

[1] In the process, many M.P.s who were neither Whig nor Tory lost their seats. Government was thus becoming more and more a party matter, with the Cabinet sharing the same party views as the majority in the Commons. Note, however, that the change of ministry took place *before* and not after the general election—a proof of how much power remained to the Crown.

stabbed by a man he was questioning in Privy Council, was for part of this year desperately ill, but St. John as St. John his deputy pressed on the negotiation without regard to the interests of England's allies. Meanwhile he also tried his own favourite scheme of an attack up the St. Law- Attack up rence on the French settlement of Quebec. The way for St. Lawrence this had been prepared by the capture in 1710 of the French province of Acadia, soon to be renamed Nova Scotia; but as the new expedition was incompetently led—among others by Mrs. Masham's brother—it failed dismally, and so ended only by increasing St. John's desire for peace. For this reason he gave little support to Marlborough, who in his last campaign in northern Marl- France nevertheless manœuvred so brilliantly that he borough's pierced the French lines without the loss of a single man. campaign

With proper support, Marlborough might now per- haps have gone on to Paris. But his home government was no longer behind him, and an important event had made the Austrians withdraw to Germany the forces under Prince Eugene. This was nothing less than the death without children of their young Emperor, the elder brother of the Archduke Charles. The Austrians were anxious that Charles should be elected without Archduke dispute as his successor, and in due course this came Charles about. It of course made nonsense of the idea of fighting Emperor to secure Spain for Charles, since he now had all the Austrian family possessions as well as the territory al- ready wrested from Louis and Philip. Charles's power, Charles too in other words, had suddenly become quite as much of powerful? a threat to Europe as that of Louis XIV. All the more, therefore, did the new government in England seek peace.

St. John's method of ending the war was to make a St. John's secret deal with Louis behind the backs of the other bargain with Allies. He agreed that Philip V should keep Spain and Louis Spanish America on condition that Great Britain had a

ENGLISH SETTLEMENTS
IN AMERICA

Settled or taken before 1660 ————
Settled or taken between 1660 and 1714 ------

generous reward.[1] Probably this was the only way to
stop the Austrians fighting indefinitely, but they and
the other Allies were naturally affronted. Among those
offended was Hanover, whose Prince George from now
on bore no love for the British Tories.

Hanover
(and other
Allies)
offended

[1] The details of this may be seen from the terms of the peace treaty,
given on page 358.

Between a preliminary Anglo-French agreement and an actual end of the war there was likely to be a long interval if the Whigs had their way. They determined to carry in the Lords a motion that peace should not be concluded until Charles had Spain. To do this they got the support of some high Tory peers who disapproved of Harley (or the Earl of Oxford, as he had now become) and St. John. It was a shady bargain on both sides. The Whigs let through the Lords a bill against occasional conformity, which they had been blocking all the reign; and the high Tories, who had previously opposed big campaigns on the Continent, then voted for "No peace without Spain"—a motion which was carried by eight votes. *[margin: Whig effort to prolong war]* *[margin: 'No peace without Spain]* *[margin: Act against occasional conformity]*

Harley, however, soon found a way round this obstacle. He persuaded the Queen to create twelve new peers. These were all men, such as Mrs. Masham's husband, who could be trusted to support the government. Thus strengthened in the Lords, Harley and St. John were able to press on with their peace policy, and—since he opposed it—to dismiss Marlborough. The reward of the man who had never lost a battle (and who had provided for his troops better than any previous English general) was to be accused of wasting his officers' lives in order to sell their commissions to others. *[margin: Creation of twelve peers]* *[margin: Dismissal of Marl-borough, 1711]*

On orders from home the British armies during 1712 now held aloof from further fighting, much to the fury of their allies. Eventually the Dutch, too, gave up the struggle, and during 1713 peace treaties with France were signed at Utrecht. The Austrians stood out for another year before they too came to terms. *[margin: Treaties of Utrecht, 1713]*

The settlement at Utrecht was thus largely due to St. John (who had now become Viscount Bolingbroke). Though arrived at by doubtful methods, its main features lasted almost throughout the 18th century. It

The Spanish empire divided recognized a division of the Spanish empire, as William III and Louis had originally seen was best: Philip V's share was Spain and the Spanish New World (on condition that the thrones of France and Spain were never united), while Charles's was the Spanish Netherlands (thenceforth known as the Austrian Netherlands) and the Spanish territories in Italy. In addition the Anne recognized French recognized Queen Anne and her Protestant successors in Great Britain; and the Dutch obtained a The Dutch 'barrier' better 'barrier' of fortresses between them and France.

So Great Britain and Holland achieved their main object—to curb the power of France. Through Bolingbroke's bargain with Louis, however, Britain also England's gains— Gibraltar etc. secured a number of valuable 'pickings'. She kept Gibraltar and Minorca (both of which had been taken on behalf of the Archduke Charles) and likewise Acadia (Nova Scotia) and the disputed West Indian island of St. Kitts. The whole of Newfoundland, too, became The Asiento recognized as hers. In addition, by a clause known as the Asiento (= Agreement) she gained the sole right to carry slaves to the Spanish New World, together with the right to send one large ship of general merchandise each year to Porto Bello, in South America. With the help of these commercial privileges Britain intended not only to earn great riches from the sale of slaves, but also to open up the whole of the Spanish New World to British trade.

*   *   *   *   *

Despite criticism from the Whigs, England as a whole approved the treaty of Utrecht. Yet within a year the Tories who made it were cast from power, and the Tory party was broken.

The Tories and the Hanoverian succession The rock on which the Tories split was the Hanoverian succession. Though their party had helped to pass the Act of Settlement, some Tories disliked the prospect of a German ruler when there was available a Stuart prince in the person of James Edward—for the 'warming-pan' story of the Pretender's origin was no longer much believed. James Edward had recently been helping Louis XIV against Britain and the Tory chiefs could not support him openly. But privately Oxford and Bolingbroke both decided during 1713 that it might be in the Tory interest, when Anne died, to bring in the Pretender instead of the Hanoverian. The main reason for this was that Prince George of Hanover was bitterly offended with the Tories for deserting England's allies, and was now surrounded by Whig advisers. If he succeeded to the English throne, the Tories would probably be out of power for long to come.

As Anne's health became worse, so Oxford and Bolingbroke felt the sands slipping from beneath their feet. Secretly they strove to arrange terms on which the Pretender might become king. But the first and most obvious condition—that he should turn Protestant— James Edward honourably refused to accept. After this Oxford had no very clear policy at all. In ill-health, drinking too much, and with his brain and speech becoming fuddled, he drifted helplessly towards disaster, carrying with him the fortunes of the Tory party. This did not suit the far more energetic Bolingbroke, who quarrelled with his chief and began to work against him. There was yet time, thought Bolingbroke, to come to terms with the Pretender. It seems too that had Bolingbroke been in control he would now have aimed to fill the main official posts, military as well as civil, so completely with Tories that the party could hardly be dislodged under any successor, Hanoverian or Jacobite.

So affairs drifted on for several weeks until at last the Queen could stand Oxford's drinking and neglect of

Tory negotiations with Pretender

He refuses to abandon Catholicism

Oxford's ill-health

Bolingbroke's policy

business no longer. Her feeling against him was cleverly sharpened by Lady Masham, who was now working on behalf of Bolingbroke. In the closing days of July 1714, Anne reached the point of dismissing Oxford from the Treasurership. For two or three days Bolingbroke, as the second man in the Cabinet, was in virtual control of the government; then the Queen's ill-health gave way to mortal illness. As almost her last action she chose as Harley's successor not Bolingbroke but the Duke of Shrewsbury, a moderate and kindly man who was practically the only Whig in the Cabinet. With the support of all members of the government, including Bolingbroke—who had had no time to complete any other plan—Shrewsbury arranged to bring over George of Hanover. On August 1st, 1714, the Queen passed to her rest and George I was peacefully proclaimed all over the country. "The Earl of Oxford" wrote Bolingbroke, "was removed on Tuesday; the Queen died on Sunday. What a world is this, and how does fortune banter us!"

The new monarch was welcomed by the country as a whole because only through a Hanoverian succession could England be sure of a Protestant ruler. This was the feeling of most of the Tory party as well as of all the Whigs. But because Oxford, Bolingbroke and other Tory leaders had played with the idea of bringing in James Edward, the Tories were for good and all regarded by George I and his son as Jacobites. Distrusted by the new rulers and hopelessly split by the quarrels of their leaders, the Tories ceased to be a great force in politics for nearly fifty years. It was under Whig government— tolerant, parliamentary, commercially-minded, and corrupt—that Great Britain now settled down to that expansion of agriculture, industry, commerce and empire which was to make her one of the foremost powers in the world.

[Marginal notes: Anne dismisses Oxford | Bolingbroke's two days in control | Shrewsbury Lord Treasurer | George I proclaimed | The eclipse of the Tories]

SOME FEATURES OF ANNE'S REIGN

CHAPTER THIRTY

GREAT BRITAIN UNDER QUEEN ANNE (I)

1. *Population, Food, and Industry*

Population

THE Great Britain of Queen Anne was still a very sparsely inhabited country. Historians estimate that only about 5,500,000 people were then living in England and Wales, about 1,000,000 in Scotland and about 1,500,000 in Ireland.

As in former times, most people still earned their living from the soil. Their chief crops were barley (especially in the largely unenclosed midland and eastern counties), wheat (in the more enclosed south-east) and oats (in Scotland and the north). Barley gave them not only food but also their main drink—the ale that was still drunk by old and young alike at every meal, including breakfast.

Crops and food

In England these crops were grown over a large part of the country. Some districts, however, such as Yorkshire, the Cotswolds, and the southern downlands, were famous instead for sheep farming; while there were also many stretches which supported neither crops nor sheep. In Wales and Scotland the proportion of barren land was much greater.

Cattle

The people had grain but few vegetables. Turnips had not long been introduced into England and potatoes were still little grown. This absence of root crops meant that most of the cattle had still to be slaughtered at the end of the harvest season, for there was not enough hay to feed them through the winter. This in turn encouraged a big trade in live cattle from Scotland and Wales to England—a trade which Ireland was forbidden to share. Living on the heaths and commons and the after-harvest stubble of the open fields, all cattle were still very small compared with modern beasts, but the days of scientific stock-breeding and rearing were not far ahead.

Because of the general slaughter of cattle at Martin-mas it was still usual for only the rich to eat fresh meat throughout the year. During the winter the middle ranks of society ate salt meat. The lower ranks (and the navy) ate this all the year round—though the high price of salt stopped them having much and the poorest rarely tasted meat of any sort. In some parts of the Scottish Highlands the nearest thing to eating meat was to bleed the cattle and eat the blood mixed with oatmeal. *Meat*

Next to the trade in sheep and cattle, the biggest livestock trade was probably in poultry. Droves of Norfolk turkeys or geese were a regular sight on the roads to London, though not many were destined for the tables of the poor. Chickens were much cheaper, as a fair-sized bird could be bought for twopence; eggs were cheap but not always available. Of the fisheries the most important were for herrings off the east coast and for cod off Newfoundland. Owing to transport difficulties fish, too, had to be eaten salted. In some districts there was a good supply of river fish. Tradition records that in parts of Scotland the labourer had to stipulate against too many meals of trout or salmon! *Poultry and fish*

All told, Britain produced enough to feed her small population, with a little over for export. Most people, however, had a monotonous and often meagre diet, and work in the open air made appetites big. If the population increased more sharply—as it was soon to do when improved sanitation and medical knowledge lowered the death rate—then drastic changes would be needed in agriculture. Already writers were pointing out that *Need for agricultural improvement* with more enclosure the country could produce more corn, new crops, better sheep and cattle. It was in Anne's reign that there flourished the first of the great agricultural 'improvers'—Jethro Tull, who secured yields far above the normal by means of a horse-hoe to keep the top soil well broken, and a seed-drill to replace 'broadcast' sowing by hand.

Jethro Tull

Closely linked with the countryside, like nearly all industries at the time, was England's greatest manufacture—woollen cloth. Mainly a domestic industry, this was still carried on in tens of thousands of cottages. Women and children did the carding and spinning; the weaving was done by a skilled man of the household or the village weaver. Cloth of a sort was made almost everywhere, but the fine cloths for export or other long-distance trade were mainly produced in Norfolk, the West Riding, the Cotswolds and the south-western counties, in or near the great sheep-rearing districts. In many counties merchants distributed raw wool round the farms and villages, and collected the made-up cloth. Dyeing and finishing were nearly always done by skilled craftsmen in the towns. The other fabric industries apart from wool included silk, made in Canterbury and by Huguenot refugees at Spitalfields in London, and linen, made in Scotland and Ireland. In addition, fabrics in which cotton was used with wool or linen were now being produced in Lancashire.

Industries

Woollen cloth

Silk

Linen

Next to food and cloth the most important products were probably coal and iron. On coal depended half the trades and most of the domestic heating of London and many other places to which it could be brought by water. Already it was mined in Scotland, Wales, and most of the English counties which produce coal today, though the workings were mainly small or near the surface. By far the biggest coalfields were around New-castle, where there were already shafts four hundred feet

Coal

Newcastle

deep and wooden rails for surface transport. Anne's reign saw the invention by Thomas Newcomen of the first reasonably effective steam pump to combat flooding, but explosions and falls remained all too frequent. The miners and their families (who in some places in Scotland were very nearly serfs) lived almost as a race apart. Newcomen's steam pump

Iron was still smelted by charcoal and so mined near the great forests. These, however, were now rapidly dwindling. Most of the woods of the Weald were gone, and the time-honoured iron industry of Sussex was giving place to foundries in the Forest of Dean and Shropshire, where there was still plenty of wood with water nearby for transport. An important new invention, however, was soon to free the industry from the forests. It was probably in Anne's reign that Abraham Darby of Coalbrookdale, in Shropshire, began to use coke for smelting. Natural coal had been tried previously, but had made the metal too brittle. Iron Darby and coke-smelting

Among other industries of national importance were London luxury goods (including jewelry, silverware, and fine clothes), shipbuilding, leather, paper, glass, and the knitting (on special frames) of woollen and silk stockings. There was also the growing industry of printing Indian calicoes. Printed cottons being gay and cheap, they were considered a threat to the woollen cloth industry and their import was forbidden—so plain calicoes were imported and printed in England. The writer Daniel Defoe records that in a riot at Colchester weavers threw nitric acid over women seen wearing the new cottons. Other industries Calico printing

2. *Trade, Transport, and Towns*

Though most counties still satisfied the bulk of their own needs, there were some trades—notably in cloth, London luxury goods, Newcastle coal and Shropshire Long-distance trade iron—that covered a large part of England. There was also a very great foreign trade. This was carried on partly by independent merchants, partly by members of the great chartered companies.

Foreign trade by independent merchants

Independent merchants managed the trade to France, Spain, Portugal and Italy, and most of that with England's overseas settlements. To these colonies they exported cloth and other manufactured articles in return for products like tobacco and naval stores (timber, masts, hemp, tar, etc.) from North America and sugar from the West Indies. The fact that independent merchants handled much of this colonial trade did not, however, mean that the colonies were free to trade as they pleased. By the end of Anne's reign nearly all the colonies had become royal provinces, with governor and council chosen by the Crown; and though the colonies were usually also allowed an elected assembly, corresponding to the Commons in Great Britain, their trade was still strictly controlled by the Navigation Acts in the interests of the mother country.

Trade with the colonies

The chartered companies with a monopoly over trade to certain areas included several founded under Elizabeth I or earlier. The most important of these was now the East India Company. This was perhaps the only company not to export much cloth (woollen garments being too warm for the Far East), with the result that its imports of silks, tea, porcelain, drugs and salt petre (for gunpowder) had to be paid for partly in gold —a fact for which the company was much criticized. Of the other companies the most important were the African Company, which tried (unsuccessfully) to monopolize the slave-trade from West Africa to the West Indies, and the Hudson's Bay Company, which imported furs from North America. All three companies had forts or depots abroad. The growth of these in the case of the East India Company later helped the

Foreign trade reserved to companies

company to become the ruler over large stretches of India.

As a trading power in the reign of Anne, Great Britain had many advantages. They included peace at home, a sound system of money, the Bank of England and the Bank of Scotland, a good position for the growing trade across the Atlantic, and the fact that after the Union England, Wales and Scotland made up the largest free-trade area in Europe. Good communications, however, were not among these blessings.

Probably the best means of transport was by sea round the coasts, despite possible waits of a week or more for a favourable wind. It was so much better than road transport that food grown anywhere near the coasts of Sussex and Hampshire always travelled to London by sea and river, just as did coal from Newcastle (whence the name 'sea-coal'). River transport, however, though improved by the making of locks and deeper channels, had one great disadvantage—only very few rivers (notably the Thames, Severn, Great Ouse and Trent) were navigable for as much as forty miles from the mouth.

Once off the waterways, the traveller had a very uncomfortable time. No hard roads had been built since the days of the Romans, and the highways were still mostly narrow tracks full of ruts in summer, mud in winter, and pot-holes at all seasons. The main road from London to Canterbury, for instance, had many stretches where only two horses—not coaches—could pass. The depth of the mud may be judged from the fact that on one occasion Defoe saw a lady in Surrey going to church in a coach drawn by six oxen, and on another occasion twenty-two oxen struggling to draw a felled oak along a road near Chatham dockyard. Each parish, of course, was supposed to maintain its roads, but few faced the labour or expense involved. On horse-back was therefore still much the best way of moving

Coaches about the countryside. As for coaches, though these had been used for over a century they were not yet common, and only the most expensive had springs. Fifty miles by coach could easily take the whole of a summer's day, even if there were no accidents or highwaymen. In winter, long coach journeys were usually out of the question.

Pack-horses and waggons For carrying goods by road there was the pack-horse, ambling along in train with perhaps forty or fifty others, or in summer the hooded waggon. The latter, usually drawn by six or eight horses and preceded by the carrier on foot, also took passengers. But though there was constant movement of goods and persons, most people did not travel at all—they stayed in their native villages, rarely journeying farther than their legs would carry

The Post them. Nor did they write many letters—though since the days of Charles II there had been an official postal service covering the main towns. Letters were carried by post-boys on horseback—from London to Edinburgh took six days—and the fee, based on distance, was met (or the letter refused) by the recipient. Within London there was already a penny post, delivered every few hours. During Anne's reign a big step forward was taken when England, Scotland, Ireland and the Colonies were all linked up in a single postal system.

Distinctive position of London London's postal facilities were but one example of the immense difference between the capital and the rest of the country. London alone had a distinctive town life largely unconnected with the surrounding countryside.

Population Fifteen times more populous than its nearest rivals Bristol and Norwich, it contained within its outer boundaries some 670,000 people, of whom almost a third lived inside the historic square mile of the City. By way of comparison Edinburgh had 20,000 inhabitants, and Glasgow (still an attractive country town though already Scotland's foremost centre of commerce) 12,000.

There were many reasons, geographical and historical, for London's importance—an importance clearly shown in the success of its opposition to Charles I and James II. As the manufacturing centre for the luxury and 'finishing' trades, the biggest buyer of food and raw materials from the rest of the country, and the port which handled by far the greatest volume of foreign trade, London had unequalled wealth and an unrivalled position in the nation's commercial life. For this reason it had secured and kept great privileges of self-government. The fact that the Court, parliament, and the main courts of law were all nearby in Westminster gave it still further fame and power.[1]

Factors in London's greatness

Several of the nobility had houses in London, especially in the newly developed and fashionable areas of Covent Garden, Bloomsbury and Piccadilly. London's real leaders, however, were the greater merchants who lived in the City—the men who held office as Lord Mayor, Aldermen or Common Councillors and occupied the higher positions in the eighty-nine gilds and companies. Such men were richer than many a noble; and very prosperous, too, were many smaller merchants, shopkeepers, and masters. Most journeymen and apprentices also enjoyed a reasonable standard of living— as did the growing body of professional men, of whom lawyers, officers and clergy were the most important. Below all these fairly comfortably situated citizens, however, there was a large class of entirely uneducated labourers living in the utmost poverty and squalor. Herded together perhaps five or six large families in a single house, they spread disease and made London the unhealthiest place in England. With their natural brutality inflamed by cheap gin (which was just becoming fatally popular) and their criminal tendencies unchecked

London's people

[1] Anne usually lived in St. James's or Kensington Palace when she was not at Windsor or Bath. The law courts sat in Westminster Hall.

by any proper system of police, they played a prominent and sordid part in London life. From them it was always possible to enlist a gang for any act of violence, from sacking a Nonconformist chapel to slitting the nose of a rival in love.

London's size and importance enabled it to enjoy pleasures which scarcely existed in the smaller towns. **Theatres** Foremost among these were the theatres, of which only two—Drury Lane and Covent Garden—were licensed to perform 'straight' plays. Since the Restoration these had been presented with women in the female parts and on a 'picture stage' with front curtain, like the normal stage of today. Among the most frequently performed works were the comedies of manners written since the Restoration by such writers as John Dryden, William Wycherley and William Congreve. In the closing years

A Carved Walnut Chair

An elegant piece in the Victoria and Albert Museum dating from about the end of Anne's reign. Note the fashionable ball-and-claw foot.

of William III's reign, however, the outspokenness or indecency of these comedies had come under heavy fire, and the favourite new dramatists under Anne—including Joseph Addison and Richard Steele—wrote in a kindlier and more moral vein. Puritan hostility to the stage, the tone of the Restoration plays, and the small number of theatres licensed for drama, together meant that play-going was now largely confined to 'fashionable' circles. The broad mass of London people, in so far as it went to theatres at all, went to

The Tea Table

An illustration to a satirical poem published in 1710. It shows the newly fashionable habit of ladies' tea-parties, where there was of course much discussion of personalities.

'Each Dame the improvement of her talent tries,
And at each sip a Lady's Honour dies.'

Two beaux try to overhear the gossip through the window; and in the background an allegorical figure of Envy, holding a serpent, drives out Truth and Justice. Note the popular tall backed chairs, the ornamented mirror, and the curved alcove for the display of the newly imported and fashionable china, etc.

places like Sadler's Wells, where the entertainment was of a 'variety' character.

One type of performance at Covent Garden deserves special mention. During the last years of Charles II Italian opera had reached England.[1] The new Italian style, with its beautiful melodies sung by single voices, English music and Italian opera

[1] At least one English opera had been performed privately under the Commonwealth.

made a refreshing contrast to the complex interweaving of parts in which the previous generation of English composers had revelled. It might possibly have eclipsed English music straight away; but at that time there was living Henry Purcell, a supreme genius who could absorb foreign influences and yet remain distinctively English. With the death of Purcell at the early age of thirty-seven in 1695, however, there was no English composer left of the same standard. When in Anne's reign there arrived at Covent Garden a new company of Italian opera-singers whose producer was the young German composer Handel, it found English musical talent on the ebb; and this, combined with the extreme skill of the Italian singers, the showy writing for very high male voices, and the great emotional power of the melodies, helped to achieve a sensational triumph for the foreigners. The result was unfortunate. At the very time when regular public concerts were just becoming established, the English public began to consider English musicians greatly inferior to those of Italy and Germany—an attitude which continued for long to come.[1]

Newspapers   Opera and the theatre were distinguishing features of London life. Another was the growing swarm of newspapers. The first regular newspaper had appeared under the Commonwealth, and later Charles II had agreed to the issue of an official paper which still continues today —the *London Gazette*. By the time of Anne there were a dozen or more newspapers published in London two or three times a week—and the *Daily Courant* could claim to be the first daily newspaper in the world. These papers consisted of a single sheet printed on both sides, and

---

[1] Handel later settled down in England as a favourite musician of George I and George II. He gave up writing Italian opera, and developed sacred oratorio—a form much more in harmony with the English temperament, and one which cast a lengthy spell over English composers.

A Japanned Bureau (*c.* 1710)

In Anne's reign japanned (lacquered) furniture became fashionable, following the introduction of pieces from the East. This is a handsome specimen in scarlet and gold. The writing bureau, or combined desk and chest of drawers, first appears in England in the later Stuart period.

sometimes folded. By the end of the reign there were similar journals in a few provincial towns.

There were also pamphlets. Floods of these had ap- Pamphlets
peared during the period of loose government control

after the defeat of Charles I, only to be checked by the Commonwealth. Encouraged by the fact that after 1695 a government licence was no longer needed for publication, the flood had now burst forth again, and the pamphlet had become a favourite weapon in the battle between the parties. Pamphleteers like Addison, on the Whig side, and Dean Swift, who deserted the Whigs to champion the Tories, though writing anonymously were real powers in the land. And when, like Defoe, they also began to air their opinions in papers appearing regularly, they helped to create a new form of journalism—the review. In this class were Swift's *Examiner* and Steele and Addison's *Tatler* and *Spectator*—the last two ranging beyond politics into literature, art and many other interests. It was in the *Spectator* that there appeared that immortal figure Sir Roger de Coverley, whose foibles were soon eagerly read all over the country.

Reviews

Coffee houses

Another great feature of London's social life was the coffee houses. These had first sprung up in the reign of Charles II for the sale of the new fashionable beverages —coffee, chocolate and tea, all of which had reached England in the early 17th century. In some of them alcoholic drinks could also be obtained, the atmosphere varying between that of a café, a public house, and a club. By the reign of Anne there were several hundreds of them, including many known as meeting-places for men of special interests. There were Whig coffee-houses, and Tory coffee-houses. White's attracted gamblers, Will's men of literature; the clergy frequented Truby's, scholars 'The Grecian'. Nearly all these places helped to spread news (which was often read aloud) and form public opinion. One of them—Lloyd's—was later to concentrate on news of shipping, and from this to develop into the world's greatest centre of marine insurance.

By comparison with London, other towns in the

The Coffee House Mob

This shows a quarrel in one of the popular coffee houses—now (about
1710) losing ground in upper circles before the rise of the club. Note the
reading of newspapers, the smoking of pipes (usually lit from the candles),
and the lady in charge at the back.

State Bedstead of William III (1695)

Note the fine 'classical' effect of the hangings
and the elaborate head-board.

British Isles had few organized pleasures, though many
had great traditions and a flourishing commercial life.
In Scotland only half a dozen towns had more than
four thousand inhabitants. Edinburgh as the capital
stood foremost, but its social life was still primitive. The
Presbyterians made sure that there were no theatres,
and a public assembly for dancing began in Anne's
reign only against strenuous clerical protests. The main
pastimes were heavy drinking and cock-fighting, together with golf and horse-racing (on week-days) on
the sands at Leith.

Edinburgh

Most primitive of all for a capital were Edinburgh's sanitary arrangements. Owing to the violence of Scottish life the capital had kept within its walls, with the result that lofty houses divided into flats had been built up to twelve storeys high. As the flats had no gardens and no water supply other than the barrels carried upstairs by 'water caddies', the disposal of sewage presented a problem. Edinburgh's solution was horribly simple. At 10 p.m. a drum was beaten as a warning to pedestrians, and to cries of "Gardy Loo" ("Gardez l'eau"—'mind the water') the dwellers in the upper storeys opened their windows and emptied their vessels into the streets beneath. Early next morning the city guard made some rough attempt to clean up the filth; but on Sundays it lay there all day long. At Perth, where there were houses fourteen storeys high, there was not even the sounding of a drum—the inhabitants cast down their refuse at all hours.

But towns, after all, occupied only a very small part of England, and still less of Scotland, Wales and Ireland. For a fuller picture of conditions we must turn back to the countryside—to its social divisions and the kind of life its people led.

CHAPTER THIRTY-ONE

GREAT BRITAIN UNDER QUEEN ANNE (II)

1. *Country Society in England and Scotland*

Social
divisions in
the countryside

A T the top of the social scale in England came the
great nobility—the dukes and others with huge
estates worth many thousands a year. Such
fortunate people could live in idleness, but in actual
The great
nobility
fact they were usually very busy caring for their estates
and neighbourhoods and occupying important official
positions. Many of them had a taste for architecture or
the fine arts, and spent vast sums improving their
mansions or filling them with paintings and sculpture
from the Continent. We can imagine their life when we
visit today some of the great houses—Chatsworth, Wilton and the like—which were already old in the days of
Queen Anne.

Lesser
nobility and
gentry
Below these, but still in a highly privileged position,
came the lesser nobility and the country gentry, ranging
down to squires of purely rustic habits and an income of
no more than three hundred pounds a year. The habits
of this extremely powerful section of society varied, of
course, with different individuals. Many were highly
cultured patrons of literature or art. Many lived the life
of fashion, coming to London for the 'season' and then
putting in a spell at Tunbridge Wells or that bigger spa
whose great days were just beginning—Bath. Others
were content with country life and company. Broadly
speaking, as a class they were interested in their estates,
their public duties—the justices of the peace, still the
real rulers of the countryside, were still chosen only

Blenheim Palace

From a print, published in 1743, of the great palace which was built for the Duke of Marlborough at public expense to celebrate his greatest victory. The architect was Sir John Vanbrugh, and the building shows his wayward and very individual but highly effective treatment of classical themes. It took a long time to build and Vanbrugh had immense trouble with Marlborough's stormy widow.

from the gentry—and such pastimes as hunting, shooting with the new shot-guns, gambling and drinking. Many a Tory squire did not consider the evening complete until claret had sent him slumped and snoring beneath the table; many a Whig squire got there even sooner on port.

Duelling Drunkenness was not confined to upper society, and in that way was unlike another bad habit—duelling. James I had made duelling illegal, but a gentleman was nevertheless still expected to defend his 'honour'. As drunkenness was so common there was no lack of quarrels and combats. Sometimes these ended fatally, but even then the survivor's punishment was usually only a short spell in prison. The fact that gentlemen always wore swords in London and the country towns encouraged the duelling habit; and great credit is due to Beau Nash, the master of ceremonies at Bath during the reigns of Anne and the first two Georges, that besides forbidding swearing and the wearing of top-boots in the public assembly rooms he also banned the carrying of swords.

The gentry not a closed caste Though the feeling of belonging to a certain 'class' was now very strong, and the gentry were very conscious of their superiority to the 'simple', it was still quite possible to enter the ranks of the gentry from below. This could be done by acquiring money (lands and a pedigree soon followed), or education, or a genteel husband (young ladies of more wealth than breeding were frequently matched with young gentlemen of more breeding than wealth). Again, some members of the gentry shared the life of folk less well-born—for many of the younger sons of country gentlemen still became apprentices in the higher trades or attended the local grammar school.

Gentle-women The women of this favoured class still lived a much more restricted life than their menfolk. The home, where two or three generations of the family often continued to live under the same roof, was almost their entire world. They got their education (reading, writing and housewifery) from their mothers, and their orders (not that they necessarily obeyed them) from their fathers or their husbands. Their chances of happiness depended very much on their luck in marriage, for there was little prospect of release—in the whole reign there were only six legal divorces. Like women of other classes they had to be brave, for they were constantly bearing children, artificial relief from pain was still unknown, and all too many mothers still died in giving birth, or (like Queen Anne herself) soon afterwards lost the infants they had brought into the world with so much suffering.

Below the country gentry but high in public esteem came the yeomen. Originally applied to the smaller owners of freehold land, in popular speech this term also covered the larger tenant farmers—who often bought a small piece of freehold land for the sake of the privileges that went with it, including the right to vote at parliamentary elections.[1] Between them, the yeomen worked perhaps a quarter of the plough land of England. Their standard of life was an enviable one for the times—as may be seen from the many fine farmhouses in stone or brick which date from Anne's reign. All the same, the small freeholder had one burning grievance. By a law passed under Charles II, no freeholder with land worth less than one hundred pounds a year—and this meant most—was allowed to kill game on his own estate. Pheasants, partridges and grouse, all had to be spared to swell the 'bag' of his richer neighbours. *The yeomen*

The game laws

Below the yeomen in esteem came the smaller tenant farmers, and below them the mass of the rural *Labourers, smallholders, etc*

---

[1] By an ancient law the county M.P.s were elected by the owners of freehold land worth more than forty shillings a year.

population. This consisted mainly of labourers (many of whom 'lived in' at their employer's farm), servants, and those who eked out a living with the help of a cottage, a small plot (or a small holding in the open fields) and a beast or two on the common. Most of this large class were very poor by modern British standards, but fairly well off by comparison with country labourers at the time on the Continent or in Scotland and Ireland. Moreover the treatment of the needy by the local authorities was generally becoming more lenient, with the result that perhaps a quarter of the population was receiving some form of public assistance. This, however, placed a great burden on the local rates, and was obviously undesirable in many ways.

Poor relief

To this growing leniency there was one big exception —the Act of Settlement of the Poor passed under Charles II. To avoid settlers from another parish qualifying for poor relief and becoming a charge on the local ratepayers, the act laid down that any man except a landowner, even if of good reputation and fully employed, might be sent back to the parish where he was born. Such a law was not only bad for industry but was also a bitterly resented restriction on personal freedom. Like the press-gang and the treatment of prisoners and lunatics, it was one of the worst features of life in the early 18th century.

Act of Settlement of the Poor

The pastimes of the lower ranks of society in the country included such food-providers as fishing, bird-snaring and the like. Among favourite sports of other kinds were football (still played as a mass game), cricket (which was just becoming popular in the villages), bowls and skittles; while for spectators there were cock-fighting and horse-racing, with all their opportunities for gambling. Except at Newmarket the race-meetings were still purely local, but during the reign a vital step was taken in the development of the English thorough-

Country sports and pastimes

bred by the importation of the three horses—two Arab and one Barbary—from which almost all Derby winners descend. Of other 'sports' perhaps the most popular was fighting, either with sticks or the bare fists; and combats of various kinds—between pugilists, or between women, or with swords—were a common attraction at fairs. Many of the ordinary folk also shared the pleasures of the chase—on foot. Of their other recreations, pride of place probably went to the inevitable drinking and smoking. Smoking was still done through pipes— Smoking often the long clay 'churchwardens'—and in some areas was almost as popular with women and children as with men. Snuff-taking began after the capture of Spanish Snuff ships laden with snuff at Vigo.

By comparison, life in the Scottish countryside was Life in the extremely backward. Everywhere, but especially in the Scottish countryside Highlands, the nobles had immense power—heads of great clans like Argyle and Atholl could command the loyalty of thousands even against the government. In the Lowlands the next in rank of society—the laird, or The Lowlands country gentleman—also enjoyed great authority. Very often he had inherited the right to hold a court and administer justice to his tenants, like the feudal lords of medieval England, and coupled with the fact that he usually granted his tenants only very short leases of a year or so, this gave him a firm hold over them—which he normally tried to merit by his care for their welfare. This dependence on the laird's goodwill, however, did not make the poorer Scot subservient. The two had perhaps shared the same classroom, and inferior continued to address superior with the frankness learnt in youth.

Short leases and the lack of fertility of much of the Lowland soil then tilled kept the whole country poor. Other handicaps were the small individual holdings and the fact that much of the tillage was still done in common. Lowland farming, though well in advance of Highland, was still very inefficient. Nine-tenths of the ploughed land was still unenclosed, rents were often paid in produce, and the tenant, like the medieval English villein, had to do certain work on the lord's home farm.

All this was reflected in the general standard of Lowland living. Only a few wealthy men had estates worth more than five hundred pounds a year, while some landowners contrived to remain country gentry with an annual rent-roll of twenty pounds. There were few fine country houses, and the typical farmhouse was a single-roomed dwelling of turf or rough stone, probably without chimneys or glass, and with the bare ground for floor. The family sat on stones or heaps of turf round the fire in the middle of the room, and the cattle often occupied the far end. Clothes, including the men's blue woollen bonnets, were homespun, and the children went barefoot. Roads were few and bad even by 18th-century standards, and many households were fifty miles from the nearest shop. There was no compulsory parish rate to relieve the needy.

Country recreations By way of recreation the dweller in the Scottish countryside usually tried to bring in something for the table. Fishing, hawking, snaring and hare hunting were favourite sports, as was stalking the red deer in the Highlands. For the time-honoured pastime of drinking, wholesome Scottish ale was still the prime favourite; but whisky, spreading from the Highlands, was unfortunately beginning to rival it in popularity. Wine was for the gentry, whose taste (formed during the 'auld alliance' with France) ran to claret and champagne. Coffee and chocolate were as yet little known outside the towns, and tea was still a medicine costing fifteen shillings or more a pound.

The Highlands If the Lowlands were centuries behind the most developed parts of England, the Highlands were centuries behind the Lowlands. Lowlanders went there rarely and Englishmen hardly at all. There was no road fit for a carriage; and the inhabitants, wearing their special dress and speaking Gaelic, normally visited the Lowlands only for such special purposes as selling cattle, fighting, or plundering.[1] The clan chief—who might be anything from a purely local figure to a great and cultured noble like Argyle—was all-powerful; his inherited rights of justice extended even to offences punishable by death. Usually he lived in idleness, surrounded by an equally idle retinue whose main task was to protect him. By contrast, most of the clansmen toiled hard to wring a living from tiny crofts leased at excessive rents from the chief's 'tacksman' or head leaseholder. Their houses were hovels of turf, their standard of comfort low almost beyond our imagination. Direct control by the government over so strange and turbulent an area was impossible. All Anne's ministry could do was to support Argyle, and through him hope to keep the Highlands quiet.

2. *Ideas, Religion, Education*

In chapter eighteen an attempt was made to sketch out some of the ideas held by a typical Elizabethan gentleman. Owing to the development of science and scientific thought during the 17th century, many of these ideas were no longer current among educated Englishmen during the reign of Queen Anne. For example, the old picture of the universe as a series of concentric moving spheres, with the earth in the middle,

[1] Defoe, in a letter to Harley, thus describes Highlanders he had seen in Edinburgh: "They are all gentlemen, will take affront from no men, and insolent to the last degree. But certainly the absurdity is ridiculous to see a man in his mountain habit, armed with a broadsword, target, pistol, at his girdle a dagger, and staff, walking down the High Street as upright and haughty as if he were a lord, and withal driving a cow."

had given place to general belief in the Copernican system, in which the earth and other planets revolve about the sun. Moreover, some of the natural laws of this universe, such as the universal law of gravitation, applying alike to heavenly and earthly bodies, had been so brilliantly propounded and explained by Sir Isaac Newton during the 1680s that the poet Pope was later able to write:

The solar system

Newton and the laws of nature

> Nature and Nature's laws lay hid in night;
> God said, "Let Newton be", and all was light.

Together, the many great advances in astronomy, physics and mathematics had given men a much more accurate picture of the physical forces at work in the universe—which no one now imagined to be pushed round on the outside by angels.[1]

In the same way, though to a much lesser extent, advances in chemistry (in which Robert Boyle took a leading part) had cleared away many of the old ideas of the alchemists. The belief that the four 'elements' made up life, however, was still strong, and there was as yet no such understanding of chemical composition as there was of physical motion.

Declining belief in alchemy

In medicine, much more was understood of the functioning of the human body, particularly since the great work of William Harvey, physician to Charles I, on the circulation of the blood. The invention of the microscope in the second half of the 17th century carried such researches still further, besides making possible a more accurate knowledge of the structure of plants and the smaller forms of life. Medical remedies, however, had

Medicine

The microscope

---

[1] Newton was not of course the first to ponder on the gravitational force of the earth. But he was the first to show that heavenly bodies obey the same laws of motion as earthly bodies. His universal law of gravitation gave the formula—that all bodies attract each other directly in proportion to the product of their masses and inversely as the square of their distance apart.

not yet changed very much, and bleeding was still extremely popular—with doctors, if not with patients.

One thing which had not greatly changed, except by the growth of more sects, was a fervent belief in religion. Religion Nevertheless by Anne's reign Church and state were at last beginning to grow apart. The Toleration Act of 1689 had allowed all except Catholics and Unitarians the right to independent worship; and already in London the Nonconformists, with about a fifth of the Toleration population, had more chapels than there were parish churches. In Scotland, too, toleration was at last introduced after the Union, for in 1712 the victorious Presbyterians had to concede freedom of worship to the Episcopalians.[1] Even in Ireland there was toleration to the extent that the Catholic majority had at least the right to hold public services.

Everywhere, however, toleration had come because it was necessary, not because people really believed in it. Anne's reign was still an age of deep and strong religious feeling, and this alone made toleration of opponents difficult. Religious matters, too, were still very much bound up with political ones. The High Church Tories, for instance, tried to deny political and educational rights to the Nonconformists not only because High Churchmen thought it sinful to break away from the Church, but also because the Nonconformists were political allies of the Whigs.

Though Christian faith was deep and vigorous, it had Magic and not yet entirely killed the still older belief in magic, witchcraft witchcraft and the like. A declining belief in fairies, ghosts and witches still lingered in the English countryside, but it was now no longer shared by those in authority. So Anne's reign saw the last time an English jury convicted on a charge of witchcraft—and even then the judge reprieved the 'witch'. He had earlier

[1] Episcopalians = believers in Church government by bishops.

remarked, when the lady was said to have sailed through the air on a broomstick, that there was no law against flying.

In Scotland, Ireland and Wales, poorer communications allowed superstition to flourish much more vigorously. In Scotland the upper classes were beginning to share the views of educated Englishmen; but superstition of all kinds was strong in the Highlands and belief in witchcraft was encouraged by many ministers, who regarded doubts on the matter as blasphemy— witches being mentioned in the Bible. During Anne's reign several Scottish women were convicted of witchcraft and executed.

The cure for superstition was education and better
Education communications. The state of communications has already been described. Of education, it is safe to say that in all probability most people still received none at all. In England and Wales there were still, under Anglican control, the universities of Oxford and Cam-
English bridge, a few public boarding schools (notably Eton,
schools Westminster and Winchester) already favoured by the upper ranks of society, and a fairly large number of town grammar schools. In all these schools the pupils' interest in Latin (still the main subject of study) was still stimulated by generous applications of the cane or birch. At a lower level there were the new 'charity' schools for primary education now being founded by the recently formed Society for the Promotion of Christian Knowledge. Over a thousand of these were started in Anne's reign alone. Outside Anglican control there were the often excellent Nonconformist Academies (which had grown up during the 17th century, and which the Church tried hard to suppress), the 'dame' schools in many of the villages (where children did well if they learned to read and write), and a good deal of private tuition in the homes of the well-to-do. There

were few schools for girls. What the female learned of arithmetic and spelling she still acquired at home.

In the Scottish Lowlands the level of elementary teaching was probably higher than in England. By law every Scottish parish was required to set up at least one school and maintain it from the rates; and most (but not all) parishes had in fact done this. The universities, however, were not up to the English standard—partly because the victorious Presbyterians had excluded many eminent Episcopalians. They were still mainly attended by those wishing to enter the ministry, but at least they drew their students from all classes of society. Many sons of poor farmers, for instance, tramped in with a sack of oatmeal as food for the term—proof of a very general belief in education. Such an interest was entirely absent in Ireland, where the great bulk of the native Catholic population got no schooling at all, and where the sole university—Trinity College, Dublin— was for the Anglican minority only.

This brief survey has mentioned only a few aspects of life in the reign of Queen Anne. It would be possible to touch on many other things, such as the growing elegance of upper-class life in southern England. We might write of the changes in dress—of the grand ladies with their hair piled up on huge headdresses and their faces adorned with rouge, mascara, powder and patches, or of the fine gentlemen with their knee-breeches and stockings and their long vests and full-skirted coats crowned by vast and flowing periwigs. We might write of the superb walnut furniture—oak was now for country or everyday purposes, and mahogany only just coming in from the West Indies—or of the delicate porcelain and lacquered ware imported from China. We might describe the great buildings of Wren and Vanbrugh, or the simple, spacious and well-proportioned houses in red brick that were adding beauty to town and countryside. We might say more of the great men of literature—of Defoe and Steele and Addison and Swift and the rising young poet Alexander Pope—or of Isaac Newton, Edmund Halley and others of the Royal Society who were adding to scientific knowledge and so creating new possibilities of health, comfort and longer life. To give some account of all these important and interesting features of the reign, however, would require far more space than is available here.

It is perhaps enough, then, to recall that the greatness of Queen Anne's reign lay in its science and literature and architecture and the increasing elegance and comfort of its social life, as well as in its political and military achievements. The danger from France averted, England and Scotland united, a population increasing in number, wealth, health and the arts and graces of life—these are good proof of how the reign of a queen, not for the first time and not for the last, furthered the welfare of the British people.

GLOSSARY OF RELIGIOUS OPINIONS

ANGLICAN: Supporter of Church of England as reorganized under Elizabeth I.

ARMINIAN (from the Dutchman Arminius). Believer in free will. Term applied by opponents to Laud and his supporters.

BAPTIST: Member of Puritan sect believing in adult baptism by total immersion. Beginning under Elizabeth the Baptists came much to the fore under the Commonwealth, and since the Act of Toleration have been one of the great Nonconformist Churches.

BROWNIST (from Thomas Browne). Early name for Independent Puritan (q.v.).

CATHOLIC (from a word meaning 'whole' or 'universal'). The Catholic Church can have many senses, but in this book, and popularly, 'Catholic' is used for 'Roman Catholic'—i.e. a member of that part of the Western or Latin Church which remained under the Roman obedience after the Reformation.

CONGREGATIONALIST. Modern name for Independent Puritan (q.v.).

COVENANTER (covenant = contract). Presbyterian supporter of the Scottish National Covenant of 1638 and the Solemn League and Covenant of 1643 (see pages 225 and 241–242).

DISSENTER (dissent = disagree). Anyone—Catholic or Protestant—who rejected the doctrines of the Church of England; but usually applied only to the Protestant sects doing this.

EPISCOPALIAN. (a) Supporter of church government by bishops as in the Roman Catholic Church and the Church of England.

(b) Member of Scottish Episcopalian Church opposed to Presbyterian organization of the official Church of Scotland.

HIGH CHURCHMAN. Member of a particular wing within the Church of England. In the 19th century and nowadays the High Churchman is chiefly distinguished by his greater use of ritual, and his belief in the Real Presence (whence sometimes they are known as Anglo-Catholics). In Anne's reign the High Churchman was one who wished to preserve all the old privileges of the Church and thought it wrong to allow Nonconformists freedom of worship.

HUGUENOT. French Protestant.

INDEPENDENT (PURITAN). Member of Puritan sect rejecting the idea of a general compulsory church and believing that each congregation should have considerable freedom to organize its own services. Like the Baptists, the Independents began under Elizabeth, flourished under the Commonwealth, and finally became one of the great Nonconformist bodies.

JESUIT. Member of the Society of Jesus, a Catholic order founded in the 16th century (pp. 109–110).

LOLLARD (from a word meaning 'mumble'). 14th-century heretical sect following Wyclif or holding similar views. In some respects they may be regarded as forerunners of Protestantism.

NONCONFORMIST. Strictly speaking, like Dissenter, a term for all—Catholic or Protestant—who refuse to conform to the doctrines of the Church of England. But usually (and in this book) applied only to the Protestant sects who so refuse.

PRESBYTERIAN (from a Greek word for 'elder'). One who rejects Church government by bishops and believes in Church government by elected elders (lay and clerical). In England the Presbyterians were the strongest element in the Puritan movement to reform the Church from within, but in the Civil War the Presbyterians became overshadowed by the Independents. Clergy of Presbyterian views were expelled from the Church at the Restoration, and Presbyterians did not receive freedom of worship as a separate sect until the Act of Toleration.

In Scotland the Church was given a Presbyterian organization during the 16th century, but James I and Charles I strove to destroy this through bishops. Under

Charles II and James II the bishops kept the Presbyterian element well under, but after the Revolution of 1688 the Church was officially acknowledged to be Presbyterian, and the supporters of the bishops were later recognized as a separate Church (the Episcopalians).

PROTESTANT (literally, those who protested against the decision of the Diet of Speir to take action against the followers of Luther, p. 40). Members of any of the Christian bodies, or their later offshoots, who renounced obedience to Rome at the Reformation.

PURITAN. Under Elizabeth and in the 17th century, one who believed that the Church of England should be reformed or 'purified' still further in a Protestant direction. The term covers many sects, including Presbyterians, Baptists, Independents and Quakers. At first reformers within the Church, the Puritans were to some extent driven outside by James I and Charles I. Under the Commonwealth they then secured control of the Church, but under Charles II were completely expelled and persecuted. They obtained official freedom of worship in their own chapels by the Toleration Act of 1689, after which they are usually called collectively Dissenters or Nonconformists.

QUAKER. Member of the Society of Friends, an extremely democratic Puritan sect founded during the Commonwealth by George Fox. In the sect there are no priests or ministers, and no form of service beyond spontaneous prayer, etc. A distinctive belief nowadays is pacificism. At first many Friends shook with emotion during their religious outpourings—hence the nickname 'Quaker'.

REFORMER. Protestant leader during the Reformation.

UNITARIAN. A Nonconformist believing in the unity of God, as opposed to the normal Christian doctrine of the Trinity of Father, Son and Holy Ghost. Unitarians were still denied freedom of worship under the Toleration Act (like the Catholics), but nevertheless attained great prominence during the 18th century.

INDEX